ALSO BY CARYL PHILLIPS

FICTION
The Final Passage
A State of Independence
Higher Ground
Cambridge
Crossing the River
The Nature of Blood

NONFICTION
The European Tribe

ANTHOLOGIES
Extravagant Strangers
The Right Set

THE ATLANTIC SOUND

The ATLANTIC SOUND

CARYL PHILLIPS

ALFRED A. KNOPF   NEW YORK   2000

THIS IS A BORZOI BOOK
PUBLISHED BY ALFRED A. KNOPF

Originally published in Great Britain
by Faber and Faber Limited, London.

Knopf, Borzoi Books and the colophon are registered
trademarks of Random House, Inc.

Library of Congress Cataloging-in-Publication Data
Phillips, Caryl.
The Atlantic Sound / Caryl Phillips — 1st ed.
p.   cm.
ISBN 0-375-40110-5 (alk. paper)
1. Slave trade—History.   I. Title.
HT985 .P53 2000
382'.44'09163—dc21   00-034917

Manufactured in the United States of America
First American Edition

for Malcolm

CONTENTS

THE ATLANTIC SOUND

PROLOGUE

ATLANTIC CROSSING

Gilbert Pyree is a tall light-skinned Creole. Thin and in his early thirties, he stands in the crowded foyer of the Guadeloupe Meridian Hotel looking anxiously about him. His face lights up when he recognizes his charge and he strides to meet me, hand extended, words falling quickly from his mouth. 'You've checked out?' I assure him that I have and that we are now free to leave. I had just gone for a walk on the beach and observed the French tourists tanning nicely in the morning sun. Among them moved the waiters and the beach boys who were all black, but French too. The people of Guadeloupe remain resolutely proud of the intimacy of their connection to Europe and Europeans.

Once we reach the car park, Gilbert quickly tosses my bag into the trunk of his Renault hatchback, and he then encourages me to get out of the sun and into the car. As we pull out of the car park and into the traffic he informs me that he has been to Jamaica, Trinidad and Aruba, but this constitutes the extent of his Caribbean travel. One of the problems of the French Antilles, he says, is that we sometimes know Europe better than our own neighbours. By Europe, I take it he means France. He looks at me and nods, aware that I may, in some way, be reproving him.

3

Guadeloupe is really two islands: Basse-Terre, which is full of hills and valleys, and the eastern island, Grand-Terre, which possesses the more desirable beaches and therefore the greater share of the tourist trade. A thin bridge links the two islands and once we have crossed it we turn off the road and enter the industrial port of Jarry. A worried Gilbert asks me if I have ever been on a ship before. I tell Gilbert that I have 'sort of' been on a ship before, but I leave it at that for I do not want to have to explain to him that forty years ago my parents travelled by ship from the Caribbean to England with me, their four-month-old son, as hand luggage. Gilbert looks at me and frames the question carefully. I am aware, am I not, that this is a 'banana boat' that takes cargo? I smile and nod, and Gilbert visibly relaxes. Then I decide that it is probably politic to take some initiative so I ask Gilbert if he has ever been on a ship. He looks partly astonished, partly disgusted by the question. 'I fly,' he says. 'It is better.'

We drive through various checkpoints and then negotiate a sharp corner and begin to speed along the broad expanse of the quay. My ship, the MV *Horncap*, stands alone. It is a large hulking vessel whose decks are being loaded with container boxes. Gilbert informs me that this ship, or one of its sister vessels, docks here every week. These days, 'banana boats' only carry a dozen or so passengers, and most people choose to board in Europe and make the five-week round trip. As Gilbert and I shake hands, he tells me that the next port of call will be Costa Rica where we will pick up bananas. Once the ship is loaded we shall set a course back across the Atlantic for Europe.

The previous day I had left the driving rain of Connecticut to fly to Guadeloupe. I changed planes in San Juan, Puerto Rico, a short stopover that proved to be more traumatic than I had anticipated. At the gate a man lay dead. I imagined him to be about seventy, and he was stripped to the waist with a portable respirator stuck in his mouth like a child's pacifier. His battered luggage was strewn all about him and passengers stepped nonchalantly around his body as they prepared to board for Guadeloupe. There was no sign of any relatives, and his white, translucent skin reflected what little light there was in the terminal. The poor man's journey was at an end.

It was some years since I had last visited the French- as opposed to the English-speaking Caribbean, so upon arriving at Point-à-Pitre airport I found myself in a state of shock. The airport was positively glowing with cleanliness, the baggage trolleys required francs (which I had forgotten to acquire) and the taxi that whisked me toward my hotel—along well-paved roads— was a new Mercedes. Quite simply, I had forgotten that the French Caribbean is the First World in tropical clothes. Having checked in to the Meridian Hotel, I could not face the thought of negotiating the crush of the dining-room, so I ordered room service and watched NBA basketball on the only television channel that had English commentary. The following morning I woke early, checked out of the hotel and then went for a walk along the beach before my rendezvous with Gilbert Pyree.

I am escorted along the quayside and up the steep gangplank by Maung Maung Soe, who introduces himself as my cabin steward. A slim, almost wiry Burmese youth, he is studiously polite. As he opens the door to my cabin he startles me with the news that the ship may also stop in Guatemala. He bows quickly then moves to leave, but not before he reminds me that in one hour it will be time for lunch. 'No lunch,' I say. The poor boy seems perturbed, so I quickly assure him that I will be taking dinner. He seems relieved, bows a second time, then closes the door behind him.

The cabin is small, but comfortable. There are two single beds, with a tall wardrobe wedged tightly between them; a desk; a swivel chair; and through a narrow door I discover a bathroom. I am pleased that the cabin has two windows, and not the porthole that I had imagined. At present the view is of the concrete platform that is the quayside, but beyond the quayside I can see grass scrubland and idling cows. Beyond the cows there is a narrow channel of water, perhaps some four hundred yards wide, which divides one island from the other. On the other side of the channel is the tourist port where three huge ships, with decks tiered like wedding cakes, have already disgorged their passengers into a world where there are telephones and shops to cater for their immediate needs, and only a short taxi ride away a whole tourist infrastructure of beaches and bistros and bars.

At dinner I meet my fellow passengers and find myself initiated into the routine of life on board the ship. The three British people sit at one table. They are Kevin, a man in his late forties who is travelling alone; and Charles and Mavis, a couple in their late sixties. The fourth chair at the table is occupied by Wallace, a seventy-year-old retired lawyer from Connecticut. Four taciturn Germans, all of whom I guess to be in their sixties, sit at another table. It is immediately clear that they are two couples, and that there is an air of thinly veiled hostility between them. They address each other, but do so coldly and only when necessary. Seated at a larger table are the ship's German officers: the captain, the chief engineer, the chief mate and the electrician. I sit by myself at a small table, and we are all served by the Burmese mess boys.

During the soup course Mavis begins to bait the Germans. She leans over and remarks on 'the wonderful purity of Elizabethan English', and then casually inquires if any of the Germans have ever been to Stratford. The Germans look puzzled. Kevin on the other hand listens as Wallace enthuses about the invasion of Grenada, describing it as 'a good invasion'. Kevin points his fork at Wallace: 'Made you feel good, did it?' I notice that the already informal tone of the messroom is further lowered by the captain who dresses in scruffy T-shirt, shorts and open sandals with brown socks. The main course menu offers either German food (fried pork chop) or Burmese (duck curry). I opt for the Burmese, a decision I am to remain loyal to for the duration of the voyage.

6

Before the coffee and cheese, the captain stands and walks across to my table. He introduces himself as the 'master' and tells me that tonight we will leave at 9 p.m. for Costa Rica. Hopefully, he says, we will reach there in three days and then after that, 'who knows?'

'Then to Dover?' I ask.

He shrugs his shoulders. 'We wait and see.'

Already I am eagerly calculating how many days I will have to endure until I return to Britain. Before we have even hoisted the anchor I am longing to see the taxi in Dover that will whisk me towards the system formerly known as British Rail. And from Dover Priory station to Charing Cross, and from there a black cab to West London. For me this will be no Atlantic crossing into the unknown. I fully understand the world that will greet me at the end of the journey, but for West Indian emigrants of an earlier generation the Atlantic crossing was merely the prelude to a larger adventure—one which would change the nature of British society.

The ship sails at night, sneaking away from Guadeloupe like a thief into the darkness. As it does so, I stand on deck and listen to the low droning of the engine, and watch the shifting patterns on the surface of the sea. Above my head the funnel spews black smoke in the direction of the stars, and in the distance the brooding hills keep their secrets. I crane my neck and can now see that out in front of us a pilot ship bedecked in red, green and white lights leads the way past the blinking buoys and markers. There is no note of lament to this departure, for this is strictly business. Only the cloying night air and the annoying buzz of mosquitoes reminds me that I am in the Caribbean. I notice that the cruise ships have already departed, and the abandoned tourist port now seems singularly uninviting. Then I realize that I am witnessing the strangest of sights: a black sea that reflects moonlight.

The MV *Horncap* is one of the world's most versatile ships.

It carries cars, trucks, containers and is refrigerated for the transportation of fruit; mainly bananas. Wallace informs me of this. He disturbs my reverie and introduces himself. He describes himself to me as 'kind of conservative'; then pauses and lowers his voice. He is worried about the Burmese crew for they appear to be treated as slaves. 'They work seven days a week for about a year, then they get a pissy four months off in Burma, then back on for a year.' He explains to me that they are Buddhists. 'You know, kind of passive. But they put a little Burmese item on the menu every night so I guess these Germans must respect them a little. Me, I don't like spices.' Wallace is getting off in Costa Rica and doing some travelling in 'that part of the world' as he has two daughters who teach Spanish. So far, the trip out from Europe has been 'a pain in the ass'. Not like Norway, where he has been on a 'working ship' four times. He likes Norway, he says. 'All those fjords and nice people.'

I soon discover that a day at sea on a freighter ship is a long day. There are no activities, no newspapers, radio or television, no cinema, no gambling, and the pool is tiny and the pitching of the ship makes it impossible to use. On this first day out from Guadeloupe the captain posts a notice informing the nine passengers that there will be a rum party at 5 p.m. in the bar. Clearly this is an attempt not only to alleviate the boredom but to foster some kind of group spirit. However, at the party I notice that the Germans keep strictly to themselves, and that Charles, Mavis and Wallace seem to be engaging each other with painfully laborious 'small talk'.

The captain takes Kevin and myself to one side and announces that in Burma the Burmese can live like kings on their $50 a month. He has been at sea since 1963, and for the past seventeen years he has held the rank of captain. A small animated man, he announces that the government in Burma has closed the universities so navigation school is a popular way for the Burmese to earn good cash and support their families. However, their agent is always accusing the Germans of being racist because they regularly have to send back crew members. 'But this is not a fucking training ship,' says the captain. Kevin agrees and orders another round of 'Planter's Punch'. It transpires that Kevin has some maritime experience, having worked the P&O ferry line after leaving school. Kevin 'graduated' as a twenty-year-old with the 'rank' Efficient Deck Hand (EDH). Since then he has worked in the airline food business until a recent heart attack brought on early retirement. He tells me that he is making this journey, without his wife, in order that he might relive his teenage years at sea and think about his future.

Charles and Mavis, having disengaged themselves from Wallace, and having failed to engage the Germans in conversation, have now returned to the fold. Charles speculates with the captain as to our speed. Formerly the second in command of Portsmouth harbour, Charles's 'rank' is somewhat superior to EDH, and the German captain clearly has a grudging respect for Charles's knowledge. Apparently we are travelling at nineteen knots which, I am disheartened to learn, means we shall be arriving in Costa Rica later than planned. The captain then confirms that we will also be stopping in Guatemala to load extra bananas, and that if we encounter any delay in the Atlantic we shall have to go straight to the ship's home port, Hamburg, to off-load the bananas before they 'turn'. This depressing news encourages me to put down my glass and retire to my cabin. Once there I discover that it is not just the low, rasping hum of the engine that makes it difficult to sleep, but the constant vibration. It is like sleeping on top of a washing machine that is stuck on the spin cycle.

After three days at sea I find myself gazing upon land. To my surprise I realize that I am taking it for granted that the low green line of trees represents the 'other' world, strange and forbidding, a world where one would not wish to linger for too long. I have become acclimatized to the sea. As we bob along the

Costa Rican coast the wind begins to pick up and it starts to rain. I look up and notice three flags flying proud and stiff. The Liberian flag, which is the flag of the country where the ship is registered; the Costa Rican flag, it being a tradition to hoist the flag of whatever country's waters one is sailing; and finally there is a bright yellow flag marked 'Del Monte Quality Bananaen'. I stand in the rain and stare at the coastline. Then, as though from nowhere, our pilot boat appears and the vegetation gives way to the ugly port of Limon. As we creep closer I can see the tall cranes and forklift trucks, and then I catch sight of clusters of anxious-looking men squatting on the quayside, all of them hoping that they might be chosen to help with the loading.

After an hour wandering about the town centre, I decide that Limon is little more than a dismal, down-at-heel Caribbean coastal port which is evidently still trying to recover from the devastating earthquake of 1991. The population is a mixture of black, Hispanic and Indian, most of whom seem to be idling the day away assiduously not looking for work. Apart from being the major Caribbean coastal port for Costa Rica, Limon also serves as the transportation hub and marketplace for the surrounding area. It feels disturbing to be once more walking on land, but despite its shabby exterior Limon does, however, boast telephone booths. After a frustrating few minutes I eventually discover one that works. Once inside the booth my attention is seized by a sign which advertises a forthcoming musical evening at the Salon El Bohio. The show features 'Daddy Banton, Ragga by Roots, Rut by Nature, Weked Boys, Getto Fabulous and the Jamming Discomovil', none of which seem particularly Costa Rican to me.

Having made my phone calls, I flag down a taxi which, seemingly permanently moored in first gear, limps back to the port. Once on board, I ask the captain about Limon.

'Limon?' he exclaims. 'It's the whole place that's the problem. Costa Rica. It's just another banana republic but it likes to think of itself as better than the rest of them.' The captain goes on to tell me that Limon differs from the rest of Costa Rica by virtue of the fact that it has a very large population of Jamaicans who first came to Costa Rica at the end of the nineteenth century, and who were largely responsible for building the railroad which links the Atlantic and Pacific coasts. Having finished their labouring, many of the Jamaicans settled in Limon and slowly began to learn Spanish. However, these days they are relearning English in order to get back in touch with their 'roots'. Apparently life is not easy for them. The captain points out that it was not until 1970 that the Jamaicans were allowed to buy the more desirable property in the hills. He sneers, then gestures in the direction of Limon. 'Fucking banana republic.'

In the evening only one security guard, plus Charles and Mavis and the German couples, are left on board the ship. Everybody else is at the local disco-cum-brothel. The lights are low and the mirror ball turns slowly, but nobody seems to be interested in dancing. The Burmese crew are splitting a bottle of Bacardi between them, while the Germans are drinking beer. The Costa Rican barman tells me that last week while one of the *Horncap's* sister ships was docking, a rope that secures the ship to the quayside snapped and killed one Burmese crew member while another Burmese man lost his arm. And then the barman shakes his head as though the sad story does not have any contemporary meaning. It has already passed into history. I notice that Kevin has developed a purposeful interest in a young prostitute who clearly has yet to pass through puberty. Her friend approaches me and whispers, 'Usually no coloured, but you I like.' As I try to uncouple insult from compliment, another girl approaches and whispers exactly the same words, in the same confidential manner.

Wallace leaves us in Limon, which means there is a spare place at the table with Charles and Mavis and Kevin. However, I decide to remain at my own table, which amuses the German officers and Burmese crew, annoys Charles and Mavis, and leaves Kevin defenceless in the face of Mavis's increasingly unlikely stories about socializing with the Royals. Eventually Kevin cracks, and having described the Queen Mother as a 'gin-swilling horse owner' he retires to the bar where he attempts to drink a barrel of Holsten lager single-handedly. The two German couples have now developed a strategy for turning up for meals either early or late in order that they might minimize the time spent with each other. Occasionally they get the timing wrong, and they have to suffer the indignity of actually eating with each other.

Two days later we dock in Guatemala which the captain, with predictable contempt, describes as a 'fucking banana republic'. The early evening air is heavy with the smell of fruit, and as the ship inches its way into the harbour and up to the quayside, I look down at the now familiar sight. Three dozen men in sweat-stained vests sit on their haunches looking up at the ship, hoping for work, ready to load all night if necessary. Behind them lies a vast acreage of transit sheds and container boxes that fan out as far as the eyes can see. The captain has made it clear that he wants to set sail soon after dawn in order that we might 'rush' back across the Atlantic. The crew are visibly tense for they clearly understand that the captain means business. For the first time I hear raised voices among the crew so I decide to go into the town of Santo Tomos De Castilla and try to find a telephone, and maybe a bar in which I might have a drink.

As I walk along the quayside, trucks and cars speed recklessly by, clearly enjoying the freedom of being beyond the codes and rules of the road. Up ahead I spot what looks to me like a group of young Americans. It transpires that they are six Christians from New Hampshire who are working on board a 'Mercy Ship'. Their mission is to 'help' the local community, but they tell me that things are getting a little nasty. The two girls among them have been subjected to constant verbal abuse, one has been 'roughed up', and the other has had her guitar stolen. One of the boys tells me that he has recently been stoned,

12

which seems to me an appropriately biblical act, although under the circumstances I decide to express nothing beyond maximum sympathy. They point me in the direction of the telephones, but as I thank them and begin to walk toward the booths they disclose the useful information that these particular telephones are out of order.

One hundred yards beyond the defunct telephones I discover the worst bar that I have ever seen in my life. It is a small shed, the size of a one-car garage, with a naked lightbulb dangling from the ceiling, a wooden counter, one makeshift table, and two chairs. Sprawled over the table is an elderly man who still clutches a long empty bottle of rum. Behind the counter a boy of perhaps fourteen is enthusiastically fondling a ten-year-old girl, while in the corner a mottled dog stirs only to disturb the fleas. I order a beer, then turn in time to see a huge rat saunter in through the open doorway. It looks around and then turns and ambles its unconcerned way out again. The only 'decoration' in the bar is a flaking Bacardi poster of 'an American blonde' in a red bikini. As I take a second slug of my warm beer I decide to abandon this venue for the relative sanity of the MV *Horncap*. However, as I make this executive decision the captain and Kevin walk in and join me in the bar.

According to the captain, the loading is not going too well, and we will not be able to leave until noon at the earliest. The captain sees the look of concern pass over my face and he puts his hand on my arm. 'Don't worry, we will still try to make Dover.' Then the captain looks about himself as though only now registering what kind of place he is in. He speaks as though to himself. 'I remember a bar like this in Rotterdam. We got twenty-eight days in jail for fighting.' He pauses. 'Back in 1967 it was not a good time to be German in Holland.' I wonder exactly when it had been a good time to be German in Holland, but before I have a chance to ask him this his mind spools back across a few more years. 'In 1963 in Chile, I walked into a bar that was full of goddamn ex-Nazis. On the jukebox there were

Nazi songs, and these bastards were trying to marry off their daughters to me.' Kevin looks at me and surreptitiously lets me know that the captain has already had a few drinks.

In the morning I walk back into town in order that I might try again to find a telephone. 'Hey, Amigo!' greets me at every turn, and I mutter back something appropriately Spanish-sounding and genial in return. Then a man on horseback, sporting a cowboy hat, rides past me down the middle of the street. I stop and look in stunned silence as clouds of dust rise in his wake. When I eventually find GuaTel, the office of the telecommunications company, I have to wait another twenty minutes before a telephone line becomes available. As I sit waiting in the lounge, another 'cowboy' strides in to GuaTel with a gun on his hip and his belt studded with polished bullets. He simply wishes to send a fax. I make my call, and as I walk back towards the ship it occurs to me that this will be my last day on land for eleven days. Whether we dock in Hamburg or Dover, this departure from Guatemala will mark the true onset of the Atlantic crossing.

The day after we leave Guatemala it becomes clear that Kevin is incapable of dealing with Mavis. He sounds me out with regard to the possibility of 'transferring' to my table, but I remain vague and non-committal. Although I do sympathize with Kevin's predicament, life by myself on my own private table is enabling me to cling to my sanity. During dinner I look across at Mavis. She is a woman with a distinct memory of an imperial past which precedes this late twentieth-century mess. I sense that it is her habit of referring to Charles as 'Charles-bear' and her description of Charles's forty-six-year-old son, Rupert, as someone who likes 'sweeties' that has finally pushed Kevin over the edge. After dinner, in the bar, Kevin reminds me, with a desperate lilt to his voice, that when Wallace left the ship all Mavis could say was 'I really don't understand, for he claims to have travelled quite extensively around the world, but the chap doesn't know how to bone his fish.' Twenty minutes later, an incredulous Kevin slides another beer in front of me and repeats the same line.

As we pass through the Florida straits the captain asks me to join him on the bridge where he is keeping a look-out for small craft, for this stretch of water tends to be 'busy'. As he scans the horizon he tells me that in 1974 he was a second mate on a ship that hit a shelf off Brazil and sank in twenty minutes. He spent almost twenty-four hours adrift in a lifeboat before being rescued. 'In those days we used to have fun,' he says. 'Fun?' I ask. The captain laughs. 'In the sixties I used to sail with a Mini in the hold so that wherever we docked I could drive myself around.' I ask him what happened to the Mini. Without taking his eyes from the horizon he says, 'I wrecked it.'

The following night the captain hosts a barbeque party on deck to mark the fact that we are passing out beyond the Caribbean Sea and into the Atlantic Ocean. Unfortunately hostilities between Kevin and Mavis have now reached such a pitch that there is precious little in the way of communication between them. Charles sips at his beer and seems at a loss as to what to do, while the two German couples find temporary solace in the grilled chops and sausages. The captain begins to dance to imaginary music and reminisce about his time in China when he drank a concoction known as the 'elevator drink', so called because you didn't know if it would go down or come up. And then he orders the schnapps to be brought out. It is cold now, and everybody wears coats and sweaters.

The Burmese boys finish clearing away the food, and the captain now demands 'real' music. A somewhat second-rate ghettoblaster is brought from the downstairs bar, but the Spanish dance music is not properly audible through the crackly speakers. The captain suddenly stands up, unplugs the machine, and hurls it over the side of the ship and into the ocean. Then he grabs his glass. The first toast is to 'women' which proves to be a popular toast. Then a second toast is proposed to the glorious regime in Burma and the former colonial power that has allowed them to be there. At this point half the Burmese crew get up and walk out. I too quickly retreat to the solitude of my cabin as I realize that free beer is no compensation for hypothermia.

The next day depression washes over me, and come night I find myself roaming the ship in an insomniac's daze. Earlier in the evening I had left the bar in despair as one of the German couples settled in for a third straight hour of Ludo. I wandered back to my cabin, but sitting on the edge of a single bed staring at the wall seemed a little too analogous to prison life. In the deserted exercise room I can see that I only have the option of darts. It is not possible to play table tennis by oneself, and the exercise bike is broken. Nighttime at sea is punishing. There is no room service, no television, and it is not possible to go for a walk or telephone somebody. Come morning I am still awake and staring through the window in my cabin. I watch the horizon rising and falling as the ship rolls lazily from side to side. This is the most depressing time, for as I witness the sun rising on the vast unresponsive expanse of sea and sky, the bleak sight only serves to remind me that there is no prospect of land for days, that there is only the prospect of another day, and the undoubted difficulty of trying to endure another night.

At breakfast the captain tells me that we might not arrive in time to land at Dover. Apparently the weather up ahead is bad and we are falling behind schedule. An unshaven Kevin appears. He announces that this morning he has taken his bed apart with a screwdriver, then put it back together again. I ask him why, and he replies, 'Something to do.' Then Kevin falls silent as Mavis and Charles arrive and join him at their table. Kevin looks as though he cannot go on, but he simply signals for the mess boy to bring him another coffee. I turn away from them and retreat to the splendid isolation of my own table. I do, however, notice that there is no sign of the German couples. Then a tired-looking captain shouts over and asks me if today I would like the chief engineer to show me the ship's engine rooms. I thank him but decline.

Back in my cabin I begin to wonder why anybody would willingly subject themselves to serving time on a ship that is primarily designed to carry cargo not human beings. Presumably the only reasons to travel in this fashion are because (a) it is cheap; (b) you have nothing else to do; and (c) perverse curiosity. But even if all three reasons are applicable, such journeys can only be made tolerable by companions of some kind *and* a purpose. I decide there is little point in my writing letters while on board ship because there is nowhere to mail them. And to write them and then save them until I get to Britain is to risk spoiling the presumed elation of arrival with the revisiting of bad times. Outside I can hear a fearful sound, and then I realize that it is only the wind howling. There is now a lot of pitch and roll and it is risky to step out on deck. Unfortunately, the Burmese crew have no choice.

In the evening I sit with Kevin in the otherwise empty bar. It transpires that one of the German women is celebrating her birthday by having a small champagne party for all passengers and officers. Kevin and I have not been invited. The Burmese barman slips us a free beer and offers to fix us up with pornographic videotapes if we are interested. I hear myself laugh out loud in a semi-hysterical manner, but I seem to be doing quite a lot of this at late. Kevin throws down his beer in one gulp, and then orders another round. It arrives and he somewhat shame-facedly confesses that he has arranged to play table tennis with Jeremiah, who is one of the mess boys. Again I laugh, and then I tell the barman that I would like a box of Quality Street chocolates, which he goes to fetch for me. Kevin is deep in thought. Then he turns to me and asks, 'What are you like at table tennis?'

The captain opens the door to the ship's hospital. There are two beds, each surrounded by an elaborate network of scaffolding for hoisting and turning. Adopting the tone of a bored tour guide he confirms that the ship's officers are trained to deal with minor accidents such as the loss of fingers. However, the suicides are the worst, and they are always related to depression. The captain has experienced two, the most distressing being a chief mate who put a rocket gun to his mouth. The gun was designed to travel three hundred metres into the air, so there was 'quite a mess'. The captain shakes his head and then adds that the officer could have had the decency to commit suicide in his bathroom rather than in his living quarters. At least in the bathroom it would have been possible just to have hosed everything down.

From the hospital we move on to the bridge, where the captain lets me steer the vessel for five minutes. The sea is heavy, and I imagine that under the circumstances I am not doing too badly. The captain looks closely at me, and then takes me out on deck and shows me the line of the wake meandering crazily as though scrawled by a drunk. Such is the evidence of my navigational ability. Back inside he points out the radar screens which display the course that we are following. Because of the danger of icebergs floating down from Newfoundland, we are travelling south of the 'great circle', the route which is traditionally the fastest. 'We wouldn't want to do a *Titanic*, would we?' grins the captain. The good news is that tomorrow we will come close to the Azores where we will hopefully pick up the Gulf Stream, and therefore time. The bad news is that it is still not clear whether we shall have to bypass Dover and head straight for Hamburg.

The captain completes the tour by taking me down into the cargo hold and showing me the jail; or, as he calls it, 'The Horncap Hilton'. A simple cage made of iron bars on all four sides; anybody held inside would feel like a budgerigar. It exists for the express purpose of holding stowaways. The captain has had problems with Cubans in particular, who will pay a guard on the quayside $100 to look the other way, and then hide in the hold.

Three days out to sea they will either emerge of their own voli-
tion or be discovered. During the day they can be treated 'properly', but at night when only two officers and one crew member
are on duty, the stowaways have to be locked up in the 'Hilton'.
Having shared this information with me, the captain looks at his
watch and offers to buy me a drink.

Two weeks into the voyage, I have now developed the habit
of sleeping until lunch-time. Once I am awake, I walk to the
fo'castle of the ship, at the very front where the bow hits the
water. To get there I have to edge past the cargo holds and under
the containers. The smell of ripening fruit is over-powering, but
once at the fo'castle I find myself in a strange and eerie world.
Being far from the engines, it is astonishingly quiet and it also
has the advantage of being a hiding place from my fellow passengers. Kevin seems to be spending most of his time attempting to tune his short-wave radio in to any station, preferably one
which has sports results. Charles has tried to make conversation
with me, and in an effort to promote his conversational gam-
bits he has let me borrow *Lloyds Ship Magazine*, which is full
of details relating to global commercial shipping. Meanwhile,
Mavis continues to speak to the Germans as though they have a
full grasp of her colloquial English. 'You sound bunged up this
morning,' she says to one of the women. I later hear her
announce to the same woman that last night she went to bed
and 'switched off and was out like a light'. The baffled woman
stared back at her.

For almost two days I manage to secrete myself away so that
I see nobody. This is relatively easy to do as I continue to sleep
in the day and wander the ship at night. This creates the slight
difficulty of my having to sneak into the kitchen and smuggle
food back to my cabin in order to eat, but this is a small price to
pay for the peace of mind that solitude bestows upon me. On
the second morning of my voluntary hibernation I stand by
myself at the fo'castle and see a pair of migrating birds skim-
ming playfully across the water, one mimicking the other. They

give me the confidence that land cannot be far off. However, I now realize that, the difficulties of dealing with my fellow passengers aside, I have actually come to like the rhythm of life on the Atlantic Ocean. I want to see land; I want to go home; I definitely want to leave this 'banana boat', but I have a feeling that I will miss the sea.

An hour later, as the sun begins to rise into a cloudless sky, and as my eyes roam the horizon for more birds, I notice a school of porpoises. As they reach the ship they begin to play, gracefully leaping and twisting as though mocking the very idea of undertaking this passage in such a large, ugly vessel. I once asked my mother what she did when she got on the ship to England in 1958. She took her time in answering, and then she said that she worked out how to get to the lifeboats with me in her arms and with her eyes closed. She cannot swim and so she needed to be sure that if there was an emergency, and if the ship was plunged into darkness, she would still know how to get off the ship. I asked her about the rest of her time crossing the Atlantic. She looked blankly at me. As I continue to stare at the porpoises playing in the strong light of dawn, I now know how she and all the other emigrants felt as they crossed the Atlantic; they felt lonely.

Having only seen pictures of the white cliffs of Dover, I was greatly looking forward to seeing them with my own eyes. Their much revered place in British history is generally connected to the Second World War, but for the West Indian emigrants of the fifties and sixties the white cliffs of Dover signified the end of a long arduous journey across the Atlantic which had brought them from one world and placed them in the heart of another. West Indian emigrants, such as my parents, travelled with the hope that both worlds might belong to them, the old and the new. They travelled in the hope that the mother country would remain true to her promise that she would protect the children of her empire. However, shortly after disembarkation the West Indian migrants of the fifties and sixties discovered that the realities of this new world were likely to be more challenging than they had anticipated. In fact, much to their dismay, they discovered that the mother country had little, if any, desire to embrace her colonial offspring.

On the final evening I stand in the bar with Kevin and the captain and I look out as the dark outline of the south coast of England goes sliding by. The radio is tuned in to the local station and after so long at sea it feels comforting to hear a 'BBC' voice. The captain is drinking soda water, as he has been for two days now. During my 'tour' of the ship he told me that because the shipping in the English Channel is particularly heavy he always observes 'Ramadan' when anywhere near the Channel. Kevin continues to peer through the window, and then he nudges me and points to the coast. 'Look,' he says, 'it's black out there, just like your country.' The captain puts his glass of soda water back on to the bar with a clatter. He is going to say something to Kevin, but I quickly raise an eyebrow to let him know that it is not necessary.

I stand on deck and watch the captain. He is staring at the white cliffs of Dover, and then beyond them to the hills whose smooth rounded shoulders easily bear the weight of the toy-like cars which snake up and down them. He holds a cigarette which is being smoked by the stiff wind. When he raises it to his lips only two draws remain, then he flicks it over the side and into the waves. He turns to watch its retreat as though this were the first time that he had ever witnessed this phenomenon. Beyond the captain is Britain. On this bleak late winter's morning, I am happy to be home. As I look at the white cliffs of Dover I realize that I do not feel the sense of nervous anticipation that almost forty years ago characterized my parent's arrival, and that of their entire generation. I have not travelled towards Britain with a sense of hope or expectation. I have travelled towards Britain with a sense of knowledge and propriety, irrespective of what others, including my fellow passengers, might think. Finally I will be able to get the taxi that will whisk me towards the station. Overhead, gulls wheel and circle as though inspecting this new arrivant; the ship, that is, not me.

I

LEAVING HOME

The African dispatches the money to the white man and his African heart swells with pride. The African hopes for a new dawn; a brighter future. Luck has not been on his side. For many years now there have been problems. But, with the help of the white man, he can once again become great. Time passes. The white man is silent. African voices begin to whisper. The African is consumed with anxiety. And then he discovers himself to be floundering in a place of despair. He remembers that not all white men are honest. He remembers that not all white men are decent. Again he hears African voices. Friends are whispering. Enemies are laughing. He is still powerful, but this ill-fortune heralds the beginning of the end. For many years the African has been respected. But now the white man has cheated him of nearly everything that he owns. Abandoning his Christian beliefs, he makes desperate sacrifices to native Gods. But they have forgotten him. His life is running aground. The African has dispatched money to the white man. And now his heart is heavy with grief.

On 28 April 1881 a tentative and somewhat frightened young man named John Emmanuel Ocansey boarded a British ship, the SS *Mayumba*, on the shores of the River Volta in the British territory known as the Gold Coast. Ocansey was bound for the world-famous port of Liverpool in England, in order that he might discover what had happened to the money accrued from goods dispatched by his father, William Narh Ocansey, during the course of the previous year. The goods, with an estimated value of £2,678, had been delivered into the possession of a well-known Liverpudlian commission agent named Robert W. Hickson.

John's father was a successful and much respected general merchant who, over the course of forty years, had pursued his business with single-minded dedication. He specialized in the export of palm oil, which he processed at his numerous factories in the upper reaches of the River Volta. Once William Narh Ocansey had accumulated a sufficient load, he would transfer his palm oil down river to the coast, where it was subsequently taken on board sea-going vessels and shipped to England. Trading in palm oil was an unpredictable business, but it was nevertheless the foundation upon which William had built his trading empire. His success as a palm-oil trader had made him famous along the full length of the Gold Coast, and merchants in all Europe's major ports knew of William Narh Ocansey.

Palm oil had been introduced to Europe as early as the 1520s, when Portuguese sailors involved in the early days of the slave trade had each been permitted a duty-free allowance of two jars of oil from their slaving voyages. The glutinous substance was becoming increasingly important in Europe, particularly in the manufacture of soap and candles. Two centuries later, with the onset of the industrial revolution, palm oil became essential as a lubricant for both industrial machinery and railway stock. As factory workers undertook increasingly dirty jobs, there was also a rapidly growing demand for soap.

William realized the value of his export, particularly to the heavily industrialized north of England, and he was forever looking for methods by which he might improve his trading practice and thereby maximize his profits. The most hazardous part of the procedure was the journey down the River Volta, during which the palm oil was floated in large casks known as 'butts' until they reached the mouth of the river. Once there, a group of local labourers were engaged to gather in the butts before they were swept away by the powerful ocean tides. William felt that if he could purchase a steam launch, like the ones owned and operated by the Europeans, then he would not only increase the numbers of butts that he was able to transfer from the interior to the coast, but he would also make this aspect of his operation significantly safer.

The great majority of William Narh Ocansey's trading was with the English port of Liverpool. The same Liverpudlian companies who, before the abolition, had been active in the buying and selling of human beings now exploited their experience and contacts in order that they might continue to trade in West Africa, albeit in a different type of local product. Liverpool traders exported the same combination of hardware and trinkets that had served them well during slavery—namely guns, strong liquors and textiles—and they soon established a virtual monopoly in palm oil for their enterprising city. In order to capitalize further upon this trading advantage, engineers and shipbuilders based in mid-nineteenth century Liverpool developed the steam-powered river launch, a vessel which greatly improved trading between Liverpool and the west coast of Africa. These modest ships, which because of their strange appearance soon became known to the Africans as 'smoking canoes', could safely negotiate the ocean crossing to West Africa. However, they were constructed so as to require only a small draught of water, which meant that they could also easily manoeuvre their way along Africa's fast-flowing rivers. Initially there were some difficulties with these vessels; the climate often proved hazardous to their good working order, and even the simplest accident could render them suddenly inoperable. Fortunately, as the years passed by, these 'teething' problems were attended to, and 'smoking canoes' soon became a familiar sight on the African coast. William Narh Ocansey was determined to acquire a 'smoking canoe'.

In late 1879 William wrote to the Liverpool commissioning agent, Robert W. Hickson—a man with whom he had previously done business—and inquired if it would be possible for Hickson to help him order a steam launch. To William's delight, Robert W. Hickson soon replied and confirmed that not only would it be possible to order the vessel, but Hickson would be happy to help in any way practical. An excited William now proceeded with confidence. He proposed to Hickson that he would export produce, principally palm oil, in order that Hickson might sell the palm oil and subsequently utilize the profits to commission a steam launch. In the meantime, William instructed Hickson that plans should be drawn up for the construction of a vessel that would be sixty-two feet in length, twelve feet eleven inches in width, and seven feet in depth; a launch that would draw approximately three feet six inches of water.

William Ocansey's formal order for the ship reached Liverpool in March of 1880, along with a large consignment of palm oil and other assorted produce. Robert W. Hickson replied immediately, acknowledging that he had received both the order and the produce, but he demanded a second shipment of palm oil to cover the estimated £2,200 that it would cost to build the launch. Hickson, however, was happy to announce to William that the ship-builders had already commenced work, and that according to everybody's calculation the vessel would be dispatched so that it might reach Addah by August 1880. In this same communication, Hickson went to great lengths to remind William that the firm of Liverpool shipbuilders whom he had engaged were adamant that they would not, under any circumstances, release the launch unless the full amount had been paid.

The news of his vessel's impending arrival caused William much joy. In a matter of months he would be an African trader who was not only utilizing the same transportational methods as

the Europeans, but he imagined that as a result of his own ingenuity his wealth would soon begin to grow beyond his wildest
dreams. During the past decade, William had suffered numerous set-backs in his business dealings, so this imminent change
of fortune was both welcome and long overdue. On a closer
reading of Robert W. Hickson's letter, William noted that the
first load of palm oil had been sold for £1,478. He quickly dispatched another large consignment, having first satisfied himself
that this shipment would easily cover the costs of completing
and fitting out the launch.

Robert W. Hickson received the second consignment of palm
oil, which he sold at a healthy profit. Together with the revenue
from the first shipment, Hickson discovered himself to be in
possession of over £400 in excess of the estimate for the purchase of the launch. In November 1880, having promised his
African 'partner' delivery of the vessel some three months earlier in August, Hickson felt obliged to write to William Narh
Ocansey. The Liverpudlian explained that although the steamer
was now finished, it would be impossible to dispatch her
because of reports of squally weather and high winds in the Bay
of Biscay. Shortly after sending this letter, Robert W. Hickson
felt compelled to write again and inform William that because
of unforeseen delays he should not expect to receive his steamer
until the first week of April 1881.

Predictably enough, the first week of April 1881 came and
passed, and a deeply disappointed William still saw no sight
of his vessel. Some among his fellow Africans sympathetically
agreed with him when he suggested that he might have been
duped. Others, who were jealous of his seniority as a trader,
were secretly pleased by the ill-fortune which appeared to have
visited their grand elder. For his part, William was not only
embarrassed by this delay, he was also seriously worried about
the financial consequences which might befall him if, as it
appeared, he had indeed been cheated. Quickly weighing his
options, William now realized that he had little choice but to

dispatch an emissary to England who might personally confront Robert W. Hickson and settle this matter once and for all. The man he chose for this task was his most favoured son, John Emmanuel Ocansey. He summoned John before him, and instructed him that he should immediately prepare himself for a long sea journey to Liverpool.

John Ocansey's relationship to the distinguished trader William Narh Ocansey was more complex than that of son to father. John was a Fulani from the interior who had for many years been a servant in the household of the prosperous trading family, the Ocanseys of Addah. The family detected an unusual intelligence in John's person and they legally adopted him and then employed him in their trading business, where he was quickly taught to read and write. Some years later, John fell in love with, and subsequently proposed to his 'father's' daughter, Salome. His 'father' was delighted, and voiced no opposition to their declared interest, and on 28 April 1878 John effectively became both 'son' and son-in-law to William Narh Ocansey. John was elevated to the position of chief assistant, and he proved himself to be an especially trusted and capable member of the family. As the evidence of this new crisis made itself known, William did not hesitate in selecting John for the crucial business venture of journeying to Liverpool.

The African dispatches the money to the white man and his African heart swells with pride. The African hopes for a new dawn; a brighter future. Luck has not been on his side. For many years now there have been problems. But, with the help of the white man, he can once again become great. Time passes. The white man is silent.

John Emmanuel Ocansey was both a devoted son and a pious Christian. The idea of being parted from his wife and his two-year-old son, Alfred John Ocansey, caused him great sorrow, but he understood that it was his duty to help his father by travelling to Liverpool. William Narh Ocansey was too old to make the journey and investigate the circumstances of this loss for himself, so John declared himself willing and happy to act as a substitute. He assured his father that he would not only solve the mystery of what had happened to his money, but he would repair any wrong that had been done to his father's good name. However, as he stepped on board the SS *Mayumba*, John's heart was heavy with grief and his mind was filled with apprehension.

It was 28 April 1881, exactly three years to the day since John had married Salome. He tried hard not to think of this anniversary as he supervised the loading of his personal cargo, which he had deliberately kept to a minimum in the hope that his stay in Liverpool might be brief. The captain of the ship, a rough bear of a man who clearly regarded Africans as little more than unsophisticated children, received John's possessions without ceremony and ordered his crew to place them in storage. Once John was satisfied that his belongings had been safely taken care of, he went up on to the deck of the ship and looked back to the shore. There, lined up on the beach, he could see his father, his dear wife and son, and countless other members of the Ocansey family, all of whom were waving in his direction. John lifted a limp hand and waved back. As he did so, he looked at their saddened features and then he gazed beyond them to the land that he called home.

It had crossed his troubled mind that he might never again return to the Gold Coast. Misfortunes upon the sea, including piracy and shipwreck, were not infrequent, and illness was also a common curse that was visited upon those who dared to confine themselves on board vessels that passed through either tropical or equatorial climates. There were also unknown dangers that would inevitably greet John in Liverpool, for it was not uncommon for an African who reached England simply to disappear from view. Rumours of kidnapping and murder were rife and as he stared down at his family John decided to stop worrying and place all his faith in his God. With his gaze now fixed firmly upon his young son, John steeled his mind so that he might give out the appearance of a man who was unconcerned by the unusual circumstances surrounding the voyage he was about to undertake.

The SS *Mayumba* departed in mid-afternoon, and began to sail west toward the British capital of Accra. Progress was slow, for every time they sighted an English ship the captain would reef in the mainsail and hail the vessel. John soon realized that there were three passengers besides himself; a young Englishman, who had apparently boarded the ship in Benin and who seemed determined to keep himself to himself, and two middle-aged Scottish ladies who, like John, had commenced their passage in Addah. They appeared to be intent upon returning to their Scottish homes as quickly as possible. John thought it improper to ask their purpose in Africa, but he imagined that they were either schoolteachers or perhaps the wives of agents based somewhere on the coast.

It took the SS *Mayumba* a little over a day to reach Accra, where it paused briefly before passing on to Cape Coast, which had formerly been the British seat of government. From the deck of the ship it was possible to see the many fine houses that lined the shore to either side of the impressive Cape Coast Castle. These houses belonged not only to the British, who continued to rule the area, but also to the local African chiefs who, like John's father, had done well in this business of trading with Europeans. Having never before left the region of his father's house, John understood that this journey would continually present him with the opportunity to feast his eyes upon sights that were new to him. He was fascinated by the six huge English men-of-war that rode at anchor at Cape Coast, sitting proudly offshore as though they were expecting trouble from foreign sources. Although John was curious about the new world before his eyes, there was nobody with whom he might form a kinship.

Accordingly, John stood alone on deck, and his many thoughts and questions bounced unanswered around his churning mind.

A little way around the coast, and with the moon now etching a path across the dark water, John saw the outline of the formidable fortress of Elmina Castle. Long since famed throughout the region as the oldest of the European trading posts, John knew that Elmina had been originally built by the Portuguese and had thereafter passed into the hands of the Dutch, although these days it was firmly under the control of the British. In the fading light, John was able to discern no less than ten English men-of-war riding at anchor, which spoke of the continued importance of Elmina. In this region the West African coastline was protected by a treacherous rocky outcrop, and so the SS *Mayumba* anchored well offshore. As moonlight pooled on the surface of the sea, John could clearly discern both the magnificence of the castle and the isolated splendour of Fort St Jago, which sat by itself on a hill overlooking the castle.

Towards the end of the following day, and while they still rode at anchor, John noticed that a small tender was bringing out more passengers. Some moments later he watched and counted as eleven soldiers and two officers clambered expertly aboard the ship, but not without making much noise and drawing attention to themselves. John stood back and secreted himself in the undergrowth of ropes and pulleys, all the while trying to make himself as inconsequential as possible. He overheard a soldier explaining to a crew member that the reason for the presence of so many warships was the fact that the Governor was currently in residence. And then, as the men went below deck to eat and drink, John discovered himself to be once more alone with only the sea for company. As the sun began to slide towards her watery grave, John looked out to sea where he saw a line of birds drop suddenly from the sky and then bank sharply towards the horizon.

Nights at sea were long and difficult, but John found solace in his faith. After his simple evening meal, which he ate at a table specially laid out for himself, John retired to his small cabin and opened his Bible. When he realized that the light was such that his eyes found difficulty in picking out the words, he closed his beloved book, lay back on his bunk and encouraged his mind to range freely across warm thoughts of home and family life. The reality was that John was concerned about the problems that he knew he would have to face upon his arrival in Liverpool. However, he had already learned that when these troublesome thoughts had the temerity to present themselves, his first response should be to banish them and replace them with sweet images of his wife and son.

On the first night out of Elmina, John lay down his Bible and turned over to sleep, but the roistering of the new arrivants kept him awake. Clearly these English soldiers were happy to be returning to their native country and their families, but as he lay in the dark it struck John that he had never really thought of the Englishman as having a family. So many of them came to Africa unaccompanied and fearful of the many diseases that they imagined might ravage their unseasoned bodies, but John speculated that some among them must have a family life to return to. As they redoubled their noise, it suited John's present purpose to conjecture that impending family reunion was the cause of their rowdy celebrations.

For the next five days, the SS *Mayumba* continued to pick its slow way to the west, closely following the line of the coast. Each day they would make a stop, usually near the mouth of a river, or by a fine sandy beach, and supplies would be quickly loaded. On two occasions, another passenger taken on board. The first was an elderly white man who was rumoured to be the superintendent of one of the gold mines in the region. He brought on board a box of gold which he imprudently announced weighed ninety ounces, and from the clenched-fisted manner in which he held the box it was clear that this valuable cargo would never leave his sight. The second passenger was an African native, who John feared might be placed in the same cabin as himself, but mercifully this was deemed unnecessary. As the man was ushered beneath deck to his own quarters, his eyes met those of John and the briefest of nods confirmed their acknowledgement of each other.

At dinner the African native was placed at a single table near to John, and some preliminary discourse between them led John to understand that, like himself, this man was making his first journey to England. Sadly, this brief conversation marked both the onset and the conclusion of their conversation, for they had little language in common. Furthermore, the man appeared to consider himself worthier than John who was, as this man made clear, merely his father's son. However, John had no reason to be unhappy with this African man's silence, for he soon observed the man's unsavoury attempts to ingratiate himself with the white men on board. Each attempt was met with scorn and rude rebuttal, which convinced John that at least there was some dignity in loneliness.

A week or so out of Addah, the SS *Mayumba* anchored off the coast of the model colony of Liberia, which John knew to be the place that 'coloured' Americans mixed freely with, and occasionally sought to dominate, the local people. Low clouds clung to the walls of the deep valleys and above the clouds rose the arched backs of rounded hills. The ship stayed only a short time before pressing on to the British territory of Sierra Leone, which boasted a harbour in which the water was as still as a mirror glass. From the deck of the ship, John observed that the capital town of Freetown was both handsomely constructed and densely populated with palm trees which shook their great matted heads as though in dispute with the breeze. The passengers were given the opportunity to go ashore, so John was soon able to see for himself the fine roads and the magical order which seemed to have been instilled into this African country.

While on shore John chose to visit the famed St George's Cathedral, a large and ornate edifice with stained-glass windows and a clock which struck on the hour. The mechanism which allowed the clock to strike by itself, unaided by any human hand, fascinated John. He remained in the church, where he attended evening prayers, and then he slowly made his way back to the ship. Once on board, John stood by himself and looked up at the broad night sky that was speckled with bright spots of fire. This break in the journey, and the opportunity of once more setting foot on *terra firma*, had pleased him greatly, but he knew that soon he would have to begin to address the problems that he would inevitably encounter in Liverpool.

In the morning, John rose with the sun and discovered that while at anchor at Freetown the ship had received not only the anticipated cargo and supplies, but also a further ten passengers. Among them was a man of the cloth, a Reverend Williams, who was a Wesleyan missionary and a practitioner of the form of worship with which John was familiar. There was also an English lady teacher, a Mrs McCarthy from one of the native schools of Sierra Leone who, in addition to the familiar boxes and bags, had contrived to bring on board a pianoforte. As the crew were manhandling it to a safe place below deck, Mrs McCarthy smiled at John which caused him to marvel at her skin, for it seemed so fair that he imagined it would bruise if touched. John was hopeful that the presence of Reverend Williams and Mrs McCarthy might prove to be of great comfort to himself and other Christians on board, for the newcomers announced that for the remainder of the voyage they intended to offer the double blessing of public worship and communal singing under their combined guidance.

Almost immediately upon their departing Sierra Leone, the SS *Mayumba* turned suddenly away from the African coastline and John found himself totally surrounded by the sea. Deciding that there was nothing to be gained by gazing at the endless horizon, and recognizing that he had made no acquaintances with whom he might profitably idle away his time, John confined himself to his cabin. A kindly crew member informed him that for four days and nights he could expect this situation to prevail, but six long nights and days somersaulted aimlessly into each other before he heard the sound of running feet overhead, and the excited cry of 'Land! Land!'

Joining the throng on deck, John felt the heavy weight of the day's heat. Although he looked frantically about him, John was dismayed to discover that, unlike his fellow passengers, he could see no sign of land. His fellow African passenger who, until this moment, had contrived to ignore John, turned and pointed. 'Look! Don't you see it above the waters?' John felt embarrassed for, although he tried to look in precisely the direction that the man was pointing, all he could see was ocean. 'Wait here,' said the frustrated man, 'and I will bring you my spyglass.' With this said, he disappeared downstairs, and some few moments later he returned with a glass, which he handed to John. When John looked through the glass he was able to see the top of a large mountain which, the man informed him, crowned the island known as Grand Canary. John thanked the man and returned his spy-glass, and then he edged his way forward to the deck rail where his view was unimpeded. As the ship sailed towards the island, John could discern houses which glistened white in the morning sun as though they had been freshly painted. They were arranged around the hem of the mountain in an orderly fashion, strung together along a narrow road as though pearls on a necklace. From the base of the mountain to about half-way up, lush vegetation and trees covered the land, but from this point to the summit the land was bare and exposed.

The SS *Mayumba* dropped anchor, but only briefly, so that she might set down an ailing passenger. The ship then pressed on to the sister island of Tenerife, which they reached on the following afternoon. Like Grand Canary, the green island appeared to be little more than a huge mountain set down in a desert of ocean, but on closer inspection John could once more see the beauty of the landscape and the grandeur of the buildings. At Tenerife, John was offered the opportunity to disembark. As he wandered the streets he was amazed to discover that the houses and the public buildings, indeed the very streets themselves, were of a quality that he had never before seen. This was a world of great privilege and splendour, and only now did John realize how far he had travelled beyond his native Africa. In some ways, he understood that his true journey was only now beginning.

Two days later the ship dropped anchor at the Portuguese island of Madeira, which to John's eyes appeared to be yet another great mountain in the ocean. He stood on deck and watched the clouds sweeping across the mountaintop, a thinning curtain being perpetually drawn back by the low sighing of the wind. Again John was offered the opportunity to go ashore, and he chose to disembark, happy as always with his own company. He wandered unhurriedly through the broad, well-maintained streets, and noted the many lighthouses. At night, John had often stood alone on deck and puzzled over the extraordinary amounts of light that lighthouses shed, which enabled them to turn even the blackest of nights into something resembling dusk.

Once back on board, John knew that the next stop would be Liverpool. According to his fellow African, the ship was now a mere three days from their destination. His countryman turned abruptly and, in a manner that John now recognized to be characteristic of this surly man, he took his leave. John ignored the man and cast his eyes upon the receding splendour of Madeira. The small Portuguese island was now only just visible beneath the broad arms of the sky, and then almost in the blink of an eye it was first a speck on the horizon, and then a memory. Sighing deeply, John retired to his cabin where, unusually for one so disciplined, he found it difficult to concentrate on the Bible in his hands. Instead, he began to worry anew about the task that his father had entrusted him with.

Leaving Home

It is said, as a joke, that the shipowners in Liverpool, where many grow wealthy through the slave trade, pray to God daily not to change the color of the Negroes.

HENRI GRÉGOIRE,
On the Cultural Achievements of Negroes (1808)

John Ocansey knew that, after London, Liverpool was the most famous British city, a place known throughout the world because of its status as a seaport. What John Ocansey probably also knew is that Liverpool was intimately involved in the slave trade. Although trading in slaves had been officially abolished in British territories in 1807, and the owning of slaves by Britons outlawed in 1834, the business relationship between Liverpool and the west coast of Africa, a relationship which had enriched families such as the Ocanseys and established Robert W. Hickson and numerous other Liverpudlian agents, had its origins in the trading of human lives—Negro human lives. The immense wealth of nineteenth-century Liverpool was based, almost entirely, upon the city's deep involvement in the Atlantic slave trade.

The first historical mention of Liverpool can be traced to a document known as a land grant that was dated some time between 1190 and 1194. In this grant Liverpool is spelt 'Lieuerpul', just one of the many variations of the name over the years. On King John's Charter of 1207, the settlement officially became a borough, spelt 'Liverpul', and, although a village of some sort was clearly in existence before this date, this Charter marks the onset of Liverpool's history. While the precise origin of the name of the city has never been properly defined, the 'Pool' almost certainly refers to a body of water known as 'The Pool' or the 'Sea Lake' which emptied into the River Mersey, but served no real purpose. The 'Liver' part of the town's name is thought to mean 'thick' or 'muddy', which the Pool was generally believed to be. As Liverpool expanded, the Pool became an increasingly redundant feature of the town, and it was eventually filled in during the eighteenth century.

THE ATLANTIC SOUND

Between 1207 and 1660 there was little growth in population or development of trade, and Liverpool remained in a dormant state. In these early days, one of the few substantial buildings of any import to be constructed was the 'pool house'. Built in approximately 1558, it was situated just south of the Castle and was the place of residence for the man who would escort individuals across the Pool by boat to the 'Great Heath'. The Pool was tidal, and unpredictable, so a boat under the guidance of a skilled pilot was the safest way to cross the water. However, the construction of the pool house aside, Liverpool remained undeveloped, and the town was perceived by most English people to be a simple northern backwater.

Liverpool finally began to grow from about 1660 when the Cromwell Protectorate ended, and King Charles II was firmly established on the throne. Once Liverpool began to develop, her growth was both spectacular and on a scale that had never before been witnessed in the history of any English town. After the Plague of 1665 and the Great Fire of London in 1666, several London merchants headed north to the relatively modest port of Liverpool in order that they might continue their profitable trade with the West Indian and American colonies. At this stage the town could barely afford to pay the salaries of its customs officers, but such was the influence of these southern merchants that by the end of the century the town was remitting some £50,000 per annum to the King in customs duties.

On 3 November 1708, the Liverpool Town Council passed a resolution which allowed for the construction of a dock at the mouth of the Pool, and seven years later, in 1715, the Old Dock opened. The dock was protected by flood gates, and its three acres of water were more than enough to contain four or five ships simultaneously. However, in the succeeding decades new docks were needed as the maritime trade began rapidly to develop. Canning Docks and Salthouse Docks soon followed, and not long after the whole of the Liverpool seafront became a maze of wet and dry docks which handled shipping from all over the world.

By the year 1800, 4,746 ships were annually entering Liverpool, which probably made it the busiest port in the world. By 1845, the figure had risen to 20,521 ships. The American author, Herman Melville, visited Liverpool in 1849 and described the vast and imposing docks in the following manner:

> I beheld long china walls of masonry; vast piers of stone; and a succession of granite-rimmed docks completely enclosed. The extent and solidity of these structures seemed equal to what I have read of the old pyramids of Egypt. For miles you may walk along the riverside, passing dock after dock like a chain of immense fortresses.

During this boisterous period, sailors from all corners of the world began to frequent the town. Press gangs roamed the streets, and if pressed on board a ship a man could expect to be treated with extreme cruelty. Drinking and prostitution were rife, and the city's ever-expanding population took up residence in insanitary courtyards or in low-ceilinged cellars, existing in living conditions that quickly established themselves as amongst the worst in the known world. The overcrowding in these hovels eventually produced a squalor that outraged doctors, priests, and those who possessed a charitable attitude towards the working class. Most visitors concluded that while the merchants of Liverpool lived like kings, the poor were encouraged to live like animals among their filth and excrement. The prevalence of contagious disease was such that the average age of death was seventeen.

African voices begin to whisper. The African is consumed with anxiety. And then he discovers himself to be floundering in a place of despair. He remembers that not all white men are honest. He remembers that not all white men are decent. Again he hears

African voices. Friends are whispering. Enemies are laughing. He is still powerful, but this ill fortune heralds the beginning of the end.

The English first began to trade with Africa in 1553, when goods were exchanged for gold, ivory and other native materials. However, some twenty years later the trade turned its attention to the more profitable cargo of human beings. The new American colonies of North America and the Caribbean required labour in order that buildings might be constructed and crops planted and harvested. The trading 'triangle' was simple. Goods, be they guns, glassware, iron bars or liquor, would be exported from England to the West coast of Africa, where they would be sold in exchange for human captives. The second leg of the 'triangle', or the 'middle passage', involved the transportation of the captives to the Americas, where they would be sold to plantation owners either for cash or for a combination of cash and crops such as tobacco, sugar, cotton, coffee or any of the 'new world' produce that was becoming fashionable all over Europe. The final leg of the 'triangle' involved a return to England, where the produce was sold to agents and merchants.

The traders made money on all three sides of the 'triangle', but the human beings who were subjugated in Africa and sold in the Americas represented the profitable heart of the trade. As early as 1572 a royal proclamation awarded an English company a monopoly to trade in slaves in all English territories, recognizing the massive fortunes that might be realized. English ships, alongside those from Spain and Portugal, were soon transporting thousands of Africans across the Atlantic Ocean every year. Although Bristol and London still controlled the largest share of the English slave trade, Liverpool had announced her intent. In 1709 a single barque of thirty tons left Liverpool and eventually carried fifteen slaves across the Atlantic to America. After this entry in the Liverpool records, there is nothing further about trading in human beings for twenty-one years. In 1730, fifteen vessels, each averaging about seventy-five tons, departed from Liverpool to participate in this new and extremely lucrative trade. By 1737, the number of ships has increased to thirty-three, and thereafter the figures climb steadily until by the end of the century Liverpool is by far the largest and most vigorous participant in the English slave trade, its docks playing host to more slave ships than London and Bristol combined.

In the year 1771 alone, an astonishing one hundred and five ships sailed from Liverpool to West Africa. In other words, one fully-laden, fully-crewed slave ship left the port of Liverpool every three to four days to undertake a round-trip voyage that could last anything up to a year. These ships delivered 28,200 slaves to the far side of the Atlantic, which of course does not take into account the many thousands that will have perished in the dungeons of Elmina and Cape Coast Castles, and the countless other slave forts along the West African coast. Nor does it take into account those who will have perished at sea, either by their own hand, or through disease, or by being simply tossed alive into the depths. A local Liverpool saying summed up the importance of the slave trade to Liverpudlians, where it would be fair to say that every man from the highest to the lowest, knew that there were great profits to be made.

> *Get Slaves honestly, if you can,*
> *And if you cannot get them honestly,*
> *Get them.*

Many a Liverpool citizen would stroll by the harbour in search of a likely sailor or even a captain, in order that he might press upon them a bale or a bandbox, or some lace, or a pair of handkerchiefs; anything in fact, in the hope that nine months to a year later, when the triangle was complete, he might be presented with some share of the profit from the black gold. Slaving ships left Liverpool packed with these goods, and upon their arrival on the African coast they would anchor and begin the process of selling their wares in exchange for human cargo. The captain might spend as much as six months bartering, during which time the sailors were exposed to many fatal diseases, and subjected to the strictly enforced Draconian code of discipline that was imposed on board slave ships.

During this process the African natives were often cheated by the Europeans, who had a tendency to tamper with the authenticity of the goods being supplied. For instance, alcohol was often mixed with water, or false heads put in kegs so that there was only a little gunpowder on top and an empty space underneath. Another frequent practice was to open up the rolls of linen or cotton and cut pieces from the middle, but as the years passed by the Africans soon became familiar with the dishonesty of particular captains. Most trading was conducted without trust of any kind, the whites bearing guns and the natives knives, but some few traders and natives were able to maintain cordial and open relationships with each other. The metal currency used in the trade was called a 'bar', although in different locales it might be called a 'piece', or a 'copper'. Originally bars were strips of iron brought from England, and although their value fluctuated over time, all cloth, guns, beer, textiles and slaves had to be measured in these units. When a price in bars was agreed upon for a slave, the African seller was able to select goods to the agreed value from an assortment that were offered up by the European trader.

Once the 'fully packed' slaving ship left the African coast there was unhappiness both below decks, where the African captives were stored in the most inhuman and abominable conditions, and unhappiness above deck where the sailors were subjected to punishments which frequently included death. As the depredations of the triangular route became better known to all in Britain, fewer sailors were prepared to take a chance and volunteer themselves. As a consequence, the quality of sailor declined, with the result that most of the crew on slave ships were refuse from prisons or drinking houses. One moment a sailor might have been idly carousing in an inn where the real 'Jamaica' was handed out free from water and in goodly measure, but upon sobering up he would realize his terrible situation, bound as he now was for Africa and probable death. Unused to any discipline, such men found it difficult to abide by the rules, and only the hard-hearted and fearless survived. Venting their anger and frustrations on the captive Africans below, although strictly forbidden (for this was valuable cargo), was an inevitable and commonplace occurrence.

Navigation across the Atlantic during the 'middle passage' was never an easy affair, for although latitude could be calculated fairly easily by measuring the height of the sun at noon, longitude was a risky business and dependent upon the use of a compass and some guesswork. For long periods the slave ships ploughed the oceans without any real understanding of where they were, until they finally made landfall at Jamaica, or Barbados, or Charleston, or some other port which would welcome an influx of human cargo in order that the local plantations might be cultivated with ever increasing vigour. Having sold the human cargo in the Americas, the Liverpool ships would thereafter return to their home port, and replenish the warehouses by the docks with sugar, rum and other American produce, and reward those citizens fortunate enough to have invested in the voyage with huge profits.

By the end of the eighteenth century, nearly half the African trade of Europe was being carried on in ships clearing the port of Liverpool. The advocates of the trade formed a powerful lobby in Parliament, and they even employed verse in defence of their cause.

If our slave trade had gone, there's an end to our lives,
Beggars all we must be, our children and wives;
No ships from our ports their proud sails e'er would spread,
And our streets grown with grass, where the cows might be fed.

The rationale behind the Liverpool slave trader's defence of his occupation was simple. He asked the abolitionist, who wished to end this trade, to consider how he would employ the seamen who were currently involved in slavery, estimating that if ninety vessels left port each year (and there were often more), then this provided employment for no less than two thousand seven hundred Liverpool men as sailors. Then there were the workmen on land to consider. The carpenters, joiners, ironmongers, painters, sail-makers, boat-builders, coopers, riggers, plumbers, glaziers, gunsmiths, bread-bakers and labourers. 'What', cried the trader, 'must become of all these people who will be left without employ?'

But the slave-trader did not stop there. He speculated as to the poverty that would befall Manchester, Birmingham and all the other manufacturing centres of Britain which depended upon the African and West Indian trade for the export of their goods, and the import of raw materials. And what of the poor West Indian planters, British citizens, whose valuable estates brought great revenue into British hands, but who were likely to be reduced to poverty by the ending of the trade and its practical supply of labour? A final argument that was fired off against the abolitionist was that even the mere mention of the ending of the trade was likely to reach the ears of the slaves and cause bloody insurrection. This would inevitably lead to the loss of many British lives, the consequences of which would have to be borne by the abolitionists. What the Liverpool 'merchants', as they liked to call themselves, omitted to mention were the huge profits that were being made by a handful of the richest among them. In the ten years between 1783 and 1793, 921 ships employed in the slave trade left Liverpool. Together they shipped to the Americas over 300,000 slaves, who were sold at a sterling value of £15,186,850. Which means that slaves were worth an average £50 'per head', and although there remained expenses from the voyage, and a 5 per cent factor's commission to be deducted, the profits to the slave-traders of Liverpool were still, by anybody's estimates, simply enormous.

The first people to openly question the morality of this traffic in slaves were the Society of Friends, or Quakers, who as early as 1727 denounced the trade. However, they were considered to be somewhat eccentric and unorthodox, and they were unable to garner much support. Other churchmen, including John Wesley in 1774, did manage to attract more support, but when former slave-ship captains such as John Newton, or former slaves such as Olaudah Equiano began to publish books which exposed the full horrors of this system of industry, then public opposition to the slave trade began to grow. In his treatise *Thoughts upon the African Slave Trade*, Captain John Newton, whose voyages emanated out of Liverpool, remembered a conversation that had taken place in Antigua in 1751. A 'gentleman', by which one might assume he meant English planter, had made exact calculations as to which might be the more profitable method of managing slaves. Either to appoint them a moderate amount of work, and give them plenty of provisions so that they might live longer. Or to strain them with heavy service and hard usage, wear them out, and then simply buy new ones to fill their place. The 'gentlemen' commented that it was generally acknowledged that working a slave to death was the more profitable method, and on his Antigua plantation it was very seldom that a slave lived for more than nine years.

Most Africans were shipped directly from the coast of West Africa and sold in the Americas, but occasionally slave-ship captains would bring Negroes back to England to work as domestics, or simply to be sold for profit. This practice was, of course, often carried out in Liverpool. An entry in Williamson's *Liverpool Advertiser*, from the year 1765, announces such a sale:

To be sold by auction at George's Coffee House betwixt the hours of six and eight o'clock, a very fine negro girl about 8 years of age, very healthy, and hath been some time from the coast. Any person willing to purchase the same may apply to Capt. Robert Syers, at Mr. Bartley Hodgett's, Mercer and Draper near the exchange, where she may be seen till the time of Sale.

The Atlantic trade in slaves fell away during the American War of Independence, for American privateers were actively engaged in attacking British ships. But in 1783, on the resumption of peace, the trade recommenced where it had left off. In 1787 the first petition objecting to the inhuman nature of this trade was delivered to Parliament by members of the Society of Friends. The Quakers objected to this 'hideous' trading in human flesh, and from this initial outcry, plus the 'evidence' of Equiano, Newton and others, grew the national movement which eventually resulted in the outlawing of the British slave trade in 1807, and the eventual abolition of slavery in British territories in 1834. During the many parliamentary debates about the abolition, the Liverpool traders had repeatedly claimed that to ban the trade would bring ruin to their city. However, after the abolition they were proved wrong, for by 1834 trade to the east, particularly to China, had been thrown open to private enterprise. Liverpool entered this trade with vigour, and soon became the chief port through which tea and rice arrived in Britain. Furthermore, the development of the Industrial Revolution and the continued improvements to canal and rail transportation meant that in the wake of the abolition Liverpool's influence as a port, far from declining, actually grew, and cotton, as opposed to human beings, soon became the port's most important commodity.

At the same time, Liverpool was also establishing itself as the chief port of emigration for the thousands of Europeans who wished to depart for the Americas and Australia. Throughout the nineteenth century, a constant flow of migrants were anxious to flee European poverty and starvation and seek a new life across the oceans, and Liverpool, with its peerless system of docks, its shipbuilding skills and its communication network by rail, road and canal, was ready to take advantage of this new trade. Countless thousands migrated from Liverpool, but while the vast majority arrived in the city determined to leave, there were many others who eventually settled in Liverpool's squalid courts and cellars, having either drunk away their fare, or had it stolen from them. In 1831 the population of Liverpool was an astonishing 205,572, but by 1881, the year John Ocansey set foot in Liverpool, it had tripled to more than 600,000.

After yet another sleepless night at sea, John Ocansey woke to the peaceful rocking of a ship at anchor. As he opened his eyes he heard doors banging and then the thundering of footsteps above his head. Experience had taught him that such a clamour on deck signalled the sighting of land, so he sat upright and then swung his legs out so that they brushed gently against the floor. Eight long days and nights had passed since the pleasant interlude of the Spanish Canaries and the exquisite beauty of the Portuguese island of Madeira. The greater part of John's daylight time had been spent on deck craning his neck at the lighthouse vessels and iron buoys with bells and anchors, all of which served as markers in the watery road. Such ingenuity lay beyond John's imagination, and he studied these inventions with a mind to introducing them into his native African world upon his return. As John rubbed the back of his hand into his crumpled morning face, footsteps continued to clatter above his head, and so John made ready to leave his cabin.

On 27 May, much to the delight of John and the other passengers congregated on deck, the SS *Mayumba* finally entered the famed River Mersey. The river thronged with maritime activity, and John realized that he had never seen so many ships in his life, both steamships and sailing vessels alike. They clogged the river and occupied the endless rows of imposing docks, the masts of the sailing vessels standing tall like a forest of leafless trees. His own ship had to pick its way slowly along the river, and negotiate not only those ships at anchor, but more importantly those that appeared to be crossing the Mersey from one bank to the other with noisy blasts from their salty whistles. A skilled pilot, who was knowledgeable of not only the water, but of the unpredictable movements of the vessels all about, was clearly necessary. Upon enquiry of a burly crew member, John was informed that there were literally hundreds of ships afloat in the River Mersey at any one time, and the evidence before his own eyes seemed to confirm the truth of this statement.

It was soon clear to everybody on board that their ship was not going to be able to dock immediately. However, in order that the twenty-eight passengers might disembark and reunite themselves with their 'home', it was decided that the SS *Mayumba* would drop anchor here in the River Mersey and the passengers would be transported to the shore aboard a smaller vessel known as a 'tender'. They were instructed to gather their belongings on deck, which they did, and then one by one they were received on board the tender, which John recognized as a small steam-powered launch with two chimneys which, although smaller, was not altogether dissimilar to the one that his father had ordered.

Once on shore they were quickly ushered into a large Customs Hall, a warehouse-sized room larger than any chamber John had ever seen. The noise and general turmoil was overwhelming, but John simply followed the others and joined the line of passengers who were being questioned by the 'custom-house officers'. In a manner that John assumed to be mean and unnecessarily harsh, these foggy-voiced men ordered each passenger to open their luggage for inspection. A kindly crew member had led John to understand that there were as many as two hundred of these men, and that it was they alone who might decide whether one was qualified to enter England. As he waited in line, John continued to look about himself in the vague hope that he might see another of his world. His fellow African passenger aside, all others around him—both arrivants and officers—appeared to be English. However, the variety of accents suggested that they came from parts of the kingdom that were far removed from each other, for at times they did not appear to be conversing in the same tongue.

When John reached the head of the line, a young man who wore whiskers that would be more appropriate on the face of an older person, looked him up and down. He enquired if John was familiar with Liverpool and John shook his head in reply. He then further enquired if John had brought anything into the country that might be deemed illegal. Again John shook his head, and then thinking better of it, announced, 'No sir.' With this exchange said and done, the man plunged his hands into John's boxes and rummaged around in them to see if there was anything of undeclared value hidden there. Having evidently decided that there was not, he then marked the boxes with a chalk cross and told John that he might go on his way to his lodgings. Thanking him most profusely, John gathered his belongings and made way for the next person in line. Before leaving the Customs Hall, John looked around and realized that this moment signalled the end of his journey. He had been fortunate in that he had not succumbed to illness or to any of the other misfortunes which were known to be visited upon men who risked their lives on the ocean. He had arrived safely in Liverpool without being robbed of his goods, or having his person sold into servitude. Now John would have to turn his mind to the task of finding his father's business partner, Mr Robert W. Hickson, and determining exactly what had happened to his family's money.

John stepped out into the bright afternoon glare, and was immediately surrounded by young barefoot urchins, all of whom appeared eager to relieve him of his boxes. 'Hey, Blackey!' was the common shout, and John's attention was seized by the behaviour of these filthy and dishevelled young beggars. Not even in the poorest village of his native Africa would a child behave in such an uncouth manner. Attempting to convey as forcefully yet as gently as possible to these children that he was presently occupied on business and would not be requiring their assistance, John picked up his boxes and began to edge his way towards a man on a carriage who first signalled with his arms and now shouted to John that he would take him wherever he required.

John pushed past the young savages, whose manner seemed to turn increasingly unfriendly as they comprehended the fact that their services would not be required. On seeing John approaching him, the man on the carriage jumped down and snarled at the young curs who instantly peeled off in all directions. 'You'll be needing help, sir,' said the ruddy-faced driver as he took John's boxes from his arms. 'Climb aboard. Don't worry, I'll watch over your belongings, sir.' Fearful that this man's cheerful demeanour might be something other than it appeared, John climbed aboard the carriage, all the while keeping a wary eye on his belongings as they were loaded, box by box.

Once he had finished loading, the driver dragged his rather obese body back up onto his seat and without bothering to turn around, he asked of John where it was that he wished to be taken. John had already arranged lodgings at a place his father had heard was a clean, tolerant and Christian household, and having taken the trouble to memorize the address, John was able to inform the carriage driver that he wished to go to 24 Oxford Street, Liverpool. John added the word 'Liverpool', unsure as to whether the man would understand that John wished to remain in Liverpool. After all, having observed the size of the city from the ship's deck, he could easily imagine that there might be any number of Oxford Streets in the immediate vicinity. The driver said nothing in reply, and he simply bellowed a guttural signal to the horses, which began to move forward.

As the carriage swayed and rocked its way through the broad

streets of Liverpool, John gazed down in amazement at the nature of the people's dress. Different stations in life were clearly represented by different clothes; there were those who dressed roughly and without care in the same manner as the urchins down by the sea harbour, and those who dressed in a high style as though about to attend a wedding or some other grand function. To John's foreign eyes it appeared as if this might be a feast day, and for a moment it occurred to him that he might enquire of the driver if this was indeed the case. However, after a moment's reflection he decided to refrain, fearful of opening a conversation that neither of them might wish to pursue. Instead, he turned again to the grand spectacle of the street, this time noticing that the ladies habitually stopped to look in the large glass windows of the shops, while the men seemed to pass them by. John also noticed that none of those who dressed in a high style, men or women, paid the slightest attention to those whose dress marked them out as being of the lower orders.

Turning his attention to the construction of the streets, John observed that they were of a type that he had never before witnessed. Generally broader than those of Africa, or the Iberian islands that he had briefly visited, he was able to discern that they were divided into many parts. The middle part was made of paving stones, while the outer extremities were also paved with smooth flags, apparently for people to walk upon. However, the parts on either side of the middle line of stones were made of sand and it was upon these tracks that the horses and carriages ran. John's attention was particularly arrested by the giant carriages, which were pulled by four horses. People not only clambered inside these vehicles, but also on top of them. John also noticed the tall and uncommonly slender houses, and he imagined that their interiors must be similarly grand. John wondered just how many people lived in this magical town, but he guessed that it would be impossible for anyone to determine. There were, however, certainly enough people for John to realize immediately that his task in tracking down Mr Robert W. Hickson would not be an easy one.

As the journey progressed, and as they moved into streets that were less noisy and somewhat narrower, the ruddy-faced driver attempted to engage John in conversation, inquiring first where he had come from and how long his journey had taken. Then, having secured what he clearly deemed to be satisfactory answers, he moved on to question John about the nature of his business. On this latter point, John deemed it sensible to say as little as possible, fearful that word might reach Mr Hickson and precipitate his rapid departure. So John, aware of what he imagined to be custom and decency of manners, leaned forward and informed the driver that he was in Liverpool in order that he 'might conduct some trade'. Under the circumstances, this seemed the most honest and appropriate answer, and it appeared to be one which satisfied the driver for he made no further enquiry of his passenger. John turned his attention back to the streets, but in these less noisy thoroughfares the severity of the grey stone edifices was not only ubiquitous, it was also somewhat depressing.

After travelling over particularly uneven stones, which caused John to be tossed about on land with more vigour than on the Atlantic Ocean, the driver pulled up outside a long row of elegant terraced houses, and for the first time since the journey had commenced he turned to look John full in the face. 'Twenty-four Oxford Street,' he announced.

It appeared, from his troubled visage, that for the past few minutes the driver had been thinking hard. Then he spoke again. 'My grandfather, he was in the Africa trade. Terrible thing,' he said, 'the way people was treated.' John watched as the man searched for his words. 'But you'll find that things have changed, you know. Folks round here don't look for difference.'

John simply stared at this man, who stared back at John as though urging his passenger to absolve him of past sins. The man looked and spoke as though the weary memory of slave ships was lodged in his soul. A puzzled John quickly reached into his pocket and withdrew a coin, which he held out hopefully. But the carriage driver, lost as he was in his own thoughts, did not notice that payment had been proffered. He continued to stare into the middle distance and then, as though appalled by some new thought, he began to slowly shake his head.

It has been the fashion throughout the Kingdom to regard the town of Liverpool and its inhabitants in an unfavourable light on account of the share it has in this trade. But I will venture to assert, as I always shall, that men more independent, of greater public virtue and private worth, than the merchants of Liverpool do not exist in any part of these kingdoms. The African trade is the trade of the nation, not of any particular place; it is a trade, till lately, sanctioned by Parliament and long continued under the authority of the Government.

WILLIAM ROSCOE, LIVERPOOL MP (1806)

John's landlady, Mrs Lyle, was a stout widow who appeared to be of good and generous heart. John's father had been led to believe that she was unusual by Liverpool standards in that she ran a clean and respectable boarding-house, which had never been tainted by any hint of impropriety or moral turpitude. She was also distinguished by the fact that she harboured no prejudice against any because of their colour, and she therefore accepted John Ocansey into her house with the same hospitality and warmth that she had shown her numerous other African guests. What concerned Mrs Lyle was one's station in life, and she was happy to be of service to any whom she judged worthy.

After the uncomfortable episode with the carriage driver, John was relieved to be in the presence of a woman who seemed both uncomplicated and lively. The rotund Mrs Lyle wore her hair tied back in a particularly severe bun, and when she smiled her teeth glistened, for they seemed to be permanently coated in saliva. She ushered John into the parlour, but on seeing how exhausted her guest was, she escorted him straight to his room. She announced that she would bring him some dinner so that he might eat in privacy and thereafter retire. She further informed John that because at present he was the only guest in her house (which when full to capacity could accommodate up to six persons), this individual service would prove to be no extra burden to her. John thanked Mrs Lyle most profusely before following her upstairs to his small room. Once there, she pointed out the fireplace with a grate full of black coal lumps, informing him that should he feel cold then he was free to apply a sulphur match. With this said, she left John by himself. On hearing the good lady close the door behind her, John slumped down onto the side of the bed.

John struggled to stave off sleep, worried that should he close his eyes then he would open them to find a new day dawning. Calculating that his landlady would be gone for no more than a half hour, John reckoned that he had time to wash his body and to change his clothes. This he did, and then he was greeted by the pleasing voice of Mrs Lyle, who rapped on the door and announced that his dinner was ready. When John opened the door Mrs Lyle handed him a large tray that was piled high with food, and then she told him that she would see him in the morning. This evening, she said, he should not bother to return the tray. John ate quickly, but with grace, remembering first to give thanks to God for his safe arrival in England, and for the fact that fate had deposited him into the hands of a kindly hostess. When John finished eating he took care to blow out the light in the room, and then he fell fast asleep and slept deeply, although his dreamworld was occasionally racked with anxiety at the thought of the mission that lay ahead of him. And then suddenly he was rudely interrupted by the sound of a panic-stricken Mrs Lyle, who was both banging loudly at his door and raising her voice.

John opened his eyes and looked all about himself, but it took him some few moments before he realized that he was not dreaming. Mrs Lyle really was bellowing at him. 'Mr Ocansey! Mr Ocansey, did you blow out the gas last night?' John rubbed his eyes, then smelt the strange pungent odour all around him. 'Mr Ocansey! Can you hear me, Mr Ocansey?'

John sat upright in bed and tried to focus in the darkness. 'Yes, Mrs Lyle, I can hear you.'

'Mr Ocansey, the gas. Did you blow out the gas?'

'Indeed I did, Mrs Lyle.'

John heard her sigh loudly.

'I thank God, sir that you did not strike a match, for if you had the house would have been blown all to pieces and everybody in it killed.' By now John was on his feet and dressing himself so that he might appear decent. Mrs Lyle continued. 'Do you not know that gas is as dangerous as gunpowder?'

John was now attired in a respectable manner and he opened the door, whereupon he saw a flustered and barefoot Mrs Lyle bundled up in a woollen nightgown. She pushed past John and into the room.

Mrs Lyle called John over to the window and then she bent down and pointed out a small screw that was fastened into a pipe.

'Mr Ocansey, when you want to put out the gas again, don't blow at it. Turn the screw this way and it will go out without danger.' John watched as she turned the screw shut, and then she threw open the window so that a blast of fresh air burst upon them. 'Mr Ocansey, it remains a wonder that you did not die in your sleep. Truly, you were blessed with some good fortune last night.'

John felt ashamed at his ignorance, and thought it best to enquire if there were other dangerous things in the room of which he ought to be aware. Mrs Lyle now smiled, and she touched John gently on the arm. 'There's nothing more that will cause you any trouble, Mr Ocansey.' This said, the good lady turned and left the room.

John sat on the edge of the bed and contemplated his luck.

He understood that Mrs Lyle raised her voice out of concern, and not anger, and that if this gas was as dangerous as gunpowder then indeed he was lucky to be alive. However, drawing himself to his full height, he realized that the new day was already announcing itself and he could not afford to dwell upon his good fortune. He crossed to the window and stared at a slow carriage, laden with passengers, that was trundling its way down the otherwise empty street. Turning from the window, John knew there was no point in delaying the inevitable, for today he would have to set about regulating his father's affairs.

When John went downstairs, a newly becalmed Mrs Lyle was good enough to give him instructions as to how he might reach the address that his father had provided him with for Hickson, Sykes and Co. Despite his ignorant mistake, Mrs Lyle was also kind enough to compliment John on the smartness of his dress, attired as he was in his English suit, and she also insisted that she would make him breakfast before he left. Although John was keen that he should cause this good woman no further trouble, he could see that a refusal of breakfast might be construed as ill-mannered, so he sat down and watched as the delighted lady began to fuss over her one guest.

When John finally stepped outside his boarding-house, he felt as though he had partaken of a feast. As Mrs Lyle cleared away his final plate, she repeated her instructions as to how he might find the offices of Mr Robert W. Hickson, and she assured him that if he walked briskly it would take him no more than twenty minutes. Should he find himself confused, then she informed him that he should ask the first decent-looking gentleman, taking good care to introduce himself by bowing slightly and saying, 'Good morning'. However, it soon became clear that Mrs Lyle's instructions were accurate, and as John turned into the final street he could feel his heart pounding. John quickly ascended the three steps which led to the door of the offices, but his spirits sank to see the nameplate of another company. Undeterred, John knocked loudly. Some moments passed, and just as he was contemplating knocking once more, the door opened and an elderly gentleman stood before him. The man looked as though he had been disturbed while in the middle of some important task and he eyed John suspiciously. Observing the man's manner, John suddenly lost his words and the two stood in silence for some awkward moments. Then the elderly man, growing impatient with this apparition before him, finally spoke up. 'Well, what is it? State your business.'

On hearing the nature of John's business, the man nodded quickly and then interrupted. He gave John the devastating news that Hickson, Sykes and Co. had recently been declared bankrupt and that on 17 June there would be a meeting of their creditors. Apparently, John was but one in a long line of persons who had been cheated by this company, and in a little over two weeks he would meet his fellow-sufferers and together they could work out what course of action to take. On hearing this news, John felt a hammer drop inside himself and he did not move from the doorstep for some moments. The man, clearly familiar with being the bearer of bad news in this regard, seemed to relax. He offered his condolences and then asked if there was any other matter on which he might offer some help. John shook his head and upon this signal the man closed the door, leaving John marooned on the doorstep.

John left the former offices of Robert W. Hickson, but he was in a daze and soon realized that he was unsure of what direction he was walking in. Then, without fully understanding how it transpired, John found himself back at the house of Mrs Lyle in Oxford Street. Upon opening the door, his landlady looked at his downcast face and asked him what had happened. As John was clearly finding it difficult to express himself, Mrs Lyle escorted him to a seat on the settee in the living-room, and she then brought him a cup of tea and made him relate his whole story, beginning with an incident in which his father lost a cargo of palm oil and thereafter decided that he should order a steam launch to be built. John continued, making it clear that he did not blame the people of Liverpool, nor the people of the European race; he considered Robert W. Hickson, and this man alone, to be responsible for the present calamity. A sympathetic Mrs Lyle listened to John, but she could offer only words of comfort and the hope that this matter might yet be settled to his advantage. She assured John that English courts were known to be fair in their deliberation, and would certainly take his side if the matter was as he related.

Having taken some comfort from Mrs Lyle's words, John informed her that he would immediately have to set about the unpleasant task of informing his father of the true extent of the disaster that had befallen them. His father would now have to consider the implications of a total loss of £2,678, in addition to the substantial disruption to his business that he had suffered as a result of this unpleasantness. John retired to his room where he spent the rest of the afternoon, and the greater part of the evening, sitting alone at his table and drafting a letter to his father, but the cheerless nature of the task made him feel so despondent that he eventually took to his bed.

For three days and nights, John lay in bed unable to complete a letter to his father which might accurately convey the facts as he now understood them. During the daytime hours, John peered at the light that leaked around the edges of the curtains and he thought about the consequences of this calamity for all of his family. His father was not a young man any more, and John had to consider the possibility that their business might never recover from this loss. This being the case, the burden would fall on John to take charge of all debts, despite the fact that neither he nor his wife were in possession of any assets of their own. Each day a concerned Mrs Lyle would walk up the stairs, first in the morning and then at night and, respectful of her troubled guest's need for privacy and his inability to talk at this juncture, she would simply leave his food on a tray outside his door.

On the fourth morning, John Ocansey woke early and as he stepped from his bed he felt the damp chill of the floor. Once again he dressed himself in his English suit, having decided that if he was going to have to spend time waiting for the creditors' meeting he would at least see some of this great city. He had finally written the letter to his father and in his recounting of the facts he had been as honest as possible. He had neither offered his father any undue hope, nor had he spared him any of the depressing details of the tragedy. He had, however, tried to reassure his father that he should not worry excessively, for every effort would be made on John's part to make sure that he recovered as much of the money as possible. With this letter written and dispatched, John had decided that the first place he would visit would be a church.

John chose to attend the Presbyterian Church in Mount Pleasant, which was very close to his lodgings. Mrs Lyle, although not a devout woman herself, had recommended it to John as a place where he might receive a warm welcome. When John entered the church he was faced with the overwhelming sight of a large body of almost two thousand worshippers, but he quietly found a seat at the back of the congregation and observed the high formality of the proceedings, which made him feel somewhat uneasy. John watched as the minister entered the church in a rather grand manner, and then he slowly mounted the steps to the pulpit while the organ sounded its sonorous notes. John had never before heard an organ, and having imagined that it would be an instrument similar in sound to that of the piano, but with more volume at its disposal, he was totally unprepared for its booming tones. Once the minister reached the pulpit he deliberately announced the number of the hymn, and people turned in their books until they found the relevant page. Thereafter the organ increased in volume and the congregation began to sing as one. The sound was overpowering and the religious fervour was of such a magnitude that John was momentarily afraid. There was little doubt that these worshippers were deeply moved, and John too felt the power of the Lord coursing through his body and shaking him to the very core.

After the service, John took it upon himself to make a visit to the Bluecoat School where Mrs Lyle had led him to believe that many young orphans, both boys and girls, are often taken in and educated. He asked a kind lady if he might see some of the grounds and buildings, and she willingly showed him the apartments where the children lived and then asked after him if he wished to attend the church service that would shortly be commencing. John thanked her and said that he would, whereupon he was ushered into yet another large building that, like the one he had attended earlier in the day, was also full to capacity. To John's untutored eyes there appeared to be about three hundred children, perhaps as many as one hundred teachers, and scores of servants and others who seemed to be connected to the school. He imagined that the other worshippers were townspeople who had come to listen to the singing, for it had been explained to John that these children were specially trained in this art. John waited as the organ played soft, sweet music, and although he could feel many eyes upon him he much preferred this atmosphere to that he had earlier experienced at the Presbyterian church.

Suddenly the organ dramatically increased its power, and the large double doors were thrown wide open. Other instruments, predominantly drums, joined with the noise of the organ, and a group of scholars began to stride into the church, two by two, like animals into the ark. They were smartly turned out in frocks with large white collars, and while the drum kept a steady beat they marched with great precision towards the front of the church. Once there, one among their number, a small boy who John estimated to be not above ten years of age, climbed into the pulpit and announced the hymn as though he had been carrying out this task for his whole life. Thereafter, the congregation immediately took to their feet and began to sing the hymn in a loud and lusty voice. At the conclusion of this performance, the congregation regained their seats. Then John watched as twelve boys came forward and lined up in front of the organ and, reading out of a book, they asked of the assembled boys many questions about the Bible. The boys answered correctly and without hesitation, and soon after the twelve interrogators stepped back. Then six girls came forward and asked a different set of questions, which the assembled girls answered with skill and without hesitation. This being done to the satisfaction of the six girls, they too stepped back.

John was fascinated by the literacy of these young children and as the next part of the service commenced, which was the taking of the collection, he studied them closely. They seemed truly devout, and to have taken the spirit of the Lord into their bodies in a most powerful and convincing manner. John watched as the generous citizens of Liverpool dipped deeply into their pockets and gave money in order that these young children might have a better future. And then, after yet another hymn had been sung, the ten-year-old boy climbed once more into the pulpit and gave the benediction with a gusto that would have shamed a veteran preacher. The final part of the service involved the swelling of the organ music and the marching out of all the children, two by two, and in great order and without noise, into the rooms where they were to eat.

The public were encouraged to follow them, and to witness the quality of the food and the general treatment that the children received at this school. The evening meal was already prepared and on the tables; bread on wooden plates, and tea and milk in tin cups. John could see on the faces of these children the gratitude that they felt for such beneficence, for having no mother or father, John understood that the expense of keeping these children was defrayed by the wealthier people of Liverpool, who saw it as part of their civic duty to give a yearly subscription in order to maintain this remarkable school. Having passed this instructive day, and learned much about his surroundings in Liverpool, John undertook the slow evening walk back to Mrs Lyle's. He would have to wait nearly two more weeks before the meeting of Mr Hickson's creditors, but John had already decided that he would spend his time contemplating his relationship with the Lord and, following the example of the young children, in the studying of his Bible.

Each day John took a short walk around the immediate vicinity of Oxford Street, where by now he had become a familiar sight to many of the local people. Mercifully, they caused him no trouble, and they simply nodded as he passed by; the truth was, John was growing used to their presence, as they were to his. Occasionally, John would venture further, principally in the direction of the docks so that he might explore the streets near to where he had first landed. In this part of Liverpool the buildings were generally large and built of stone or marble, or some combination of both, and the broad streets were commonly thronged with people, all of whom hurried about as if they had much business to conduct and very little time in which to carry it out. John particularly enjoyed the exhilarating activity attendant upon both the arrival and the departure of the ocean-going vessels, and the river seldom failed to present him with this spectacle of joy. At night, gas lamps lit the streets, but John seldom remained long enough to witness the full effect of this illumination. At this time of the evening he preferred to walk in the quieter parts near to his lodgings, for after dark he did not feel safe in the hustle and bustle of the docks.

Most evenings, John sat alone in his room where he continued to spend long periods of time contemplating the consequences of his father's loss. However, there was little more that he could do except pray that upon receipt of John's letter his father might not take the news as a mortal blow. The loss appeared now to be a fact, and John had relinquished all hope into the hands of fate. Each night, before turning off the gas, John would simply beseech the good Lord to guide him safely through the next few weeks, and deliver him back to Africa and into the loving care of his good wife and child.

On John's second Sunday, he chose to attend the Methodist Free Church on Russell Street. As it happened, this day was the fifth anniversary of the Church's Sunday School, and the young boys and girls were arranged on a platform at the front of the church, where they led the singing both sweetly and with enthusiasm. John felt more at ease in this church, for he knew some of the hymns, and the manner of conducting the service was very similar to that of his own Wesleyan church on the African coast. There were, however, some important differences, chief among them being the employment of what appeared to be two ministers. The first was a man, who gave out the hymns, and prayed and read lessons from the Bible. The other was a woman, about forty years of age, and dressed severely in black. Miss Pooke, as she was named, wore a man's haircut and had a roll of fat around her neck which hung as heavy as a necklace. However, she gave out her text in a fluent and excellent style, and was at least as convincing as any man that John had witnessed in the pulpit. Her text was on 'Abraham offering up Isaac, or personal sacrifices for God'. As delightful and instructive as it was to listen to this woman, John knew that the introduction of such a custom into his native Africa would never be tolerated.

The Methodists seemed happy to have John among them, and at the conclusion of the service he was invited to dine with the minister of the church at his house at Mount Vernon Green. Not knowing the practice in such situations, John took a chance and accepted. Thereafter, he enjoyed a most pleasant lunch and a delightful afternoon with the minister and his family. Among the other guests was a Mr George Quilliam, with whom John immediately struck up a friendship. Mr Quilliam was a watchmaker who lived on Elizabeth Street in Liverpool. He was an exceedingly kind and obliging man, and John decided that he should be ranked among those he might call a friend. However, he thought it best to not share with Mr Quilliam, or any other beyond Mrs Lyle, the purpose of his visit to Liverpool for fear that they might consider him prejudiced against the Englishman.

Over the next few days, John tried very hard to be both diplomatic and patient with his new friends, many of whom were hospitable enough to invite him back to their various houses. One among them was kind enough to introduce him to his children, two little girls and a small boy, who John found both charming and polite. However, during the course of the evening one of the girls unexpectedly turned to John and, her eyes lighting up as she spoke, announced that when he returned to Africa she would like John to send her a small black boy so that the boy might carry her books to school for her. At first the child's father showed some sign of embarrassment, which manifested itself by his extreme silence. John tried to smile at the young girl, and in this way remove some of the tension, but all the while he was waiting for the father to intervene and suggest to the girl that she was incorrect in her statement. Eventually, the father spoke: 'Mary, my love, what are you saying? Suppose I give you to Mr Ocansey, and he were to take you off to Africa, you would then have to carry the books for the black boy.'

The father smiled somewhat smugly, feeling pleased that he had delivered a riposte of suitable vigour to the child and rescued his guest. However, the girl did not seem in the slightest bit troubled by this announcement from her father. She spoke smartly and said, 'But father, I shall not go to Africa, for the sun will make me a black girl, and you said yourself that they have no good schools in Africa.'

Hearing this, the father sighed outwardly, and John hurried to change the subject. While he knew that the attitudes of the child were clearly formed by the attitudes of the father, he had no wish to subject either person, father or daughter, to any more conversation based around this thorny subject.

After this incident John was increasingly careful about those homes that he was prepared to enter. It was not that he lacked a desire to mix among these Liverpudlians, for clearly by doing so he was learning much about their society, and about England in general, and he imagined that this information would be useful to him in his future trading life. However, John understood that there were certain attitudes about Africans which still prevailed in this city, attitudes which were at best uncomfortable, at worst insulting, and he had no desire to put himself into a position where he had either to defend his people, or chastize his hosts for their uncivilized behaviour.

On another occasion, John learned of the complex nature of Liverpool life while simply pursuing his daily business. One evening he was walking down a broad street with a trusted church friend who had invited John to his home, and in order to reach their destination they had to turn in the direction of the docks. As they did so, John and his friend were approached by a poor white boy who came and ran alongside them. He seemed down on his luck and composed his face into a picture of complete misery. Then he requested that they press a penny upon him, and John began to feel compassion for this poor young urchin who was as thin as a communion wafer. However, he noted that his friend showed no sign of wanting to stop, and so, torn between his desire to talk with the boy and his desire not to offend his friend, John walked awkwardly on his way.

The boy, however, having noticed that John's affections were torn, continued to press his case, so much so that John asked him what it was that he really wanted. 'A penny, please!' said the boy, and the use of the word 'please' so affected John that he stopped and began to put his hand into his pocket. At this his friend also stopped and, raising his voice to make himself heard above the continual rumble of heavy wheels, he ordered John to desist. 'No!' he said, 'Do not do it. You encourage begging, but we want to put it down. The fact is, no one in England need beg if they are honest and willing to work, for there are jobs for all, particularly the young and able-bodied such as this wretch.'

His friend turned and began to walk off, and John was left with no choice but to follow him. The poor boy continued to track John and beg for his penny, and John looked at the boy and found it difficult to think of the urchin as either able-bodied or strong enough to endure a full day of labour. After some minutes of this torture, John quickly reached into his pocket and pressed a single penny into the palm of the boy. The boy beamed with gratitude and, his mission complete, he scampered off down the hill toward the docks. John's friend observed what had taken place, but he said nothing. For some moments the two walked on in silence, and then John's friend felt compelled to speak.

He explained to John that in England every man who lives in a house is taxed to keep the poor, the sick and the cripples in a large place called a workhouse. When the workhouse is too full they are free to give more to the poor people, or they can simply take them into their own homes. John listened, unable to believe that such a system of unbridled generosity could exist in the world, but he was not going to question this man's word. His friend further admonished John by informing him that the reason he had suggested that he should not give any money to this boy was because the boy would either spend it on drink for his own consumption, or he would give the money to his parents, who were no doubt lurking nearby, and they would spend it on drink. According to John's friend, strong drink was the root of most of the trouble in English society, the implication being that John had just contributed to the problem. The evening that followed was soured by this 'mistake' on John's part. His friend introduced John to his wife and his two children, but the time passed very formally and with little laughter or light-hearted humour. A despondent John returned late to his lodgings, his way lit by gas lamps. Once there, he discovered a tired-looking Mrs Lyle, who was sitting up waiting for him. He thought about asking her advice with regard to the social mistake that he had just made, but he was too miserable to burden this good lady with his worries. Instead, he simply exchanged a few words of greeting and then retired to his room where he tried in vain to find sleep.

The following day was Sunday, which was by far John's favourite day of the week. He lay in bed for a few moments and listened to the pealing of the great number of church bells, which together sounded like a chorus of heavenly splendour, but he dared not linger for long. On this morning there was a particular focus to his day, for he was anxious once again to attend the Methodist Free Church which he now regarded as his second home. John hoped that this day might pass in peace and with good cheer, for at its end he would have to prepare himself for the forthcoming week, which would feature the meeting of Robert W. Hickson's creditors, and hopefully some conclusion to this difficult business.

On the Tuesday afternoon, John, together with half a dozen other anxious creditors, presented himself at the offices of the lawyer representing the interests of Hickson, Sykes and Co. However, after waiting for nearly an hour, he was disappointed to learn that rather than settle out of court, Robert W. Hickson had placed John and the others in the position of having to take him to trial should they wish to receive any money. It soon transpired that such a trial could not take place until the end of July. Disconcerted by this news, John thought about returning immediately to Africa and reporting to his father that all was lost and that there was no reason to expect any financial recompense whatsoever. However, later in the day, when he suggested his plan to his friend Mr Quilliam, he was met with such an outburst of indignation that he immediately backed down. Mr Quilliam made it clear that he suspected that John was ready to abandon his claim because he did not trust the system of justice that operated in Liverpool. His friend therefore explained to John how the judicial process worked, taking particular care to point out the fact that it discriminated against nobody and offered justice on the basis of fairness to all, irrespective of racial, religious or national background. John listened patiently, but assured Mr Quilliam that although he had faith in the system, the outcome was still likely to produce no material gain for his father. John was worried that he might simply be wasting time that could be more profitably spent helping his family back in Africa.

At this point Mr Quilliam lectured John, laying particular emphasis on the fact that justice is more concerned with principle than with material gain. He pressed his argument with vigour and three times he repeated his belief that when a man is taken to court it is the principle that he is wrong that is of primary importance, not the size of the settlement or the length of any sentence that might be passed down. Mr Quilliam insisted that should John drop his case, Mr Hickson would be able to disseminate the falsehood that there had been some mistake on the part of the African, and that John had withdrawn from the case before embarrassing himself. On the other hand, by staying and seeing his case through to its conclusion, John would not only be establishing that his family were in the right, but henceforth all would know Mr Hickson's true character and he would never again be in a position to dupe anyone. Long before his good friend had finished his deposition, John was convinced that he should remain and wait for the date of the trial. He now knew that it would be wrong of him to return to his father without the matter having been properly settled. For his part, Mr Quilliam agreed to help John pass his days with sightseeing trips and other pastimes that would be both educational and pleasurable. John, thinking again of the young scholars of the Bluecoat School, privately resolved to spend a great part of his time in Bible study.

Despite the efforts of Mr Quilliam, the days passed slowly. John enjoyed his own company, and that of his Bible and a few other religious texts that he had managed to acquire, but being exiled from his wife and child caused him to feel increasingly heavy in both body and mind. One day, while out walking with

Mr Quilliam, they happened upon a crowd of people who were gathered around in a circle and closely watching something or somebody. On pushing their way through the throng, John and Mr Quilliam saw a man who had taken too much drink, for he could neither stand nor walk and he appeared to be lolling about on the ground to no great purpose. The aspect on the faces of those who looked on was that of intense disapproval. John commented to his friend that he had been in Liverpool for some time now, but this was the first time that he had seen somebody drunk, but Mr Quilliam pointed out the unfortunate facts. He informed John that there were many people in Liverpool who over-indulged in drink, particularly sailors and those who inhabited the hostels and streets close to the docks. Powerful spirits were used by those in all stations of life, but the poor seemed incapable of doing so with any kind of moderation. The surprise being expressed by this crowd was not that the man was drunk, but that he had collapsed in a street that was normally frequented by those of a higher station. Hence the numbers that had gathered about him to witness his disgrace.

A few moments later a policeman appeared, although it was not possible for John to discern if this policeman happened to be passing or if he had been summoned by one among the crowd. The policeman, a great burly fellow, as seemed to be the case with all the English policemen that John had observed, reached down and pulled the man to his feet. Thereafter he dragged him away, much to the approval of the crowd, who continued to converse long after the man had disappeared from view. John's friend explained that the man would be placed in jail, and in the morning, having had the night to sober up, he would be brought before the magistrates who would probably fine him five shillings and costs for being drunk. John confessed to Mr Quilliam that one of the most miserable of the many ills that afflicted Africa was this addiction to strong drink that some grown men, and not a few women, seemed all too keen to indulge in. Mr Quilliam suggested that the use of strong liquors in the trading process had probably helped to accustom the otherwise passive African people to a taste for dangerous drink. John agreed, but went further, saying that if he could learn anything in England that might help him to rid his countrymen of this addiction to strong drink, then he would return home a happy man.

One morning, while idling over breakfast, John realized that there was much shouting and rowdiness occurring in Oxford Street. He leapt to his feet in a state of mild alarm and Mrs Lyle looked at him as though he had taken leave of his senses. It shocked John to hear people arguing, for Oxford Street was a quiet part of Liverpool and raised voices traditionally played no part in the daily order of things. Curious to know who the participants in this unholy clamour might be, John crossed to the window and peered out. It was then that he saw two stout women with large baskets on their heads, shouting at each other. John found it impossible to discern whatever it was that they were shouting, but from his vantage point they both appeared to be angry. As he watched, Mrs Lyle explained to John that, far from arguing, these women were merely selling their produce. Suddenly a door opened at the house opposite and the serving woman emerged and bellowed something to the two women. Immediately they rushed across to the house and set their baskets down at her feet. Mrs Lyle explained that in one basket there was fruit, and in the other vegetables.

Once John understood the nature of the procedure, this mobile market seemed a novel idea and he marvelled at the ingenuity of the women. After all, in this manner goods could be easily distributed to those who did not have the time to make the journey to market.

A few days later, John was taking a walk when he discovered another of the traditions of Liverpool. A small boy approached him, touched his cap in salutation, and then began to run alongside. At first John thought this boy was merely in search of a penny, and having listened to Mr Quilliam on the subject, he felt himself prepared to not only refuse the request, but to deliver a short sermon suggesting to the boy that he should find himself some work and avoid the evils of drink. However, John misread the situation. As the boy ran alongside John, he kept touching his cap and pointing at John's feet. Eventually the mystified youth was forced to utter the words, 'Shine Sir, only a penny!' and only then did John fully understand the nature of the boy's presence. Upon closer inspection John noticed that the boy was in possession of blacking, brushes, and even a little stand upon which to rest his client's boots. To John's way of thinking, this seemed an altogether more industrious and sensible way of earning a living than the scandalous begging that he had hitherto been fooled by.

One feature of Liverpool life that John became particularly familiar with was the gangs of scruffy children with dirty, wrinkled faces, both boys and girls, who earned an honest living by selling newspapers. They were quick to see potential customers in the afternoons, but especially quick in the early part of the evening, when they received delivery of their 'final editions'. When they saw an individual without a newspaper they would rush up to that person and try to impress him with their patter, and being a man who always enjoyed reading, John saw no reason why he should not indulge in this 'English' habit. Newspapers contained information which might prove useful to him, and he also knew that through reading the newspaper it was possible that he might receive news of events in his part of the world. The first time John tried to purchase a newspaper, he put his hand into his pocket to see if he had a copper, and at that moment at least a half dozen of these young wretches tore towards him and implored him to buy a newspaper from them, 'Please buy from me!' 'Good sir, be kind as to take mine.' John looked from one to the other, and wondered what on earth had influenced them to be so aggressive in their manner. Would John's penny truly make a difference to their daily earnings?

Such ferocity of competition, and between ones so young, was alarming to John. Thrusting his copper into the nearest hand, John seized his newspaper and moved off swiftly.

And so, in this manner, most of John's Liverpool days passed by, with constant exposure to new ideas and experiences. John regularly walked abroad and studied what was happening in the world of Liverpool. He was no longer surprised by the poor, who often wandered bareheaded and barefooted, and sometimes he would see a whole family begging, the woman with an infant in her arms and children tugging at her dress, raising her voice in a discordant wail in the hope of attracting pity and charity in equal portion. The streets of Liverpool presented a constant rush of energy which appeared to be undimmed by either the hour or the quality of the street. John learned to read his newspaper before the evening meal in Mrs Lyle's parlour, and then after the meal he would read his Bible and write to his father and to his wife. He remained frustrated at the delay in settling his father's affairs, but having decided to remain in Liverpool he had little choice but to keep his mind occupied and to continue to attempt to learn from this adversity.

14 July 1881 marked a significant change in the fortunes of John Ocansey. An earlier letter from his father had informed him that he should be aware that there was a possibility that his childhood friend, Christian Jacobson of Quitta, might well be coming to Liverpool to conclude a business transaction. John's heart leaped at this news, and each day he closely studied the passenger lists of the ships coming to harbour. On the early evening of 14 July, John read in his newspaper that the African steamer *Lualaba* had arrived in Liverpool, and that a Mr Christian Jacobson was a passenger on board. Although he had not eaten, John threw down the newspaper and, muttering some hurried apology to Mrs Lyle, he fled her house and started in the direction of the docks.

Running at full tilt, John reached the docks just as the light of the day was beginning to fade and be replaced by the artificial light from the gas lamps. The policeman stationed at the gate to the docks, being there to observe the comings and goings of strangers, and prevent thefts, asked John to state his business. Having listened to the African's story, he allowed John to make his breathless way to the Customs Hall, where John enquired if any there had seen his friend. One among the English men said that he knew the man to whom John was referring, because this same man had made enquiries after John. The kind man then suggested that John go to the Alexandra Hotel on Dale Street, which he remembered to be the destination of the newly arrived African.

Unsure of the location of this hotel, John secured the help of a carriage and driver, and within a few minutes he was deposited outside the Alexandra Hotel. Such was John's excitement at the possibility of being reunited with his childhood friend that on approaching the desk he could hardly pronounce his words. Fortunately, this proved to be unnecessary for the desk attendant seemed to understand who it was that John was seeking. He smiled, then asked John to be patient and stand to one side. A few minutes later John fell into the arms of his best friend and the two Africans began speaking as though one, so that neither could fully understand the words of the other. On this first evening the two of them ventured no further than the lobby of the hotel. They sat together, and John listened as he received information about his family. It appeared that his wife and child were safe and happy, apart from the natural anxiety of being separated from the head of the household. However, with regard to John's father, things were not good. Apparently William Narh Ocansey's health had declined, and the news of a probable financial calamity as a result of Robert W. Hickson's bankruptcy had done little to alleviate his problems. John felt somewhat depressed on hearing this sad report, but then he realized that he was in the presence of his friend and that there would be time enough for him to brood when alone.

After this most welcome and surprising evening, John

returned to Mrs Lyle's house where he was pleased to discover that his kind landlady was still awake. This gave him the opportunity to announce the news of his friend's arrival, which he did, but before he could continue with his recollection of the evening he found that Mrs Lyle had anticipated the direction that his conversation was going to take. She interrupted John, and wondered if his friend might wish to come and stay with them at Oxford Street. This pleased John enormously, and he said that he felt sure that his friend would be happy with this arrangement. John suggested that he would put this to Christian in the morning, and if he was agreeable then perhaps he might move in some time during the following afternoon.

John retired to his room, confident that his friend would soon be dwelling under the same roof as himself and therefore offering John the rare opportunity of conversation about familiar landscapes and people. However, the nature of his friend's journey to Liverpool, being very similar to his own, caused him some new dismay. It transpired that Christian had been trading with a Messrs Taylor and Co., of 72 Virginia Street, Glasgow, and he had sent to them African produce to the value of £183. After receiving the produce and realizing cash for it, the firm sadly failed, but without returning either produce or cash to Christian. They impudently suggested to Christian that they had an account due to them by 'some people in Grand Bassar', another place on the coast of Africa, and that Christian might secure payment from these people. The insulting suggestion that Christian Jacobson, a young man new to the trade, might collect his debts from another party, and one not involved in the initial transaction, was patently ridiculous. What was even more galling to both Christian and John was the ignorance of these Glasgow traders, who seemed not to understand the size and extent of Africa. Grand Bassar was a full sixteen days from Quitta by mail steamer, and furthermore there was no history of trade or dealings between these two different peoples. One might as well send a Frenchman to collect his English debt from a Turk. Being an enterprising young man, Christian journeyed to Sierra Leone by ship, where he continued to press his claim directly with the agents of Messrs Taylor and Co. He was informed by these agents that they were unable to help him, but they warned him that should he follow the 'Scottish suggestion' and reach Grand Bassar, then he would discover that the territory did not even fall under British protection of any kind. In fact, should he attempt to travel there and claim money from the native people, he ran the serious risk of being attacked and robbed, or even killed.

On hearing this news, Christian Jacobson had determined that he would travel to Britain and seek recompense. He therefore wrote to the trading company in Glasgow and told them of his impending arrival, but on arrival at his Liverpool hotel he had been met with a letter from the self-same Glasgow merchants which simply informed Christian that there was nothing that they could do for him. They had paid a partial compensation to some creditors, and the rest, including Christian Jacobson, would simply have to consider themselves unlucky. It was with much sadness that Christian told his friend John that he was not only now accustoming himself to a loss of £183, but he was resigned to losing the £54 that he had paid for his return passage, in addition to all the valuable time that he had invested in chasing this debt. John worried that this unhappy trading experience was bound to influence the way in which Christian thought about Englishmen in the future, and he remained baffled as to why men should wish to inflict injury upon their own race by behaving in such a low and unnecessary manner.

As they journeyed by carriage to Mrs Lyle's boarding-house, John tried to persuade Christian not to brand all Englishmen alike. He pointed out that he had now tarried for some time among them, and while there were undoubtedly those who were villains and thieves, the African trader had little choice but to send his goods to them. As far as John was concerned, the best way forward would be to learn their ways and therefore know better the nature of the people with whom they were dealing. John suggested to his friend that if he could learn from this journey to England, and apply the knowledge gained to some service in the future, then his sojourn in Liverpool need not be seen as a false investment of time and money. Further, he warned his friend that it made little sense to allow one's opinion of the general to be tarnished by the immoral behaviour of the few, and that while in England he should never allow himself to become either poisoned or bitter by listening to other people's low opinions of the African.

Noting that his friend did not immediately object to his suggestions, John pressed on and ventured that Christian might 'baptize' his time in Liverpool by recommitting himself to the ways of the Lord. John reasoned that if they must both suffer by the loss of worldly goods, then they should both also hope that in the future the Lord might recompense them in some other way. John insisted that they should strive to achieve the spirit of Job who, when he lost everything could still say: 'For we brought nothing into this world and it is certain we can carry nothing out; and having food and raiment let us therewith be content.' As they approached Mrs Lyle's house, John returned to an earlier subject and tried once more to convince his friend that many Englishmen of the city possessed great faith in Africa, and were sure that it would soon become one of the great continents of the world. Christian, respectful of his friend's experiences and opinions, said nothing, although to John's eyes he remained outwardly sceptical.

After introducing Christian to Mrs Lyle, and making sure that he was settled comfortably into his room, John proposed that they should walk the streets. It was, after all, part of John's declared plans to acquaint Christian with some of the many English sights and customs with which John was now familiar. They set out in their Sunday clothes, and John was pleased to note that although there was an evident struggle between sunshine and shadow, blue sky held the advantage. He took his friend down to the marketplace where he showed him stalls filled with butchers' meat, and all kinds of fowls, and fruit, and flowers, and vegetables. Thereafter, they visited the area around the docks where every building was either a warehouse or a shop or an office that was in some way connected with trade and commerce, while those that dwelt hereabouts were either merchants or servants of merchants. By revealing such sights to his friend, John hoped that Christian would be able to observe the organization of the Englishman, note the various degrees of men and women, and make a mental record of their trading actions. As it transpired, Christian seemed pleased to have been exposed to this particular 'lesson', and by the end of their first day he seemed satisfied that together they might usefully pass their time in Liverpool.

On the following Sunday, 17 July, John and Christian were invited by Mr Quilliam to attend an 'open-air' service. While John knew that such services were not the common practice in England, he realized that Mr Quilliam probably thought that this might be a good opportunity for the two Africans to see the 'darker' side of English life where those of a lower station—some of them fatally addicted to drink—found a place to worship. Such people were unlikely to find their way to a church, and it was therefore deemed to be the responsibility of the church to come to them, hence these so-called 'open-air' services.

En route, John stopped at a baker's shop, where he was able to point out to his friend the unique construction of the interior. The long and narrow shop possessed a counter that ran its full length, and customers stood to one side with the baker to the other. On the white countertop there was a huge pyramid of fresh butter, and to the side of this construction there was a pile of hot rolls fresh from the oven to which the customers were busily helping themselves. Mrs Lyle's breakfasts were substantial affairs, which besides muffins, crumpets, and Dundee marmalade, also featured smoked haddock and freshly boiled mackerel. This being the case, neither John nor Christian felt the urge to indulge themselves at the baker's counter.

The 'open-air' service was to be conducted at Gill Street market, a place with which John was familiar. To reach their destination the two men had to pass by an alehouse, and although Christian suggested that they might enter to observe the Englishmen at rest, John made it clear that having observed some of the refuse that emanated from such places he preferred to tarry on this side of the threshold. He did, however, share with Christian his knowledge that the Englishman, and woman, was particularly fond of a drink called 'swipes' that was known to possess a musty, sour taste and be made from the washings and rinsings of old beer barrels. Christian looked at his friend in disbelief, and he suddenly seemed relieved that John had taken the decision that they should bypass the alehouse and continue to the service.

Once there, the two men observed that there were almost a thousand people present, and that the vast majority of them were improperly attired. Clearly these were not regular chapel people, for some attended without their coats or hats, and could be seen to be smoking pipes. In addition, there were scores of untidy women with babies in their arms, and drunken, careworn men who were clad in their regular clothes without any allowance being given to the sacred nature of the assembly. However, these same individuals were soon weeping and seen to be deeply moved by the nature of the service, and to John's eyes they all seemed to possess a quality of patience which bordered on the tragic. Many of them wiped their eyes with their rags as a fair sermon was preached, and then they joined in wholeheartedly, if somewhat discordantly, to the singing of the hymns. Christian was greatly taken by the whole scene, and looked in awe at the wide range of people on display. As John tried to explain to him some of the goings-on about them, they were approached by a toothless and begrimed coloured man who styled himself 'Abraham'. It appeared that this man was very popular and well known, particularly among the young boys who freely addressed him with an intimacy that shocked the two friends. The coloured man was clearly pleased to see two fellow 'Africans', and in a transport of delight he fell to his knees, announced that he was from New York in America, and embraced the feet of both John and Christian. Then, climbing quickly to his full height, the dewy-eyed negro began to boast that in his country they have many fine churches, and he seemed keen to engage his 'brothers' in conversation.

Neither John nor Christian had anything to say to this man, whose dirty clothes and pungent breath announced that he was clearly existing at the lowest level of society. They noticed his chapped, raw hands, and Abraham quickly explained that during his years at sea the constant action of the salt water and the friction of sandy ropes had caused this disfigurement. Eventually Abraham withdrew, and a disturbed John found Mr Quilliam and made inquiries about this dark apparition. It transpired that Abraham earned his living as a 'knocker-up', which meant that in the mornings he would go by the residences of people who needed to be roused early in order that they might do business, and he would hammer loudly at their doors. For this menial service they paid him by the week. John felt intensely ashamed of this Abraham, and sensing John's discomfort Mr Quilliam quickly changed the subject and the three men thereafter retired to the house of the minister who had conducted this service. Once they reached the minister's house, John and Christian were encouraged to sing a hymn first in English, and then offer some entertainment by singing in their native language, which they did to the great amusement of those present. In this way the rest of Sunday passed quite agreeably, although John began to feel the dark cloud of depression once more sliding over him. The proposed day of the trial of Robert W. Hickson was drawing ever closer, and John could not help but think about the waste of time and money that this process was causing his family. True, he was broadening his understanding of the world, and he now had his dear friend for companionship, but John's heart remained heavy and his spirit miserable.

The day after the 'open-air' service, and without discussing the matter with John, Christian chose to return to Africa on a steamer whose captain had suddenly announced that he possessed a spare berth. Although John was disappointed to lose his companion, Christian's flight hardly surprised him. After all, what did his friend have to stay for? There was no pending trial in his case. At night John now lay in bed and found it impossible to think beyond his present predicament, while during the day he found it difficult to stir outside the confines of the house, for he no longer possessed the appetite to mix with people. What, he wondered, could he really expect from this trial? The sad truth was Robert W. Hickson had squandered his father's money. John constantly reminded himself of Mr Quilliam's reasoning on this matter, but as the trial drew ever closer, John realized that his one remaining hope was that this whole situation might now reach a speedy conclusion, which would enable him to return to his family in Africa.

For many years the African has been respected. But now the white man has cheated him of nearly everything that he owns. Abandoning his Christian beliefs, he makes desperate sacrifices to native Gods. But they have forgotten him. His life is running aground. The African has dispatched money to the white man. And now his heart is heavy with grief.

On the morning of Tuesday, 26 July 1881, Mr Justice Lopes presided over the opening of the Liverpool Assizes. It was determined that the business of the Assizes would commence at eleven o'clock, with Lord Chief Justice Coleridge presiding in the Civil Court, and Mr Justice Lopes in the Crown Court. As John left Oxford Street and briskly walked the mile or so to his lawyer's office, he hoped that his case might be presented early in the court's sitting, and dealt with swiftly. However, his lawyer had already informed him that there might well be unavoidable delays which he would be expected to tolerate. When John arrived at Mr Carver's office he was delighted to discover that everything was prepared, and that his lawyer was now confident that their case might be one of the first to come before Mr Justice Lopes. Mr Carver handed John the indictment, and suggested that he take a seat and read it at his leisure.

> Robert W. Hickson, Ship Owner, (trading as Hickson, Sykes and Co.), Insurance Broker, and Manager of the Mersey Marine Insurance Company, Carlton Buildings, 3, Rumford Street, Liverpool, charged with having, at Liverpool, on the 28th May, 1880, and subsequent other days, been entrusted by John. E. Ocansey and others, as a Merchant or Agent, with certain securities for the payment of money, with directions in writing to apply and pay the proceeds thereof for a certain purpose, specified in such directions, did, in violation of good faith, and contrary to the terms of such directions, convert to his own use and benefit such proceeds.

John handed the document back to Mr Carver, and informed his lawyer that he was ready to do whatever he deemed necessary.

On the following morning, 27 July, John Ocansey presented himself at St George's Hall, where he noticed that a sizeable crowd of people had already gathered on the steps. On making enquiry he discovered these people to be other individuals who had cases in the court, witnesses, jurymen, solicitors and their clerks, and a host of others, including those simply curious to see the proceedings unfold. At precisely ten o'clock, John noticed a commotion across the street where a carriage drawn by four splendid horses, their harnesses decorated with gold, drew up outside a hotel. The elderly driver was gaudily dressed in fine livery, as were his two footmen, and they waited by the main entrance to the hotel. As people became aware of the arrival of the carriage, they began to swarm towards the hotel, abandoning their previous vigil on the steps of St George's Hall.

John joined the rush, and as he crossed the road he was astonished to see that between twenty and thirty men, all dressed in large cloth coats, and with long pikes in their hands, were busily clearing a path from the hotel door to the carriage. Among them were three men with silver trumpets who, upon a secret signal, began to play. Dressed in his black gown, and with a broad band of scarlet cloth decorating the front of his robe, and a large powdered wig upon his head, the judge then emerged from the hotel and entered the carriage, which then easily negotiated the small distance between the hotel and St George's Hall. John rejoined the masses who were now making their way back across the road, and being a petitioner he was quickly ushered into the building and directed towards the courtroom.

Once in the courtroom, John looked around and saw a large chair upon a platform, which he assumed to be the place where the judge would eventually take his seat. John was struck by the order and hierarchy which surrounded the arrangements of the chamber. The public seating was to the front and set out in a semi-circle, while below the judge there were chairs for the officers who were in charge of preparing all the business, such as the swearing in of the jury, and calling out the names of the prisoners. Next to the chairs for these officers were two rows of seats for the barristers who, like the judge, were also known to wear black gowns and white powdered wigs upon their heads. Behind the barristers was the dock, where the prisoner stood while the trial was proceeding. John noticed that the dock was railed and guarded by policemen, and he could see that one could only gain direct access to this area from the cells below the courthouse. As the public began to filter into the courtroom, John sat quietly and waited for events to unfold.

After a long process of deliberation the twelve jury members were selected, and the officers called out their names from white cards as they took their places and were sworn in. Mr Quilliam had already told John that any jurors who failed to appear were immediately fined and that once the jury was sworn in, none but the judge or the barristers were allowed to address them directly and even then their every utterance had to be audible in open court. Once everything was in place, a pair of large folding doors was thrown open and the judge entered his domain. As he did so, everybody stood and bowed and the judge acknowledged their presence with a small bow of his own. The judge was a handsome man, with grey hair, a strong brow and dominating eyes. John understood that English custom was such that these ceremonies would be repeated on every morning that the court was in session, but as fascinating as he found these rituals, he longed for his own case to begin.

The greater part of the morning passed by with a mystified John unclear as to what he was expected to do, so he simply observed the proceedings and waited for instructions. He was eventually rescued from this state of ignorance by a clerk of the court, who approached and directed John to a room where he was told that he would have to appear before something called the Grand Jury. It transpired that this was a body composed of twenty-four merchants and gentlemen whose job it was to see that the charges against the prisoners were proper and lawful, and to make sure that the prosecutor and his witnesses were adequately briefed and prepared. By following this procedure it was understood that time could be saved and confusion avoided.

When John entered the room he was somewhat overwhelmed by the formality of the occasion. He saw that these men sat by themselves around a large table, assisted only by a small group of barristers. On the table before them, John saw all the letters and documents pertaining to his case, and then, without warning, the men began to ask him questions, but John was confident that he would be able to satisfy the men with his answers. The Grand Jury then summoned before them the lawyer representing the person who should have built the steam launch, and another lawyer who claimed to be acting on behalf of the broker who sold the Ocansey family's goods. Having questioned each party in turn, the Grand Jury decided that the case was properly prepared and instructed John to appear in court at ten o'clock the following morning.

John left the room of the Grand Jury, and then St George's Hall, relieved that this matter now appeared to be reaching a speedy conclusion. He walked back across the city to his lodgings, his mind attuned to his family, and in particular his wife and child back on the Gold Coast. It was many months since he had last seen them, and his heart, far from growing accustomed to their absence, was increasingly troubled by loneliness. John walked with his head bowed, for during his time in Liverpool the sights of the city had grown so familiar that he no longer felt any necessity to gaze about himself. He knew that he could never exhaust the complexity of Liverpool in one short stay, but the truth was, John no longer found the city about him of any interest. That night a disconsolate John lay in bed, his arms and legs knotted clumsily into the white sheet, listening to invisible dogs barking in the distance. As the poignant misery of dawn broke upon him, he watched closely as the shadows began to define themselves as a chair, a tall wardrobe and then a small table.

John dressed quickly, ate breakfast and then rushed to the Liverpool Assizes, where he was told that the case before the judge was murder and that in all likelihood it would last the whole day. The following morning being Friday, John again presented himself at the opening of the court, where he remained until noon, when the court officers announced that he should come back the following week. On Monday, John once more presented himself, but the case before the judge was a complicated one which concerned two men who were accused of attempting to blow up the Town Hall. Some officers of the court were convinced that John's case would be heard later this same day, but others said that he should return the following day. As John was feeling unwell, and it was by no means certain when his case would be heard, it was arranged that should he be needed then an officer would come for him at his lodgings. However, Monday afternoon and all of Tuesday passed with John ailing in bed, but no officer knocked at the door to 24 Oxford Street.

On Wednesday morning John presented himself in court, and the court officers were certain that his case would be brought this day. John waited until noon, when he was given the crushing news that his case had now been postponed until Thursday. A feverish John once more left the court, but when he returned the next day he heard the clerk call out for 'Robert William Hickson'. It was soon discovered that the aforementioned man was not in the courtroom, which caused John's heart to sink, but a gentleman quickly announced that Mr Hickson was temporarily indisposed and a policeman went to fetch him. A few moments later, John watched as a stout, nervous-looking man with a thick black moustache and a wave of silvery hair entered the dock and clung to the railing with both hands. As he did so, Hickson's wife rose from her seat and crossed the floor so that she might greet her husband with a kiss.

John looked closely at this man, whose demeanour seemed to betray a surprising lack of confidence. During the week-long delay, John had occasionally noticed a haughty Mr Hickson and his barrister as they whispered and planned. For his part, Mr Carver had originally advised John that Mr Hickson was thoroughly confident of acquittal, and thereafter he might even consider suing for false imprisonment. Mr Carver also informed his African client that Mr Hickson had employed the services of the most celebrated barrister in Liverpool, a man of cool and dispassionate demeanour named Mr J. B. Aspinall, who was also the Recorder of the City. However, as the week had passed by, and Mr Aspinall had apparently seized the opportunity to look more closely into the case, he had, according to Mr Carver, suggested to his client that there might indeed be a case for fraud. In fact, it was now Mr Aspinall's opinion that the best course of action might be for Mr Hickson to plead guilty and claim the merciful sentence of the judge. Having spoken with his client, Mr Aspinall had then sought out Mr Carver and pleaded hard on his client's behalf, but Mr Carver pointed out that if such cases were allowed to go unpunished then those Africans who were engaged in trade with England might be forever subject to being cheated. Mr Carver sought to convince his fellow barrister that there was nothing vindictive about John Ocansey's prosecution, and he concluded by informing Mr Aspinall that the case was prepared and must follow in the normal circumstances. Acknowledging all of this, Mr Aspinall then claimed that he believed there were extenuating circumstances and he hoped that these might excite the merciful consideration of the court. And with this said their conversation reached a conclusion, and they both adjourned in order to make final preparations for the trial which was set to be heard before Mr Justice Lopes.

On the appointed morning Mr Carver appeared on behalf of John Ocansey, while Mr Aspinall, QC, and a Mr Walton were for the prisoner. The charges, which were read by the clerk of the court, were as follows: Robert William Hickson was charged with having, on the eighth day of July, 1880, falsely pretended to John Emanuel Ocansey (trading under the name of W. N. Ocansey and Sons, native merchants, carrying on business at Adahpoah and other places on the West Coast of Africa) that he had entered into a contract under which a steam launch was to be built for the firm, by means of which false pretences he afterwards, on the 8th August, obtained a bill of lading for sixty-three bags of kernels, to be shipped in the steamer *Ethiopia*. The charges having been solemnly read out loud, Mr Hickson, the prisoner, pleaded 'not guilty'. A further charge was then read out, that on the twenty-eighth day of March, 1880, and subsequent other days, Mr Hickson was entrusted by Messrs Ocansey, as an agent, with securities for the payment of money (the proceeds of the sale of casks of palm oil) but he converted them to his own use and benefit in violation of good faith, and contrary to the terms of the directions, which he received in writ-

ing, to apply the proceeds. Having heard this particular indictment, the prisoner did not hesitate before pleading guilty as
charged.

What then followed was, as far as John could understand,
unusual even in an English court of law. To the first charge, to
which the prisoner had pleaded 'not guilty', it was decided
between the barristers that the prosecution would offer no evidence. Therefore, the judge addressed the jury and said, 'This is
an indictment charging the prisoner with obtaining money by
false pretences, but as the learned counsel for the prosecution
offers no evidence, you have only one course to pursue, and that
is to say that the prisoner is not guilty.' A formal verdict of 'not
guilty' was then taken. With regard to the second charge, to
which the barristers had agreed that Mr Hickson would plead
guilty, it now fell upon the defendant's barrister to make a case
in mitigation of punishment, and Mr Aspinall spoke to this end.

He began by trying to outline the way in which business was
generally conducted between Mr Hickson—a merchant who he
claimed was a man of some standing and reputation—and his
African 'partners' on the coast. Much emphasis was placed upon
the manner in which Mr Hickson credited his accounts with
goods received from Africa, and debited them with the value of
the consignments of goods that he shipped to Africa. Apparently, from time to time balances were drawn up to indicate the
state of play between both parties, but it was admitted that
there was no consistent pattern to this accounting. The barrister
then went on to make clear that the prisoner's produce broker
had a balance against the prisoner, and bills of lading for produce
that were sent to the broker were pledged against whatever balance there happened to be. In other words, the lines of credit in
this manner of trading were both complex and relied totally
upon trust. The scope for fraud was great in the ordinary course
of such business transactions.

Mr Aspinall claimed that his client had two establishments
on the coast of Africa, both of which were seriously damaged by

considerable fires in May and June of the previous year. The difficulties which Mr Hickson then experienced with insurance payments, which were inexplicably delayed, caused him to fall into debt which was then acted upon by the produce broker in England. Mr Aspinall stressed the fact that the goods that should have paid for the launch ought to have been set aside, and he acknowledged that Messrs Ocansey had been, through no fault of their own, the losers of £2,678 11s. 8d.

John listened to what the learned counsel for the defence had to say, and then it was the turn of his own barrister, Mr Carver, to present himself before the judge. Rising to his full height, Mr Carver referred the judge to all the papers pertaining to the balance of accounts between the two parties. One particular item was to be focused on, which was a letter of March 1880, in which specific instructions were received from Messrs Ocansey that the proceeds of all the produce sold by Hickson, through his agent, Messrs James Bowden and Co., should be set against the launch which Mr Hickson claimed to have ordered. In fact, said Mr Carver, Mr Hickson did not order the launch until December 1880, at which time more than sufficient consignments had been made. However, by this time, Mr Hickson had already pledged these consignments into the hands of the produce broker, who had settled Mr Hickson's account with the proceeds. By December 1880 there were no proceeds left with which to pay for the launch.

John was impressed by the clarity of Mr Carver's arguments, and the occasional nod and general assent of the judge suggested that he too was happy with the manner in which things had been laid out. At this juncture, Mr Aspinall sought to take the opportunity of once again arguing a case for his client's having slipped unfortunately into this present state through ill-advised business practices, but at the prompting of Mr Carver the judge clearly understood that by not carrying out the specific instructions to set aside the profit from the consigned goods against the price of the launch, and by not ordering the launch at all, the defendant had gone against the law of the land. Mr Aspinall claimed that the charge of fraud that had already been dropped suitably covered all the questions concerning the delay in ordering the launch, but the judge would hear nothing of this plea.

The judge pointed out that Mr Aspinall could not claim that his client had merely drifted into the situation, for it was clear that he purposefully neglected to order the launch. Further, the judge forcefully dismissed Mr Aspinall's repeated attempts to place the matter within the confines of the case of fraud that had already been spoken to, and he also dismissed Mr Aspinall's 'new' claim that the delay in ordering the launch was related to discussions between Mr Hickson and the boatbuilders with regard to the character and price of the vessel. Again the judge pressed Mr Aspinall to explain why his client should lead Messrs Ocansey to believe that the launch had been ordered in March, when in fact his client chose not to do so until December. Having tried once more to invoke the argument that such a question belonged properly to the dismissed case, Mr Aspinall finally relented and admitted that an untruth had been told to the Ocanseys. However, he soon changed tack, and now claimed that the launch had not been ordered because, in fact, there were not sufficient funds presented by the Ocanseys, and Mr Hickson was not prepared to take on a huge debt for the launch without having the money to hand. But Mr Aspinall did not stop here.

He returned again to the question of details that had to be settled with the boatbuilders, and handed to the judge a sketch that had arrived from 'the people in Africa' who, according to Mr Aspinall, did not know much about launches. He claimed that such a sketch, and the accompanying instructions, would not much help an English boatbuilder. Mr Aspinall persisted, and again he stated that 'in the normal course of business' there was nothing in the defendant's balance sheet, as late as 30 September, that gave any rise to questions relating to his ability to pay for the launch. John was by now somewhat tired of hearing this barrister repeat tedious and inaccurate details of his case, and clearly the judge felt similarly. Having once more listened to Mr Aspinall's argument, Mr Justice Lopes simply stated, 'I will read over the deposition again, and call the prisoner up for sentence.' And so the trial was over.

The prisoner was immediately led away by a policeman to the cells below the dock, and John was instructed by his lawyer that he should remain in the building for the judge might wish to ask him a few more questions by way of explanation. As instructed, John waited, but to no real purpose for at the end of the day a clerk of the court told him to go home and report back in the morning. Frustrated and exhausted, John left St George's Hall and made his slow way through the crowded streets of Liverpool towards his lodgings. Once there, a kind Mrs Lyle welcomed him with a newspaper and a hot meal, after which John read his Bible and fell into a deep but restless sleep.

In the morning, John discovered that, for the first time, he could not stomach Mrs Lyle's breakfast. She appeared to understand John's dilemma, and made it clear that his inability to eat in no way offended her. A grateful John left her house and began the familiar journey across Liverpool to St George's Hall. Once there, he joined his lawyer in the courtroom, where they both noticed that there was a new tension about the judge's demeanour. No longer was he relaxed and confident; he appeared now to be impatient. In fact, there was a sternness about his deportment which alarmed John. He turned to Mr Carver, but his lawyer did not appear to be in the slightest distressed by this change of manner and encouraged his client to remain calm. John, however, felt a cold film of sweat begin to line his palms, and he moved uneasily in his seat.

The unshaven prisoner was brought up before Mr Justice Lopes, and without any hesitation the judge turned swiftly to face him. He addressed the prisoner in the following words.

Robert William Hickson, you have pleaded guilty to having misappropriated a large sum of money which had been entrusted to you as an agent. You were also indicted for obtaining a very large sum of money by false pretences. No evidence was offered on that indictment, and you were acquitted. I desire to say that if that indictment had been proceeded with, and you had been convicted, I should have felt it to be my duty to direct you to be placed in penal servitude for a considerable time, because the offence would be a most serious one. The offence to which you have now pleaded guilty is also a most serious one. Everything that could be said in your favour was urged by your counsel in palliation of the charge against you, and that charge is that you misappropriated something like £2,600. It has been said that you got into difficulties, and that you drifted into this act of dishonesty. It appears that in the month of March, 1880, you received special orders to purchase a steam launch for your employers in West Africa, and it also appears that you did not order it until December of that year. In the interval money enough had come into your hands to pay for it, the whole of which you did not apply to the purpose you were directed to apply it, but devoted it instead to your own purposes. I am desirous, as far as I possibly can, to give effect to any extenuating circumstances which I can find in your favour; but I cannot help saying that I find great difficulty in discovering any in this case, and I can pass upon you no other sentence than that you be imprisoned with hard labour for fifteen calendar months.

John Ocansey listened carefully to every word, and once the sentence had been pronounced he felt as though a great burden had been lifted from his person. His thoughts immediately turned to his father, who he knew would be relieved that he could now look to the future and put this unhappy incident behind him. It transpired that Mr Hickson's affairs were in a worse state than John had imagined, but a delighted Mr Carver shook his client's hand and informed him that when everything was settled Hickson's many creditors, including John, would receive something in the region of two shillings and sixpence in the pound. In other words, a considerable loss. John thanked his lawyer, who had served him honourably during the full extent of the trial and, casting a final glance around the courtroom, he stepped out of the chamber and into the lobby of St George's Hall. For what he imagined to be the last time, John Ocansey began the familiar walk across Liverpool towards his lodgings. With each successive step it became increasingly clear to John that this long and murky chapter was finally closed, and he could begin to put Liverpool behind him. However, this realization did not ease his passage. He walked slowly now, burdened by sorrow as he began to regret the months that he had been forced to endure apart from his wife and child.

When John arrived at his lodgings, the dark look on Mrs Lyle's face gave him cause for grave concern. Without even inquiring after the results of the day's proceedings, she simply handed him some letters, the most prominent among them being an envelope with a black border which indicated bereavement. John swallowed deeply for he could see that this letter had originated in Africa. He knew that death was the door through which everybody had to eventually pass, but his hands trembled as he fumbled at the seal. A nervous Mrs Lyle touched his arm and she asked if he would like some water. John shook his head, and then he prayed that his God might give him the strength of mind and body to suffer whatever news he was about to receive. On opening the letter there was relief, albeit guilty relief, for the letter announced that it was his seventy-six-year-old grandmother who had gone to her eternal rest. John felt the dampness beneath his collar, and his landlady grasped his hand and encouraged him to take a seat. Thereafter, she went to fetch him a glass of water, and John wiped his brow with a large white handkerchief. He pictured his grandmother, her eyes cloudy with cataracts, her leathery skin furrowed with the ridges of old age. She was watching him. She was still watching him. Mrs Lyle handed John the glass of water and stood to one side. She was watching him. John knew that it was time to go. It was time for him to return to Africa.

John sat in his room and looked out of the window. It was a warm English summer's night, and even at this late hour people ambled back and forth going casually about their business. John wiped the mist from the window with the back of his hand, but everything still appeared to be opaque and indistinct. He realized that his eyes were brimming with tears. His mind drifted back to a beach. He remembered how everyone had crowded together and waved him goodbye as the SS *Mayumba* began to depart the coast. As he remembered, John fell to his knees and prayed that his Lord might preserve him in health so that he might return home safely. As John knelt in this small bedroom in Liverpool, it occurred to him that perhaps he would have seen this city in a different and more generous light had the troubles of his father's business not dominated his mind. However, he was grateful for the few friends that he had made, and the kindnesses that he had received. In the morning he would make preparations in order that he might leave Liverpool as quickly as possible. Thereafter, he would set out on the long journey home.

The African dispatches the money to the white man and his African heart swells with pride. The African hopes for a new dawn; a brighter future. Luck has not been on his side. For many years now there have been problems. But, with the help of the white man, he can once again become great. Time passes. The white man is silent.

POSTSCRIPT

Yet, how calm, innocent, how staid Liverpool looked in the June sunshine! What massive and solidly built buildings! From my train window I could catch glimpses of a few church spires punctuating the horizon. Along the sidewalks men and women moved unhurriedly. Did they ever think of their city's history?

RICHARD WRIGHT, *Black Power* (1954)

As the train pulls in to Liverpool's Lime Street Station, I am struck by the satanic quality of the station. Pigeons fly overhead, darting in and out of broken windows. The station is a throwback to an era of Victorian expansionism when huge arches and long black platforms were the norm. Somehow Lime Street's crumbling grandeur seems appropriate for a city which has long recognized itself as being in a state of decline. I decide to take a taxi from the train station to my hotel, although I suspect that it is not very far. This is confirmed as I slide into the back seat of the cab and announce my destination. The taxi driver spins around in his seat and looks at me in disbelief. 'Something wrong with your legs, whack?' The driver starts to laugh, his shoulders shaking as though independent of the rest of his body. And then he turns back round and begins to drive off. I look in his rear-view mirror and can see that he is muttering to himself and shaking his head. But he seems happy and his eyes are bright. This encounter is, I presume, an example of the famous Liverpool humour.

We drive through a city centre which has clearly been subjected to the irrational urban planning that characterizes most British cities. Overpasses, underpasses, roads that have been randomly deemed 'one-way', unnecessary pedestrian zones and narrow streets that suddenly bloat into four-lane highways. Although I now know that the hotel is very close to the train station, the journey seems to be taking for ever. I peer anxiously out of the window of the cab, eager to see two things. First, black faces. I was surprised that at Lime Street station there was a distinct absence of black faces. At most major train stations in Britain one expects to see black porters or ticket collectors. My father, when he first came to England in the fifties, worked as a labourer on the railways and some childhood reflex in me has always associated British train stations with black faces.

I also find myself looking for the sea. I half-expected to step out of Lime Street Station and on to a seashore promenade, so closely do I associate Liverpool with the sea. But as the cab spins its circular way through the city, and the taxi driver begins to sing in a loud and discordant voice, I can see nothing that is even vaguely maritime. And then suddenly, at the bottom of a steep hill, I see the River Mersey. A wide, murky river, it appears—at least to my eyes—to be singularly uninspiring. On the far bank of the river is the middle-class enclave known as The Wirral, and somewhere beyond The Wirral lies the open sea. The cab swings past the huge Cunard building, and then the architecturally ambitious Liver building, both of which I recognize from my guidebook, and then we turn inland again, and I am deposited at my hotel.

I stand idly at the hotel desk while the receptionist pro-grammes the key to my room. Then she quizzes me about how long I am staying and which newspaper I want in the morning. I am somewhat puzzled by the nature of the accent. Her high voice has a melodious quality that is noticeably different from the elongated flattened vowels that I traditionally associate with the north of England. There is, in fact, an undeniably upbeat trill to the sound of the woman's voice. As I am finally dispatched to my room, programmed key in hand, I realize that I am actually looking forward to my time in Liverpool.

I first sensed that there was something disturbing about Liver-pool when, as an eleven-year-old boy, I stood on the terraces watching my team, Leeds United, play against the Liverpool-based club, Everton. At that time Everton, in common with most football clubs in England, possessed no non-white players.

In fact, when the occasional non-white player did have the temerity to run out onto an English football pitch, he would invariably be subjected to a volley of racist baying. Every time he touched the ball the crowd would erupt in anger, and it was extremely common for bananas to be thrown at the black players. Such was Britain in the sixties and seventies. I remember my palpable discomfort as I watched West Ham United's Bermudan striker, Clyde Best, on his annual visits to Leeds United. For the life of me, I could never determine why he put himself through this hell. With Everton, there was never any danger of their fielding a black footballer. In fact, as time wore on, and club after club capitulated to the inevitability of signing non-white players, Everton held out. They were the last of the elite football teams in Britain to sign a black player.

On this particular Saturday afternoon, I found myself standing on the terraces next to a group of a half-dozen Everton fans. 'Lads' in their thirties, with cigarettes permanently pasted to their lips, scarves around their necks, and beer bellies protruding over the waistline of their jeans. I listened to their Liverpudlian banter, and was lulled into a false sense of security. One of them asked a question about a Leeds United footballer that the others could not answer. I answered the question. Almost as one, they turned in my direction. 'Fuck off! We're scousers and we don't talk to niggers.' For many years afterwards, I was always careful to distinguish Liverpool from Manchester, or any of the other northern industrial cities. In my mind, Liverpool was a place to be avoided. A dangerous place.

In the early eighties, Liverpool was one of the British cities that exploded in a fury of inner-city violence. The damage in Liverpool was so extensive that the government appointed a special minister to deal with the problems of Liverpool alone. In 1985 Liverpool football club (Everton's cross-town rivals) signed John Barnes, the most talented footballer in Britain. He happened to be black. Many in Liverpool, including Liverpool fans, were not happy about this development, and the rancour and bigotry that was unleashed was shocking to many outside of the city. During the late eighties, Liverpool found it difficult to stay out of the news. In 1985 rioting Liverpool football fans contributed to the violence which resulted in the death of thirty-nine Italian fans at the Heysel stadium in Belgium. In 1989, ninety-four Liverpool football fans were killed in a dreadful crush at Hillsborough football ground in Sheffield. As Margaret Thatcher's Britain split, and became in essence two nations—one to the north and one to the south—it was clear that Liverpool, the former grand industrial city of the north, was succumbing to the prevailing blight of violence, unemployment, poverty and depression at a rate that was far in excess of other British cities.

By the early nineties I had determined that I should go and see this place for myself, but I hesitated. And then, during an extended period in the United States, I found myself reading article after article about the regeneration of the north of England, including Liverpool. One day I turned on the television and saw a football match between Liverpool and Everton. A local derby, full of all the tension and passion that characterizes such encounters. However, what struck me forcefully was the fact that not only were there countless non-white faces on display, but the captain of Liverpool was a black man. What had happened to the shouting and the name-calling? The banana-throwing? Had Liverpool really changed? I did not recognize this suspiciously multiracial Liverpool.

In the evening, Stephen, my guide to Liverpool, arrives at the hotel and I suggest that we first have a drink in the bar upstairs. To my horror, the bar turns out to be 'themed' along the lines of a ship. As I wait for the drinks, I stare out of the window at the uninspiring skyline of Liverpool. Beyond the rooftops and chimneys I can just about glimpse the gloomy waters of the Mersey. And then the bored and lavishly over-scented barmaid hands me my change, and I detach my beer and Stephen's orange juice from the sticky bar top. The bar is empty, apart from two businessmen in suits, who are concentrating with great intensity on their video game. However, as I cross the carpeted space with the drinks, they both look up. Stephen eyes them as he takes his orange juice. 'You'd think they'd never seen black people before.' I suggest that perhaps they are not used to seeing black people in this particular hotel. Stephen laughs dismissively. 'Listen, man. This is the end of the twentieth century.' I look over at the two men, but they are once more concentrating on their game. 'They were staring at us like we're gonna nick something.' Stephen sips his orange juice, but he appears to be getting angrier by the minute.

Stephen is a strikingly tall young man of twenty-three. He left school at sixteen and began to work, but although he is erudite and clearly interested in literature, he never went on to university. His passion is Liverpool's hidden history; its black history, and in particular the city's relationship to the slave trade. Some months earlier the BBC in London had arranged for Stephen to travel to West Africa with a radio producer in order that he might record a personal documentary about going 'home'. In Stephen's case 'home' was deemed to be Elmina in Ghana, a small town which contains one of the best preserved of the many West African slave forts. Stephen visited Elmina Castle and talked about its significance as 'a place which reminds us of where we came from'. His programme, which he entitled *In the Belly of the Beast*, generated media interest and attracted a respectable audience.

Shortly after returning to Liverpool, Stephen was asked to participate in a local radio programme in which he was interviewed about the experience of making his personal documentary. In the ensuing discussion, the question of Liverpool's 'African' history emerged. Apparently a local councillor had decided that it would be a good idea to rename The Goree, one of the main streets of Liverpool, and call it Lottery Way. He argued that the name 'The Goree' was 'embarrassing' because it referred to the infamous island off the coast of Senegal where a slave fort, like the one at Elmina, was located. Stephen objected to the councillor's suggestion, and pointed out that by renaming the street in this manner the city would be endorsing the historical amnesia which already prevailed. When the phone lines were opened up the councillor in question called in and made his case, and the programme then descended into a 'discussion' that only just stopped short of a blazing row. Having been sent a taped copy of both Stephen's original documentary and the local radio programme, I had decided that I would like to meet Stephen.

'You see,' he begins, taking another small sip of his orange juice, 'Liverpool people don't want to acknowledge their own history. They don't want you to know what built this town, and how the exploitation of black people has formed the basis of all the wealth around here.' Again he looks beyond me to the two businessmen. 'These guys, all of them really, they have a kind of guilt problem. They don't know what to do about us, because we're not going away. We also remind them of stuff they don't want to think about.'

I wonder aloud if such people really do feel guilt, or if their discomfort is based on something else? Perhaps something as simple as curiosity? Or perhaps something as profound as hatred? I cannot be sure, but I suggest to Stephen that offering up guilt as a reason for their discomfort appears to me to be surprisingly generous.

'No, no, no,' insists Stephen. 'You see, they're guilty because they know. That's the thing. If they didn't know, then it would be just a matter of what you're saying. But they know. You can't help but know in Liverpool.'

'Know what?' I ask.

'Know that they've been involved in slavery, but they just want it to go away so they don't have to deal with it. That's what I'm saying about guilt. It's really bad news, but everyone around these parts has got it because people don't talk. It's a segregated city. The whites have their bit, and we have our bit, and that's it. Which is weird for a place which has one of the most multicultural histories of any town in Britain, right?'

I listen to Stephen, and then I decide that I will order another round of drinks. I want to see if the two men will talk to me, or even acknowledge me, as I walk by them to the bar. I also decide that tonight I will not venture out into Liverpool with Stephen as I had originally planned. I want to listen to him talk about his city, and to discover more about his feelings for its history. Stephen is wound tight, like a metal coil. I have met young men like this before, intelligent men who exist in a liminal zone where the line between creativity and self-destruction is etched vaguely into the sand.

I pass quite close to the two men, but although they stare, neither man actually says anything. The fragrant barmaid makes no secret of the fact that she finds it irritating to have to deal with an order that consists of one small beer and an orange juice. However, she manages to paste a smile to her face as she hands me my change, and I am almost grateful when I hear her sing-song voice tell me, 'There you go, love.' Once more she takes up a perch on her stool, and she continues to watch her television programme. I walk slowly by the two men, but again they merely stare. I put down the drinks in front of Stephen, who looks at me, then across at the two men, then back at me. He shakes his head.

In the morning I get up early and decide to go for a walk around Liverpool before the day stirs. It is already light, and clouds race across the still visible moon. Walking through the city centre I pass Dixons, Woolworths, Boots the Chemists, McDonalds; in fact, all the familiar stores are laid out along both sides of the ubiquitously dull pedestrian precincts. In the bleak morning haze, the odd pedestrian slouches by with collar turned skyward and hands thrust deep into their pockets. It seems too early to be going to work and it is definitely too late to be coming home from a club. Peering down the full length of one precinct, I see the strange sight of a boy with a skateboard practising by himself. As I walk towards him the deafening clatter of his skateboard grows louder. I secrete myself in a shop doorway and watch him. The boy's sallow, grim features are contorted into a mask of concentration as he tries again and again to perform a single trick—a trick which he appears to be incapable of mastering. I stare at him as though I have a vested interest in his success or failure. Sadly, the predetermined conclusion of his strange labour appears to be that he should repeatedly fall from his skateboard and watch it glide away from him and into the concrete base of a Liverpool City Corporation planter.

I cross a broad street, recognizing it as one that the taxi drove along the previous day. I walk up to the Cunard building and can see that carved into its façade are the names of the major ports in the world that this huge shipping company has done business with over the years. The word 'Africa' leaps out at me. Ships to Africa. The multiple ports of this huge continent are represented by this one word. Behind the Cunard building are the medley of docks, one leading to the other, which together create a formidable bulwark against the river. Huge concrete structures, they now lie empty like vast swimming-pools. I walk past Salthouse Dock, and then Albert Dock, and then I take a seat on a wooden bench. Overhead the gulls are wheeling lazily, riding the now stiff morning breeze. Behind me the Mersey lies silent. In front of me cars are beginning to ease their way along the road. Morning is breaking. Another Liverpool day is about to begin. Never before have I seen a day brighten to grey with more undisguised reluctance.

My mind drifts back to the previous evening. I had asked Stephen about the councillor with whom he had had the disagreement on the local radio programme. Our conversation then quickly broadened into a discussion about local politicians in general, Jewish politicians in particular. 'You see, it's the Jews', said Stephen. 'Everywhere they go they just take from the black community and they give nothing back.' Sipping on his orange juice, a focused Stephen continued. 'We've got a guy here in Liverpool who's always talking about how blacks and Jews ought to stick together, a Jewish guy, that is—a politician—but when it comes down to it he does nothing for us.' I told Stephen that I thought his analysis was at best simplistic, at worst offensive, but he looked at me as though I were the pitiful victim of some awful brain-washing experiment.

'The Jews', he continued, 'are our worst enemy, but they always play at being our friends. Malcolm said this, and he was right.' By now I was becoming exasperated and I tried to point out the dangers, to say nothing of the ironies, of making such judgements, but Stephen persisted. 'They were involved in the slave trade. They used us back then, and they're still using us now.' Being familiar with the fallacious argument that the Jews were somehow largely responsible for the slave trade, I decided to listen and see if Stephen presented any evidence for his assertions. Predictably, he did not, and my evening in the bar with Stephen collapsed as he became increasingly frustrated with my inability to acknowledge Jewish culpability, and I grew increasingly worried that I had perhaps chosen the wrong person to act as a guide during my time in Liverpool.

My reverie is disturbed as the traffic increases in volume. Sitting on a bench down by the docks, I imagine that I must seem an odd sight to those trudging their way to work. I decide that it is time to move on. I cross the street and head back towards the centre of Liverpool, but unsurprisingly it starts to rain. I stop and buy a newspaper, and then I find a small café. As I push open the door I hear the tinkling of a bell, and then I feel the pleasing rush of warmly scented air. I take my chipped mug of black coffee to a seat in the far corner by the steamed-up window, and only now do I realize that this is a place for derelicts. But this is fine by me, for I feel surprisingly at home. I am not seeing Stephen until the evening, so I have ample time to read the newspaper and then plan how I am going to spend my day in Liverpool.

Having had a second cup of coffee, I step purposefully out of the café and into the light drizzle. I begin to walk in the direction of the Town Hall, but after some panic-stricken moments I stop and unfold my rudimentary map. For a city supposedly mired in problems of unemployment there seems to be a great deal of resolve to the manner in which the pedestrian traffic is charging through the busy maze of narrow streets. Understandably, nobody has time to stop and help this disorientated stranger, and the stranger himself is, of course, too proud to ask.

Eventually, I approach Liverpool Town Hall from the rear. I turn off a main street, and then pass through a narrow alleyway and find myself standing in a huge square that I know from the map to be the Exchange Flags. It is here that trading was conducted in the eighteenth and nineteenth centuries, and the chief topic of conversation on these Flags would have been the current prices of cloves, sugars, rum, spices and other exotic commodities. Hundreds of the traders would meet daily and mill about so that this open square was in many respects the stock exchange of its day. On this wet, overcast morning, the Exchange Flags is abandoned. I look around and can see that on three sides the square is bounded by tall office buildings, and on the fourth side is the back of the Town Hall. It is clear that this deserted square has long outlived its original purpose.

I walk to the middle of the square where an imposing monument occupies pride of place. Around a fountain, which was built to celebrate Admiral Nelson's victories at sea, there is a powerful sculpture of four semi-clad and chained men. Each French 'prisoner' is meant to represent one of Nelson's significant sea victories; however, it is impossible to look at this fountain and its sculpture and not think of the slave trade. In fact, when Herman Melville visited Liverpool and laid eyes on the monument, he remarked that the four figures reminded him of the slaves of Virginia and Carolina. On this dismal morning, the fountain is not actually working, but the impact of the monument is no less striking because of this. I walk around it in a slow circle, and then my solitude is interrupted by the clicking of high heels as a solitary woman strikes her hasty way across the square.

To approach the Town Hall from the rear is to be immediately struck by its huge grandeur. Built in 1754, it is a testament to the immense wealth of the Liverpool trading merchants. I circumnavigate the building and can see that high up near the roof there is a frieze that 'subtly' depicts the images that were central to the development of Liverpool's trading empire: llamas, cocoa pods, a Native American woman with a bow, an elephant, an African face, a rhinoceros and so on. I had read, in my guidebook, that it is not possible to view inside the Town Hall, except on official business or on a guided tour, but as I reach the front of the Town Hall I decide to take a chance and wander in.

Once inside the doors, the traffic is magically muted and I find myself in a lobby with a huge vaulted ceiling. There is nobody in sight, and the building appears to have been abandoned. As I walk towards another set of doors, which promise to lead me into the interior of the building, a uniformed security guard emerges. I know, however, by his untucked shirt, and the tie that hangs helplessly beneath his top button, that this man is not going to prove a major obstacle. When I tell him that I am from London and that I merely wish to look around, he says that this will be all right. But not before he has glanced furtively about him, as though checking to make sure that nobody is eavesdropping on our conversation. The exterior of Liverpool Town Hall, although undeniably grand, gives absolutely no hint of what is contained inside. I discover the building to be a truly spectacular repository of marble, crystal, oil paintings and gilt. I pad my way from one room to the next, feeling increasingly glutted with the visual evidence of excess, until I finally succumb to a strange feeling of disgust. I decide to seek fresh air.

From Liverpool Town Hall I make my way back across the city centre towards St George's Hall, which my guidebook has led me to understand was built in 1841 as a public meeting place for the citizens of Liverpool. To get there, I have to cross some of the precincts that I had passed through earlier in the morning. The skateboarder is no longer there, but there are countless young people camped outside buildings, holding pieces of cardboard on which are written signs of pathetic brevity. 'Hungry'. 'Need food'. 'Homeless'. 'Spare change'. I find it surprising that the greater number of these young people seem to have a dog with them, invariably a scrawny-looking mongrel on the end of a piece of frayed rope which seems to be much happier with life than its owners.

St George's Hall is an enormous neo-classical edifice that was built with the express purpose of rivalling Athens's Acropolis. Flanked by lions, and supported on a seemingly endless row of columns, it is one of Britain's truly great buildings. My guidebook sternly informs me that St George's Hall is only open to the public for a few days each year, but I am hopeful that I might be able to pull off the same coup that I managed at the Town Hall. I present myself in front of the huge wooden doors and find myself face to face with an elderly woman who, with arms folded and piercing eyes, seems determined to discourage me from making any inquiry. I ask, as innocently as I can, if I might just take a quick look inside. She looks me up and down, and then relents. 'The floor's covered up, but you can still see a part of it.' She assumes that I want to see the famous mosaic tiled floor, which is the building's chief attraction, but in order that I might glean some insight into the former imperial splendour of Liverpool, I am actually hoping that I might be able to see the whole of the hall.

Whether out of a sense of pity, or whether she is simply puzzled by this rain-sodden stranger clutching a guidebook, she nods her head and says that I can take a quick look around. However, she insists that there is not much to see at present because the building is being renovated. She leads me into the main hall, which I am astonished to discover is about the size of a football pitch. The mosaic floor is indeed covered over by protective wooden boards, but a small corner is exposed and it is possible to see the immaculate quality of the finishing. With arms apparently permanently folded, the woman takes the lead, shuffling along and all the while attempting to keep me informed. She offers no facts, only opinions; 'I like the way the light comes through those top windows.' She gestures with her head. 'Up there.'

Eventually she escorts me to the only other part of the hall that is open to view, which is the law courts. There are, in fact, two courts, one at either end of the main hall, but the one she shows me has the distinction, so she claims, of having played host to one of the last hanging cases in England. The darkly lacquered wooden panelling, the carefully described semicircle of seats for the public, the prisoner's dock to which one can only gain access from the cell below, the high platform for the judge, all of this instils the chamber with a sonorous sense of decorum. We stand in silence and look around, and then my guide asks me where I am from. When I say 'London' she looks at me half in amusement, half in pity. 'Oh, down there, love', is all she can think of to say. Then, as a coda, she adds, 'I prefer it up here myself. I've never been one for travel.'

I decide to have lunch in a city-centre pub. I step through the door and my feet sink into the beer-stained carpet which still has enough cushion in it for me to know that, despite its appalling condition, it must have been recently installed. Linoleum would have been a better option in this pub. There are a half-dozen people scattered about the public bar, all concentrating on their newspapers and sipping at their solitary pints of ale. On closer inspection I am able to discern that they all appear to be reading the same publication. *The Racing Post.* They grip small pencils with which they occasionally mark the newsprint, and then they take another sip of their beer and resume their studying.

For some bizarre reason, the juke-box is blaring out a Christmas tune. John Lennon is singing 'Merry Christmas, War is Over'. A Liverpudlian voice, so at least this aspect of the 'entertainment' makes sense. At the bar I order a pint of lager, but having surveyed the menu (scampi and chips, or tuna bap, or cheese and pickle), I decide to forgo the food option and eat at my hotel. The barman has a solid boulder for a stomach, and as he pulls my pint I realize that I have now spent a whole morning walking, sitting and talking in Liverpool, and aside from a few solitary faces in the street, I have not encountered a single black person. Where on earth is the Liverpool black population? I take my pint to the corner of the pub, near the window, so that I can look at the midday shoppers and office workers. Why does everybody seem clinically depressed? I take a sip of the warm beer and then gently place my pint back into its watery circle. And then another Christmas song comes on the juke-box ('Merry Christmas Everybody' by Slade) and it occurs to me that I felt more at ease in the derelict's café. I resolve to leave the pub after this one pint.

When Stephen walks into the hotel I am sitting in the lobby in a well-upholstered armchair, eager to get on with the business of seeing Liverpool. A jovial Stephen, hands pushed deeply into his pockets, asks me where I have been, and I tell him. Much to my relief there appears to be no hint of the acrimony of the previous evening. Uninvited, Stephen slumps into the sister armchair with a proprietorial ease that causes both the bellman and the woman behind the desk to look over at him, and then glance at each other. I catch their exchange and understand what they mean by it. Although I am anxious to leave the hotel, I decide that we will sit for a while longer until Stephen is ready to make a move. He asks me what I think about the Town Hall and St George's Hall, both of which he describes as 'incredible'. To Stephen's way of thinking, it is not so much the physical evidence of the wealth as the 'secret' manner in which it has been accrued that is 'incredible'. It greatly concerns him that people do not know the true story of how and why these buildings came to be built. It is beginning to concern me too. On this we can agree.

We eventually leave the hotel lobby and Stephen begins to drive towards the university area to the north of the city centre. He wants to show me Liverpool's Georgian architecture; the terraces, squares and crescents that are reminiscent of Bristol, Bath and London. Liverpool contains more listed buildings than any British city except London, but Stephen tells me that these days the elegant Georgian neighbourhood is largely dominated by the university, and that many of the houses now host university departments and administrative offices. The place that Stephen seems particularly keen to show me is a building that he claims effectively served as the confederate embassy during the American Civil War.

Even before we enter 19 Abercromby Square, I can see the evidence of a southern history. Eight stars representing the eight rebel states are embossed around the twin columns which flank the door, and above the entrance there is a single white star which represents the state of South Carolina, the first state to secede from the Union. There is a regal southern grandeur to the architectural design, which suggests that the building was constructed with status in mind. I step inside the door and look up. The ceiling of the lobby is decorated with a painting of a cabbage palmetto, the state tree of South Carolina. Stephen points out the immaculate spiral staircase that on the first-floor level boasts the sculpted heads of Carolina panthers. He then informs me that this house was originally built for Charles Kuhn Prioleau, a financial agent for the American confederate government who originated from Charleston. I look around and see that Mr Prioleau's house is now dominated by filing cabinets, coffee machines, and the humdrum business of university life. I ask Stephen about other houses in Liverpool which speak of the connection between Liverpool and the southern states during the American Civil War, and he shrugs his shoulders and tells me that if I wish to see more then he will take me, but it will mean going back in the direction that we have just come from.

Stephen dips quickly into a rare parking space and then straightens out the car. I look around and immediately recognize the street as being close to my hotel. As soon as we step from the car, my guide points to the various doors that are decorated with the flags and emblems of the different southern states. The houses of Rumford Place were reception houses for those from the south. 12 Rumford Place was Charleston House, but these days it is the office of Gerald Eve, Chartered Surveyors. At the outbreak of the Civil War, Charleston was the fourth largest city in the United States, after New York, Boston and Philadelphia. By the end of the war Charleston lay devastated and in decline. Like Liverpool, the city of Charleston also possesses a hidden history that is centred on the slave trade. While eighteenth-century Liverpool was the most important slave port in Europe, Charleston occupied the same position in North America. Discovering Charleston in Liverpool is strange, although the logic of this discovery is, of course, perfect.

By now it is getting dark and I ask Stephen if he would mind driving me around Liverpool 8, which I have been led to believe is the district in which most black people in Liverpool live. As we wind our way out of the city centre, Stephen begins to explain that 'Liverpool Born Blacks' (LBBs) are 'a slightly different breed' from those blacks that I might find in other parts of the country. Apparently, LBBs do not take kindly to black outsiders, for they consider their own long and continuous history in Liverpool as evidence of a certain authenticity. For instance, Stephen informs me that he can trace his own family back to 1842, during which time they have moved about five miles, from the dock area to Stanhope Street. In 1842, Stephen's great-great-great-great-great grandfather married an Irishwoman called Hannah Stubbs in Liverpool's Church Street. This is how far back Stephen can trace his 'roots', and his voice swells with pride as he gives me this information.

Stephen is adamant that because of their 'longevity', LBBs do not recognize themselves as being part of the 'recent' wave of post-war Caribbean migration which is generally known as the 'Windrush' generation (the SS *Empire Windrush* being the name of the ship that conveyed the first boatload of Jamaicans to Britain in 1948). This antagonism towards 'new arrivants' has meant that blacks from other parts of Britain have often been made to feel uncomfortable in Liverpool. I suggest to Stephen that this seems somewhat bizarre, for I cannot see that there is anything in the city about which LBBs might feel particularly proud. Stephen shrugs his shoulders. 'Liverpool blacks are pretty uneducated as far as solidarity and stuff is concerned. I'm one myself, so I don't like to say it, but they can be really ignorant.' He pauses and shakes his head. 'A lot of people leave and go to Manchester or London because they can't take the crab-eat-crab attitude of the Liverpool ghetto. Sometimes it's just too much, man.'

Liverpool 8, or Toxteth, appears to me to be no different from scores of other British inner-city areas that have entered a stage of terminal decline. Stephen and I drive down streets and along avenues that were clearly once grand, and we pass by elegant single-family residences that have, over the years, been divided up into units which now provide immigrants with shared accommodation. The white population has withdrawn to other parts of the city, and it is clear that the social services now pay scant attention to cleaning and upkeep. The present-day 'immigrants' are from both Africa and the Caribbean, and they have slowly, but not without some considerable difficulty, attempted to blend in with the proud LBB population, a population which was originally made up of West African seamen, former slaves from the Americas, and others connected to trading in both goods and humans. As we drive down what Stephen describes as the 'main drag', he points out Toxteth's newest arrivants, who are war refugees from Somalia whose relationship with the LBBs is as problematic as one might expect.

As we continue to cruise the streets of Toxteth, I can see that the neighbourhood is dominated by boarded-up houses and general convenience stores encased in large metal grilles. The sidewalks are peopled with scruffy individuals who loiter aimlessly. Stephen seems bitter that about 80 per cent of the black community are out of work. 'We're going backwards in Liverpool. We just don't get employed in shops, not even McDonalds. Whites won't deal with us, and although loads of European money pours in to Liverpool, none of it seems to come to us.' In the evening gloom the perennially unemployed scrutinize us, and although I am being 'minded' by an LBB I still feel a palpable sense of menace in the air. Behind the decay it remains easy to imagine that these streets were once highly desirable, but it is equally easy to imagine that once this pattern of 'decline' set in, just how quickly this area slipped into the present abyss.

Stephen suggests that rather than get out and walk—which had been our original plan—it might be better if we just circle around for a while so that I can 'get a feel for the area'. I nod enthusiastically, and as Stephen continues to drive I peer sheepishly through uncurtained windows where whole families appear to be perched on the edge of sofas watching television. Gardens are almost invariably full of rubbish that is piled high, and outside an off-licence I see a cluster of men who say nothing to each other, but who are all smoking with a ferocious intensity. Further down the same street, we stop at a junction. I see another group of men leaning against a slightly battered car. A blue Ford of some kind, although the front nearside panel is a dirty brown which suggests it must have been recently replaced. One of the men looks into Stephen's car, and then he flicks a cigarette butt, which briefly flies before plummeting to the ground. It is the kind of sudden dramatic action that is designed to inculcate fear. We move off and pass a large building that looks as though it once served some kind of ceremonial purpose. 'What's that?' I ask, turning around in my seat to stare at the receding image. Stephen smiles. 'The synagogue.' He glances across at me. 'But then the Jews all moved out, if you know what I mean.' Indeed, I do know what he means. The Liverpool Born Black is making his point with undisguised glee.

Back at my hotel, I open a pictorial history of Liverpool that I had bought earlier in the day. The book confirms that the very same streets that Stephen and I have been driving along were once the main thoroughfares of a highly desirable residential area. The neighbourhood was tree-lined and featured parks and playgrounds, and I stare in disbelief at the black-and-white photographs which proffer evidence of a happier, more manicured, era. Liverpool 8 has undeniably changed, but as I turn to other sections of the book it is clear that over the years the city of Liverpool has undergone a major transformation.

There are numerous photographs of the courts and cellars of the nineteenth and early twentieth centuries, insalubrious areas where the poor and underprivileged lived like animals. A great number of these people were emigrants who had arrived on ships from all corners of Europe, ready to depart for Australia or America. In the one hundred years between 1830 and 1930, 9 million people, predominantly Irish, Scandinavians, and Germans, passed through the great English port. Inevitably, once in Liverpool some would lose their savings, or have it swindled from them, or simply drink it away, before they had a chance to get on board ship. Condemned to a life of poverty in the hellish quarters of the city, they endured unspeakable deprivation. These disturbing photographs are all that remain of the courts and cellars for, unlike Liverpool 8, the actual buildings have long ago been destroyed.

I had hoped to be able to spend some more time with Stephen and meet his 'activist' friends in the black community, but in the morning I receive a phone message that he has been called away 'on business'. He had warned me that this might transpire, so I am prepared to spend my final morning alone before heading back to London. I decide that if I am not going to be able to meet Stephen's friends, then I ought to visit the Maritime Museum's permanent exhibition that is dedicated to the slave trade. The exhibition opened in 1994, but for many years before this there had been a strong lobby from both the black and white communities of Liverpool, who argued that the Maritime Museum should at least acknowledge Liverpool's deep involvement in the slave trade. Stephen had told me that as a young boy his visits to the museum were characterized by being exposed to people dressed as sailors, who played the hornpipe and encouraged the black and white children to sing sea shanties.

I walk back along the docks and notice that a slither of sunshine has managed to find its way through the clouds and momentarily brighten up what promises to be yet another dull day. I pass the bench on which I had sat the previous morning, and then I turn seawards toward the Albert Dock. In a complex which includes restaurants, pubs, galleries, the Beatles Museum and the northern extension of the Tate Gallery, I discover the Maritime Museum. Located in a huge old warehouse, the museum features exhibitions which deal with customs and excise, emigration to the United States and, in the basement, a collection of material relating to the African slave trade. Although the permanent exhibition dedicated to the slave trade is hardly high-tech 'interactive' in the tradition of some London museums, it does feature succinct and accurate explanations, in pictures and words, of the complicit involvement of Liverpool in this trading in human lives.

I follow a group of young white schoolchildren, and listen to their bearded and somewhat over-earnest teacher's explanation of the various exhibits. However, it is clear to me that the children are unsure of what they are being told. When their teacher stops speaking they are encouraged to read, but they do so without absorbing any meaning. Their poor faces are clenched in concentration, but it is not their fault. This visit to the museum is woefully premature. Beyond the children I notice an elderly couple, who I assume to be from Liverpool, and who stop at every reference to the founding fathers of the city having made their money from the slave trade. As they position themselves in front of yet another cabinet, I peer over their shoulder and look at a silver plate that Liverpool Town Council presented to a James Penny in 1792. Four years earlier, in 1788, Mr Penny had been given the freedom of the borough, along with other 'witnesses', 'for the very essential advantages devised to the trade of Liverpool from their evidence in support of the African slave trade, and for the public spirit they have manifested'. Penny, a prominent Liverpool slave trader, had given evidence to a parliamentary inquiry into the trade. The elderly woman, coming face to face with her history, and noticing me on her shoulder, turned to her husband. 'Oh dear, there's a lot to be ashamed of, isn't there?' Her husband ignored the question and nodded in my direction, and I felt duty-bound to nod back.

Once outside the museum, I rediscover my bench overlooking the Albert Dock, and I take a seat. I think back to my childhood, and to the time when I first read Emily Brontë's novel, *Wuthering Heights*. Near the beginning of the novel, Cathy and Hindley's father, Mr Earnshaw, comes down to breakfast one morning dressed for a journey. He announces that on this day he will be going to Liverpool, which lies some sixty miles distant. He does not disclose the purpose of his journey, but he does ask his two children what they would like him to bring for them, warning them that it should be something small for he intends to walk both ways. Three days later a clearly distressed Mr Earnshaw returns. He throws himself into a chair 'laughing and groaning', and breathlessly announces that the walk nearly killed him. Mr Earnshaw then peels opens his greatcoat and offers his wife 'a gift of God, though it's as dark almost as if it came from the devil'. The dirty, ragged, black-haired child who 'stared' and repeated 'some gibberish that nobody could understand', was named Heathcliff.

Mrs Earnshaw immediately chastizes her husband for bringing another child into the house when they already have two of their own to feed, but although he is 'half-dead with fatigue' the master explains. He describes seeing 'it starving, and houseless, and as good as dumb, in the streets of Liverpool where he picked it up and inquired for its owner'. Presumably motivated by a sense of charity, Mr Earnshaw decided to bring 'it' home with him. This seven-year-old dark stranger, whom Mr Earnshaw 'rescued' from the streets of Liverpool in 1771, was one of the first literary characters to seize my imagination. There is no textual evidence of Heathcliff having any negro blood. In fact, during the course of the novel he is referred to as a 'gypsy', as 'dusky', a 'Lascar', an 'American or Spanish castaway', not 'a regular black', and so on. However, with each rereading of the novel, it has seemed increasingly ironic to me that this 'dark alien' should find himself adrift in the streets of Europe's major eighteenth-century slaving port. From the vantage point of my bench, I look around and am suddenly convinced that it must have been down here, by the docks, that Mr Earnshaw spotted the scrawny dark apparition named Heathcliff. And, not for the first time in my life, I close my eyes and try to solve the puzzle of this seven-year-old boy's origins.

I open my eyes and look around. I now realize that I have just about enough time to dash across the city to Lime Street Station. I take out the map which, although it is falling to pieces, has not failed me, and I determine the quickest route. It begins to drizzle so, turning up the collar on my coat and hunching my shoulders, I half-walk, half-jog away from the docks and the River Mersey. As I pause to cross a main road, the rain-bearing wind lashes into my face. And then, as though materializing out of nowhere, I am approached by a young man who is dressed in a thin jacket, which is a pathetically inadequate gesture to the suddenly inclement weather. 'Wanna help the homeless?' he asks, thrusting a newspaper in my direction. I buy it and he thanks me, telling me that he is hoping to get his 'life together'. Apparently, there is a chance that he might have a horse-chestnut stand for Christmas. I wish him luck, but wonder just what is it with Christmas in this city? First the juke-box, now this man. It is May.

As I turn into the skateboarder's pedestrian precinct, I am struck by how the tall dark buildings of a bygone era, and the ugly, concrete and glass ones which represent supposed progress, are all uncomfortably tethered together. I notice the long glum faces of the shoppers, the same miserable aspect which seems to be etched across the faces of most of the people I have encountered in Liverpool. In this city, the past casts a deep shadow, yet the present seems grubby and inadequate. I take a shortcut through a narrow alleyway. Again it begins to rain, light, insincere rain. And suddenly I am alone on a back street. A man stumbles into view. He staggers. He sits on a step that leads to a padlocked warehouse door. His hair is dishevelled, his brown jacket is stained, and between his legs he clutches a pint glass. It is half-full of beer. Has this man wandered out of a pub by accident? Perhaps lost his way en route to the bathroom? His large black eyes stare up at me. A curiously engaging stare, as though he wishes to ask me a question. But this man's mind will not function. Where a man keeps his memories is the place he should call home. As I hurry past, I wonder about this man's home. I suspect it is not Liverpool.

At Lime Street Station I sit and wait for my train. As the minutes tick by, I watch the pigeons circling high in the roof of the station. The world's first passenger railway service was inaugurated in Liverpool, but what a farce. As the train moved off, it ran over and killed the Liverpool MP who had been officially observing. A history hitched to tragedy. A train pulls in and I can hear the uncivilized braying of football fans readying themselves for a Saturday afternoon of revelry. I am glad that I am leaving. It is disquieting to be in a place where history is so physically present, yet so glaringly absent from people's consciousness. But where is it any different? Maybe this is the modern condition, and Liverpool is merely acting out this reality with an honest vigour. If so, this dissonance between the two states seems to have engendered both a cynical wit and a clinical depression in the souls of Liverpool's citizens. As I sidestep my way around the fat-bellied football fans and move to catch my train, I silently wish everybody a happy Christmas.

II

HOMEWARD BOUND

A friend told me a story about a Ghanaian man he knew who, apparently through 'no fault of his own', had ended up in a British prison. He paused. I waited. He had just returned from visiting his friend in prison and the accumulated fatigue from the journey, plus the disturbing experience of seeing the man in confinement, was beginning to tell on him. He sat down. He began to tell the story again, this time more wistfully. OK, so perhaps his friend was culpable to some degree. He was a young Ghanaian man who had ostensibly come to England to study but he had managed to overstay his visa. He had also managed not to study—or rather, he had 'studied' but earned neither a diploma nor a degree. In all likelihood he would be deported back to Ghana with a stamp in his passport that would effectively make it impossible for him to return to Britain. I listened to my friend's new version of the story, which was identical to the first version except this time I learned the man's name. Mohammed Mansour Nassirudeen, prisoner number HA1000, would soon be returning to Ghana without his formal education, and with a mark of shame. He would be a convicted criminal.

'You know, he wants to be a writer.' I looked across at my friend. 'He's been writing, and he's just got a prize for an essay.'

My friend reached down into his smart new briefcase and retrieved a file of papers. He flicked through them and then handed me a five-page essay entitled 'A Day in My Life as a Detainee'. I looked at the creased, dog-eared pieces of paper, then put them to one side. I would read them later. I asked, 'Is he likely to get any kind of last-minute reprieve and be allowed to stay?' My friend rubbed the back of his hand into a tired and lined face. 'No chance', he said. 'He'll be going back to Ghana on a one-way ticket. After all his effort to get here, after everything that he's been through in Britain, they'll just put him on a plane to Ghana and kick him out. As simple as that.'

In the evening, after my friend had left, I picked up the crumpled essay and began to read. The structure was conventional enough. It simply traced the contours of Mohammed Mansour Nassirudeen's 'prison day', which began at 4.30 a.m. with Muslim prayers, and ended at 9 p.m. with more prayers. The 'day' that sprawled from pre-dawn to post-dusk was characterized by Mansour's apparently insatiable hunger to attend educational classes in order that he might improve himself, and his dedication to prayer. Mansour's narrative successfully resisted the impulse to explain just why he was serving time in Haslar Detention Centre but, this glaring omission aside, there was an admirably stoic determination to his tale—as told by himself—which was betrayed by only one piece of special pleading.

The morning session of education ceases at 11.30. During the interval I keep myself mentally active as much as possible. My mind is constantly occupied with new ideas which I have organized in my Database. That leaves me little room to think about my problems of being locked up in detention when I have committed no crime during the eight years that I have lived in Great Britain and paid my taxes. Nevertheless, I see my situation not as a problem but as an 'opportunity'. I certainly don't know why I am here. But it has to be for a reason which only God knows. Even prophets like Joseph, Yusuf, have been in jail, and other dignified people like Nelson Mandela. Life is full of paradoxes, I feel physically that I am in detention, though spiritually I am not.

Six weeks later Mohammed Mansour Nassirudeen was escorted on to a British Airways flight to Accra, Ghana, his passport having been suitably stamped so that it would be clear to any immigration officer at any immigration point in the world that this man had been deported from Britain for being an illegal immigrant.

Through the open window of the car the warm night wind strokes my face. We are racing further into the heart of a city. As we do so, the houses begin to multiply on either side of the road, thickening into neighbourhoods that reach back to the low-lying hills. A forest of flickering lights suggests the density and extent of the hidden population. Despite the late hour, traffic streams relentlessly, and noisily, along the black ribbon of the highway. Through the cracked and spidered windshield, I can see that we are following a large truck whose red tail-lights blink with ominous unpredictability. As the truck brakes, we too brake, often with a sudden violence which throws me forward so that my outstretched arm is all that prevents me from careening into the back of the driver's seat. African driving. First, a somnambulant dog and then a disorientated cow wander aimlessly across this main road. They provide us with further obstacles to be screeched around. Mercifully, the driver slows down as we enter the heart of Accra. As we do so, the streets broaden with a majestic moonlit flourish and announce themselves as the streets of a capital city. At all the major intersections there are clusters of vigilant, gun-toting policemen. Young policemen. Boys really. Mansour twists around in the driver's seat. 'Nearly there,' he says with a broad smile. 'You will soon be at your hotel.' He is proud of his country, and he is clearly enjoying the role of trusted driver. I settle back in my seat and let the warm night wind continue to stroke my face.

I am sitting at a filthy plastic-topped table that is littered with abandoned packets of white and brown sugar, discarded plastic stirrers, a shallow puddle of coffee, and the sticky remains of some sweet orange drink. The plane is delayed and I have suddenly been presented with an extra six hours in Gatwick Airport. They say travel broadens the mind. I had asked the airline's representative a polite question. She looked disdainfully at me. 'Mechanical problems, love.' I was hoping for something a little more specific than this. No, I cannot have my luggage back and take a flight on the following day. Apparently my checked bag has already been 'processed' and is lurking somewhere in the inner bowels of the airport. Like the other one hundred and fifty abandoned souls, I have been presented with a £15 voucher, haven't I? There are, she tells me, a whole network of shops and restaurants in the terminal 'which rival any inner-city High Street'. So what is my problem? Shamefaced, I hurry away and sit at the filthy plastic-topped table.

'United revel in goal spree.' I am reading the story for a second time when I am interrupted by a tall, slightly stooped man who, on the evidence of his heavy tray, has clearly spent his £15 with enthusiasm. 'Do you mind if I join you?' Of course not, I say, both signalling him to please take a seat and gesturing helplessly towards the tabletop. 'I am used to Heathrow,' he says. He takes a bite out of his egg and cress sandwich. I know what he means. I too am used to Heathrow. Suddenly choice opens up for me. I can go and spend my £15, I can have a conversation, or I can return to my newspaper. I choose the latter. 'United revel in goal spree.'

I had awoken at dawn to the unusual sound of birds singing. In my London neighbourhood the sound of an articulated lorry rumbling by is the usual signal that the day is breaking. The alarm rang out, but having turned it off I lay in bed for ten minutes watching the light creep around the corner of the curtains. Eventually I went downstairs, made a cup of black coffee, and stared intently at a cat who was sitting on top of a wall staring intently back at me. As usual, I would lose this face-off. My bags were packed. I was leaving for West Africa, a significantly shorter journey than the more familiar ones to the United States or to the Caribbean, but a journey which none the less always suggests both distance and otherworldliness. My minicab driver raced through the empty streets of south London, then burst into the open Surrey countryside. He hurtled past mist-shrouded green fields, negotiated knotty junctions where one motorway threaded into another, and then he delivered me to Gatwick's South Terminal. 'Thirty quid, mate,' 'Mechanical problems, love.' 'United revel in goal spree.' 'Do you mind if I join you?'

I sip at a beaker of warm white wine whose contents both look and taste like a urine sample. Then I screw the top of the small bottle firmly into place, unsure as to whether I will ever open it again. I have spent my £15 on white wine, coffee, and a 'baguette', the contents of which defy description. At least somebody has deigned to wipe the top of the table clean with a wet cloth. I look around and can see that the airport is becoming increasingly populated with travellers who, having spent their vouchers, are now both frustrated and angered by this delay. At the airline counter I see an African businessman who is attempting to check in a pair of spectacularly oversized boxes, with addresses scrawled hastily across them in felt-tip pen. In addition to the 'boom-box' stereo and the computer equipment that he apparently wishes to take on board as hand luggage, there is also a fridge. It is a small, white, mini-bar size fridge, but nevertheless it is a fridge. The bewildered look on the face of the woman behind the counter is eloquent. I unscrew the top from the bottle of wine.

When the captain announces that we will not be landing in Nigeria I breathe a sigh of relief. I want to get to Ghana as quickly as possible. I stop the flight attendant as she saunters down the aisle, but her explanation for overflying Kano alarms me. She perches on the armrest of the seat across the aisle, and then begins to explain in a muted whisper. It transpires that the British authorities have recently banned Nigerian aircraft from landing at any British airports, claiming that the planes are not being properly serviced. The Nigerians have understandably decided to respond in kind by not allowing any British aircraft to land on their soil. The flight attendant smiles weakly and says that she imagines that the situation will soon be resolved. She seems, however, painfully unconvinced.

As the flight attendant moves off down the aisle, the man next to me reaches below the seat in front of him and withdraws his attaché case. He is a small bullet-headed man, with a curiously large white shirt collar that seems intent upon climbing over the lapels of his purple jacket and declaring itself independent of the rest of his shirt. He snaps open the attaché case and produces a bottle of Johnnie Walker Black Label Whisky, which, nodding in the direction of my plastic cup of water, he offers to me. 'Whisky, my brother?' No thanks, I say. Having caught a whiff of his breath, I am sure that my 'brother' is already several drinks past drunk. He seems puzzled. 'Muslim?' Not really, I say. At this point he decides to ignore me and pour himself a drink. Perhaps he is celebrating the fact that we will not be landing in Nigeria. I close my eyes in an attempt to drift off to sleep.

'Where are you from?'

The abruptness of his whisky-scorched question shakes me out of my reverie. The bullet-headed man appears now to be fully libated and eager for conversation. 'Yes please, my friend. Where are you from?'

The question. The problem question for those of us who have grown up in societies which define themselves by excluding others. Usually us. A coded question. Are you one of us? Are you one of ours? Where are you from? Where are you *really* from? And now, here on a plane flying to Africa, the same clumsy question. Does he mean, who am I? Does he mean, do I belong? Why does this man not understand the complexity of his question? I make the familiar flustered attempt to answer *the* question. He listens, and then spoils it all. 'So, my friend, you are going home to Africa. To Ghana.' *I say nothing.* No, I am not going home.

'My name is Ben.' He extends his hand in a gesture of fraternal welcome. *(No, I am not going home.)* His knuckles are callused, and his firm grip makes me wonder if he has ever been a boxer. He smiles at the question, careful not to deny his former 'occupation'. He then offers me another opportunity to share his whisky. 'Water's fine,' I say, 'or maybe a beer when they next come by with the drinks.' Ben seems relieved that I have at least acknowledged the possibility that I might drink something alcoholic.

'I go to England to do business, maybe three times a year. That is all England is good for these days. Make some money and leave. They don't want to know us any more.'

'Any more?'

'Since independence. We have to survive by ourselves.'

'But isn't that the purpose of independence?' Ben seems momentarily offended, so I press on. 'Britain's primary relationship is now with Europe. That's just how it goes.'

'But what about us?' Ben twists around in his seat to face me. 'You think it's fine to just forget us?' He throws out a helpless arm. 'You think it's fine to forget the Commonwealth?'

I shrug my shoulders. Ben is drunk, but his indignation is focused. I recognize the anger as having its roots in parental abandonment. The jettisoning of a truculent child who demands respect, yet craves love.

Ben trades in foodstuffs and hair products. The foodstuffs he exports to Britain, where they are sold in specialist groceries, while the afro hair products are manufactured in Britain, but sold in Ghana and throughout West Africa. For five years Ben has been flying this route, but his dream is to make enough money so that he can settle in Ghana and not have to bother with Britain any more. In the meantime, he tells me that he enjoys having access to the material goods, the television sets, the CD players, and the video recorders that he can buy in London. He always brings a few of each back with him to 'distribute', and in this way he easily covers the cost of his flight. 'What about customs duty?' I ask. 'Isn't there an import tax levied on all of these goods?' 'Yes, but even after the tax I make money.' Ben laughs. 'And I pay the damn tax.' He points in what he imagines to be the general direction of Nigeria, through the window and down beneath the clouds. 'Not like those Nigerian people down there. How can a country develop when everybody is helping themselves and nobody is helping the country? You tell me that?'

Long before the plane begins its descent into Accra's Kotoka International Airport, Ben is asleep, his mouth open, his head thrown back, his attaché case tucked safely underneath the seat in front of him. The flight attendant stalks the aisles, encouraging passengers to fasten their seat belts and put the back of their seats upright for what remains of the flight. Ben fails to respond to her urgings, so I lean over and strap him in. I wonder about the quality of hurt that remains damned up in Ben's soul? In our short time together I have listened to him sing a discordant anthem of indignation. Like me, he is the product of British imperial adventures. Unlike me, he is an African. A Ghanaian. A whole man. A man of one place. A man who will never flinch at *the* question, 'Where are you from?' A man going home. Stupefied with drink and despair, Ben is returning home. And, in spite of his present predicament, I envy his rootedness.

We're related—you and I,
You from the West Indies,
I from Kentucky.

Homeward Bound

Kinsmen—you and I,
You from Africa,
I from the U.S.A.

Brothers—you and I.

LANGSTON HUGHES

From the air, the earth of Ghana appears to be unnaturally red. One cannot call it soil for there are great bare patches which suggest that the land is incapable of being cultivated. Scattered among this barren landscape are clumps and clusters of green, and the occasional thatched roof of a mud hut. The pejorative term always makes me feel uncomfortable, but that is what they are. Mud huts. All of this I remember from a previous visit some seven years earlier. Now it is dark—we left six hours later than planned—and through the window all I can see is the vast blackness of the earth speckled with an occasional light from a house or a shop. As though the wide night sky, with her shimmering stars, has suddenly been painted on the ground.

The night air is stiflingly hot and humid. An airport bus of a decidedly earlier vintage transports us the one hundred or so yards to the terminal building. Once there, we are politely encouraged to quickly disembark and enter the terminal, please, so that the bus can sweep a wide arc and return for the remaining passengers who are marooned on the sticky tarmac. In fact, politeness is everywhere. As I step into the terminal building, a uniformed man in his fifties smiles and says 'Hello'. At 1.30 a.m. this seems a strangely calm and understated greeting. The cursory inspection of yellow-fever documentation precedes immigration. Both procedures are swift and efficient, but the baggage hall is something else. The 'conveyor-belt' is a wooden bench on which luggage is randomly piled, which means that in

127

order to retrieve my bag I have to temporarily abandon both my trolley and my hand luggage, and dive through a thick crowd of people. Having identified my bag, I tug at it as though pulling a cork from a bottle. I burst backwards and stumble into clear space where I am surprised to discover that my trolley and hand luggage are where I left them. To my left a pinch-faced Scotsman addresses a khaki-clad baggage-handler by shouting, 'Get me a trolley!' He appears to be angry about something—the collapsing colonial condition, I imagine. The baggage handler politely waits until the apoplectic man has turned away and begun to shout at somebody else, and then he laughs.

Customs control involves hauling my bag on to a counter and then producing my passport. By now I am anxious to escape the turmoil of the customs hall. The most cursory of glances indicates that I am to open my bag, which I do. The young man looks at my passport, and then he looks at me and asks if I have had a good flight. I confirm that the flight was fine, largely because I did not have to stop in Nigeria.

'Ah, so you are happy,' he says as he hands me back my passport and nods in the general direction of my bag. I begin to zip it up. He asks again, 'So, my brother, you are happy?'

'I am happy to be in Ghana.'

'You're welcome.' He chalks a large 'X' on my bag, and then there is a significant pause. I imagine that I am being silently invited to reward him with a present of what is known as 'prior appreciation,' but I decline the invitation.

'Akwaaba.' I look puzzled, but the final gatekeeper smiles. 'In the Twi language, it means "Welcome back home".'

I pick up my bag. Thank you. No, *I am not going home*.

The triple rite of passage: health check, immigration control, customs. I am familiar with these three third world gates. Long lines of people; businessmen and backpackers, and those simply returning home with a small fortune in used notes secreted about their person. Health check, immigration control, customs. And then the disorientating humidity, the new smells, the cloying heat, the strange eager faces, the proffered hands, the anxious waiting, the exchanging of cautious glances. As I step into the night I look around for Ben, but I cannot find him. I do, however, see the red-faced Scotsman, who is now sweating profusely. I imagine that his visit to Ghana will, in all likelihood, prove to be problematic for both himself and those he encounters.

Outside the terminal building the crowds are bathed in floodlights and held behind barriers at a safe distance across the road. A policeman who struggles to control a muzzled Alsatian at the end of a short chain asks me if I need a taxi. No thanks. 'You're welcome,' he beams in reply. Good system, I think. And then I see Mansour standing next to a soldier. He has on a black jacket and a clean, crisp white shirt. I see him point in my direction and I imagine he is asking the policeman if he can cross the road and approach me, and it is clear that permission is readily granted. Mansour is a dark, stockily built man of about 5'7". He takes my hand and welcomes me to Ghana. In the same sentence he asks about my family. Only when he is satisfied that everybody is doing fine does he then suggest that we can move off.

Mansour secures a trolley, deposits my bags on it and then steers it across the road. I discover that he is not alone. I am introduced to his younger brother, Amin; his sister-in-law (for one of his older brothers); and her two children, an infant and a small boy. All are dressed in their Sunday best, and they do not appear to be in any way flustered by the fact that it is now after two o'clock in the morning. Mansour seems determined to push the trolley so I take the hand of the five-year-old boy who has on a green jacket with a matching bow tie. As we walk along, it occurs to me that I have been welcomed into Africa by a family. There is something surprisingly reassuring about this.

Some weeks earlier I had telephoned Mansour from London. This involved calling a neighbour, and letting him know that this was an overseas call and that I wished to speak to Mansour. I was then informed that I must call back five minutes later. I imagined the neighbour quickly pulling on something respectable, then dashing out into the yard and shouting over the fence, whereupon Mansour quickly donned something equally respectable and dashed over to wait for his call. When I called back I introduced myself as a friend of his friend in London, and then I asked Mansour if he might arrange for me to rent a medium-sized car as I would soon be visiting Ghana. I also inquired if Mansour would be available to act as my driver for a few days. Although we had never met before, Mansour seemed eager to help and happy for the work. I asked him how we would know each other at the airport, but Mansour laughed into his neighbour's telephone and assured me that there would be no problem.

The five-year-old tugs at my hand. He seems excited by the car, but I am not. The clapped-out green Mercedes is not what I would call 'roadworthy', but I deem it best to say nothing about my fears, or the eighty dollars a day that the car is costing me, until I have some *prima facie* evidence to confirm my suspicions. This does not take long. Having bundled everybody into the car (I insist that Amin sits in the front seat next to his brother), and placed the luggage in the trunk, Mansour is unable to start the vehicle. I watch sweat cascade down the back of Mansour's neck as the rasping sound of metal on metal becomes increasingly desperate. The engine refuses to turn, but before I have a chance to sympathize with Mansour and reassure him that these things happen, a rugby scrum of men emerges from the darkness. They begin to shove and push at the Mercedes as Mansour frantically engages and then disengages the clutch. Eventually, some two hundred yards down the road, the engine roars to life and the now exhausted men burst into applause and laughter. The tired five-year-old boy joins in with the applause, while a beaming Mansour and Amin both turn around as if to say 'Told you it would be all right'. No problem, right? Except I can smell diesel, the engine sounds like a 747, and as Mansour attempts to negotiate his way through a series of tight curves it is clear that he is having serious difficulty distinguishing between first and third gears. The ten kilometres from the air-port to the city are beginning to look increasingly distant. Mansour asks my permission to take his family home first. Of course, I say. His sister-in-law is pale with fear, and she clutches the infant to her chest. She relaxes a little as Mansour turns back around so that he is now looking in the direction that he is driving. The five-year-old has calmer nerves; he is slumped sound asleep next to me.

Through the open window of the car the warm night wind strokes my face. Mansour brakes sharply, then he pulls the car over to the side of the road. The family—Amin, their sister-in-law and the two children—seem embarrassed that they have fallen asleep in front of their guest. They line up by the side of the road and wave as Mansour drives away with his guest still seated in the rear. Through the open window of the car the warm wind strokes my face. We are racing further into the heart of a city. As we do so, the houses begin to multiply on either side of the road, thickening into neighbourhoods that reach back to the low-lying hills. A forest of flickering lights suggests the density and extent of the hidden population. And soon after I am swept away by sleep, which in these circumstances represents the comprehensive triumph of fatigue over both comfort and vigilance. We are racing further into the heart of a city.

In the morning I hear a tentative rapping on my door. I knock over the alarm clock as I try to see what time it is. Again I hear a hammering against my door, but this time the rhythm is more urgent. I pull on a pair of jeans and stumble in the dark towards where I imagine the door to be. When I open it I see a middle-aged man with a teenager's features. With both hands he proffers a basket of fruit.

'Welcome to Ghana. Some fruit, please.'

Back in the room I pick up my now broken alarm clock. It is 1 p.m.

I look out of my hotel window, but the day seems surprisingly dull, the sky a London grey. Then I realize that the glass has been tinted with a dark stain, presumably to protect the visitors from the African glare. This hotel is part of a large European business chain; most of their guests do not come for African sun. I can smell the fruit which, despite the loud hum of the air-conditioning, already seems to be ripening in the room. And then I look across to the crumpled bed and notice that the pillow is stained with a damp patch. I have had some kind of an anxiety attack, my dreams undoubtedly fuelled by disorientation and fatigue. However, I can remember nothing of whatever it was that caused me this discomfort. Suddenly I am aware of the rumble of construction and I turn again to the window. I watch as a tall, angular crane describes a wide sweeping arc. Large black kites swoop in the opposite direction. Ghana is on the move.

By the elevator I notice the shoe-shine machine. Although my white tennis shoes do not need a layer of either black or brown polish, I still push the button. I want to see if the machine is working. It is. Brushes whirl in a crazy circle. This is a business hotel. The advertisements in the elevator introduce the three restaurants—café, terrace, grill. As the doors open onto the lobby, I am greeted by a familiar scene. Deep carpet beneath my feet; shops selling local carved sculpture and jewellery; the newspaper shop with *Time*, *Newsweek*, *Le Monde*, the weekly *Telegraph*, and a few copies of English Sunday newspapers. I change money at the front desk, and in exchange for $50 I am handed an unlikely bundle of cedis. I divide the thick wad of notes into two and push a fistful into each trouser pocket. However, it is impossible to disguise the fact that I look as though both pockets are stuffed with paperback books.

The lobby is full of sofas and easy chairs in which dozens of

Ghanaian men appear to have taken up residence. The men are slumped down deeply in the chairs as though waiting for somebody who has either forgotten to show up, or somebody who is not due to turn up for hours. They have transformed the lobby of the hotel into an airport terminal. Some of the men are blissfully asleep, and nobody seems to want to move them on. I have time on my hands. Time to go for a walk and eventually find some place where I might sit and have a drink. But I know what will greet me the moment I leave the hotel. Third world travel imposes patterns upon one's life. There is a stubborn predictability to the encounter, which is only enlivened by different languages, different sights and different smells. Otherwise the pattern remains much the same.

Beyond the tinted glass doors, I will meet the man who will be my driver. Taxi? You need a car? It is not good to walk. And then the man who will change my money at a more advantageous rate than any I might obtain at a bank or bureau. Dollars? Change money? Best rates. Please, my friend, let me help you. A little further from the hotel I will meet the street vendors who will be eager to sell me anything from toothpaste to hand-held plastic fans (AA size batteries are extra). And then I will meet the beggars, most with children, all with palms outstretched. Some will touch, others will rely upon a well-cultivated expression of pathos. Finally, I will meet the limbless beggars, some hauling themselves along the street on wooden boards, others just strewn across the pavement in a double attempt to block one's path and arrest one's conscience. The negotiation of the third world.

Seven years earlier I had arrived in Ghana to undertake a lecture tour. I remember a park in which there was an outdoor café which served beer, coffee and light snacks. I took lunch there nearly every day, and I am convinced that I can find it again. As I step out of my hotel I negotiate the plethora of third world obstacles with a confidence born of memory and intuition, but after fifteen hot and humid minutes, I soon resign myself to the reality that I am lost. The teeming streets flow seamlessly one into the other, and I can see nothing that is familiar, although I am careful to keep the tall concrete and glass block of my hotel in sight. I realize now that I should have taken a map, but it is too late. It is also too suffocatingly hot to be walking about like this.

Ahead of me I see another modern-looking hotel, the sun flaring dramatically along the edge of the glassed-in upper storeys. Unable to tolerate any more proffered hands, and exhausted by the heat, I flee through the doors and find myself in a high-ceilinged lobby. Mercifully, the place is free of the lounge lizards who populate my hotel, and I am able to have a whole sofa to myself. As I sit the cushions exhale with a long, somewhat audible sigh, which causes me to feel momentarily self-conscious. The atmosphere is a curious mixture of old and new, the wooden ceiling fans suggesting a nod to the past while everything else about the hotel announces its relationship to the present—Hertz desk, tourist information, and business centre. A young woman in a bright blue dress, and carrying an empty ashtray, takes my order under the watchful eye of a man in a dark suit. Moments later she returns with a plain white cup of hot water (no saucer), and a sachet of Maxwell House coffee. Clearly I will have to do the engineering of the drink myself. I smile gratefully. I am left in peace to mix my own coffee and contemplate how I am going to circumnavigate the melancholy throng on the return journey to my own hotel. But all of this will be in the future.

By ten o'clock the sun is already blazing down. I am sitting by the pool, under the shade of a large green umbrella, eating my breakfast. I have decided to opt for fruit and juice, unsure as to how quickly my body will adapt to solid food. Mercifully, the coffee is of the pre-made variety. In the pool a French mother plays unconvincingly with her two young children, a boy and a girl, who are fearlessly splashing water everywhere. The mother seems principally concerned with not getting her hair wet. I imagine that her husband is already in some air-conditioned office doing 'business'. Beyond the French family, I see a young Ghanaian man with a brush, and what looks like a fishing net, standing in the shadow of a palm tree. A silent, dusty statue, he too is watching the French family at play.

The waitress refills my coffee with one hand and simultaneously takes up my plate with the other. Again I am left by myself. I sip at the black coffee, which reassuringly blades into me. The French mother has already had enough of this 'playing', and she leaves the pool and lies full length on a lounger. I turn my mind back to the previous day. I had arranged to meet Mansour in the lobby of the hotel at seven o'clock in the evening so that we might plan for the next few days. I also wanted to settle some money upon him for the expense of the car, and for his time and trouble. My friend in London had led me to believe that since his deportation from Britain, Mansour had been unable to find work. I disliked the idea of Mansour being out of pocket for a minute longer than was necessary.

By seven o'clock in the evening, most of the lounge lizards had disappeared. In fact, the lobby of the hotel appeared to be vaguely inviting. There were empty tables and chairs, and neatly liveried waiters were hovering all about. I walked to the bar and ordered a local beer, which the barman served with what I detected to be a degree of reluctance. As I carried the beer away from the bar I realized that the waiters would have preferred me to have sat at a table and ordered from them, as presumably there is a mark-up on drinks ordered from them, as well as the hope of a tip. I would remember. The buzz of the air-conditioning was cut by the light tinkling of a piano emanating from speakers that were recessed into the ceiling. Unbearable music, just one step short of supermarket music, it was no doubt a gesture to jazzy western sophistication.

I looked at my watch and realized that Mansour was already

fifteen minutes late. There were three other people in the bar, all European men, and all sitting together. They occasionally burst into laughter which would then quickly subside into short, staccato-like conversation, and then silence. Their outbursts of communal joviality only served to increase my sense of isolation. Mansour was now thirty minutes late, and I could only assume that the car must have finally given up on him. I tried to read a playscript by a Dr Mohammed Ben Abdallah, a playwright whom I had arranged to meet during my stay in Accra. However, my anxiety with regard to Mansour's absence made it difficult for me to concentrate, so I ordered another beer, this time from the grateful waiter. While I waited for my beer I wandered over to the newstand. The last copy of the weekly *Telegraph* had already gone, so I handed over a fistful of cedis and returned to my table with *Newsweek* magazine.

Mansour eventually turned up an hour late. I wanted to buy him dinner, but I suggested that we bypass the air-conditioned fridge that was masquerading as a dining-room, and eat outside on the terrace. As we took our seats I could see that Mansour's brow was beaded with sweat. He was panicking.

'The car?' I suggested. Mansour nodded and then downed a glass of water in one gulp. The waiter reappeared and refilled the glass.

'But the car is all right?' I asked.

'Everything is all right, but many problems.'

I handed Mansour the menu and decided that, unless it was strictly necessary, I had no desire to know the fine details of these 'many problems'. Being both a Muslim and dependent upon my hospitality, Mansour seemed nervous about being confronted with a menu. I suggested that he might like the fish, but I told him to order whatever he wanted. A mixed message. No wonder Mansour looked puzzled.

After the waiter had taken our order, and while I continued to sip my second beer, Mansour cleared his throat and began to speak. He told me that he was grateful for the books that I had brought for him. The eclectic pile of paperbacks included an anthology of African short stories, novels by Ousmane Sembene, and the journals of Stephen Spender. I suggested to him that if he really wanted to write then it was important that he should read as much as possible. He nodded, and then his eyes lit up as he thanked me for the package of creative writing brochures and pamphlets that I had also brought to Ghana for him. He assured me that he had already been assiduously studying them. The waiter reappeared with some bread and set it before us. As he withdrew, Mansour seized the moment and decided to state his case. 'I want to live in America.'

Mansour stared at me, his eyes brimming with water as though he might at any moment cry. The sentence had obviously cost him dearly, addressed as it was to a stranger. And then, as though unsure if I had fully registered the import of what he had just said, Mansour repeated himself. 'I want to live in America. I just need somebody to write me a letter.'

Suddenly it did not seem appropriate to be eating, but we both persevered. A sad-looking Mansour explained that without a letter he could not obtain a visa. There would be no point in his going to the United States embassy without a letter. What he needed was a letter from somebody in the United States inviting him to visit, then everything would be all right. I listened, but I could immediately see two problems, the one more serious than the other. The first was that being only a United States resident, and not a citizen, it would serve little purpose my writing the letter for him if, as I assumed, this is what he was obliquely asking of me. Second, Mansour could only visit the United States as a tourist for a few weeks. Permanent migration to the United States is a complex procedure involving a great deal more than a letter of invitation. Mansour listened and nodded, his state of agitation becoming increasingly apparent as I spoke. He stopped eating and placed the roll of bread back on to his plate. Then he leaned forward and gently touched the back of my hand. 'But I can travel as a tourist for I will not be coming back. I want to disappear.'

I too placed my roll of bread back on to my plate. I was angry with him.

His face brightened into excitement. He could, he suggested, get a place to live, then a job and study. He had a few Ghanaian friends in New York and New Jersey, but he quickly stressed that none were in a position to write him a letter. Some, he said, were doctors who, having studied medicine in Turkey on Islamic scholarships, were now trying to gain proper medical accreditation in the United States. Mansour insisted that once he reached the United States his friends would help him, and then he would be able to study Creative Writing. His excitement was temporarily muted as he dropped his voice. 'I can't afford the fees that are set out in the books you brought for me, but I can save.' Again his eyes lit up. 'I just need contacts and then I'll be fine.'

'You'll be fine?' I asked. For the first time, Mansour detected that perhaps I was not sharing his enthusiasm. He decided that he must be more explicit.

Ghana, he told me, is a very complex place. It hurt him a lot that he had to leave Britain and return to Ghana without a degree of some kind. He assured me that if he had obtained a degree in Britain, then he would never again have wished to leave Ghana. After all, his ultimate dream is to build a mansion and look after his family. Mansour lowered his eyes and stared vacantly at the tabletop. Apparently, the brother that I met, Amin, has had to drop out of university because of money problems. At the moment he sells ladies' cosmetics. Furthermore, the house in which Mansour now lives belongs to his older brother, who is a customs officer in the north of Ghana. Things are very difficult. Mansour was very keen to stress this point. Things are very difficult. Mansour insisted that he needed to do some business and make some money. And in order to do this properly, he must leave Ghana.

I stared at him, but Mansour would not meet my eyes. Perhaps it was wrong of me to be angry with Mansour for dreaming of life beyond Ghana. Perhaps it was wrong that I should be in any way judging this man who had not had the opportunities that I had. I decided that I would not judge him. I would try to help, as I had already tried to help by bringing him paperback books and the brochures from various universities. However, I wondered now if I had in some way encouraged him down this ludicrous path. Here before me was a man who had served time in a British prison for being an illegal immigrant, asking me to help him to become an illegal immigrant in the United States. According to Mansour, he had, during his time in Britain, enrolled at the University of London, while at nights he had stacked shelves in a supermarket. He claimed to be only one year from graduation when he was deported. However, the overwhelming fact about Mansour's time in Britain is that he spent eight years there and he returned with nothing. And now, unemployed in Ghana, he was dreaming of leaving again. Another eight years in the United States? Or Canada? Driving a taxi? An illegal African, enjoying the trappings of a car, a television, a stereo, and harbouring hopes of becoming 'qualified'. He looked across at me and I told him that we could talk of his situation at a later time. Tonight I was tired. Mansour smiled with relief.

I am still thinking of this encounter as I watch the French children cavorting in the pool, their mother having long since fallen asleep on the lounger where she lies basking in the sun. Mansour had promised that he would be at the hotel by noon, for he would need some time in the morning to check on the car. I had already shared with him my concerns about the reliability of the car, but Mansour had explained that this was the only car he could get access to. He had also assured me that he had negotiated the best possible deal, and I had thanked him for doing so. I check my watch and note that Mansour is already half an hour late. Having long since finished my breakfast, I turn again to the play by Dr Mohammed Ben Abdallah. A visit to see him will be the first of the two appointments that I have arranged in Accra, for I am keen to meet somebody who has been active in the field of Pan Africanism. And then, later in the day, I have arranged to meet an African-American who has settled 'back' in mother Africa. Having made my Accra 'house calls', tomorrow I will leave for Elmina and the famous castle. However, contingent upon Mansour's arrival, ahead of me lies a busy few hours in the capital.

As Mansour snakes the bulky Mercedes in and out of the crazy traffic of downtown Accra, I ask him if he has ever read any of the plays of Dr. Mohammed Ben Abdallah.

'No, but they are very popular.'

I say nothing in reply, and a somewhat puzzled Mansour takes his eyes from the road and looks across at me. 'I know people, many people, who have seen them performed.'

I do not doubt this, but I have found the plays hard to read for they seem clumsily constructed and rather transparently didactic. I do not tell this to Mansour, for Dr Mohammed Ben Abdallah appears to be something of a local hero for him. Not only is he a playwright, he teaches at the School of Performing Arts at the university and he is also a former high-ranking official in the Ghanaian Ministry of Culture. According to Mansour, Dr Ben Abdallah resigned from his government post on principle when somebody he deemed unworthy was promoted over his head. Now this fact seems impressive.

We arrive at Mohammed Ben Abdallah's residence at the agreed time but there is no sign of the good doctor. On the spacious veranda of his large wooden house there appears to be some kind of cottage industry in full flow, for the place is packed with women seated behind sewing machines. They are assembling clothes of some sort, while another group of women is ironing the finished products, and yet others are folding the clothes and sliding them into transparent packaging. A woman, whom I presume to be the playwright's wife, tells us that we can sit inside and wait, but she does so without letting us know how long we might have to wait. In fact, she barely bothers to look up from her work. Mansour and I squeeze past the workers and into the living-room of the house.

Choice FM radio is blasting out from the deep bass speakers which flank the big-screen television. The muted television is tuned in to ESPN, but the taped highlights of the American All-Star baseball game seem curiously at odds with Choice FM. In one corner of the room an exercise bike stands half-buried under a pile of women's clothing. The furniture in the room is either wooden, or wicker, the most impressive pieces being two solid mahogany chests and a dresser. The décor is completed by random pieces of a hi-fi system, African bronzes, wooden carvings, and numerous huge cardboard boxes that are crammed full of 'packaged' clothes. It is clear that the room has been haphazardly thrown together without any consideration for aesthetic appearance. The primary concern is for the practical. Whether African or western, all the goods are being utilized. I imagine that the flickering television set suggests some kind of a window on the world.

Mansour and I sit on a wicker sofa and watch as a whole procession of women pass in and out of the room. It is like a Whitehall farce, for we can never be sure which door will open next and who will appear. Through the unshuttered windows I stare at the blank expressions on the faces of the women who work assiduously while listening to Choice FM. The female disc-jockey announces that at 2.30 p.m. they will be talking about 'Women who seek attention in very dangerous ways, and how to curb that habit'. Clearly she is some kind of Ghanaian Oprah Winfrey, complete with fake American accent. I look up and am alarmed to notice that a series of large holes have been cut into the ceiling, exposing the rafters and beams underneath. I assume that there must have been a spate of leaks at some point in the past. And still more women pass through the house, some of whom I imagine must be related to the doctor. I am witnessing the place where the extended family meets family business.

When Dr Ben Abdallah finally appears it is immediately clear to me that he has been sleeping. A small, slightly overweight man, he wears a trim beard and is dressed in a freshly laundered white shirt and khaki pants. Mansour greets him as an old friend, and Dr Ben Abdallah smiles broadly. However, he shakes my hand in a rather formal manner and suggests that we 'visit' the garden. I remember that I am in the presence of a former politician, a man used to trading on the imagined charisma of his name. As we walk towards the shade of a large palm tree, he explains that within the next year he will have to leave 'this large and magnificent garden' for this is a university house which will soon have to be demolished. He points to the high-tension electricity cables directly overhead. 'Radiation,' he says. He encourages us to sit on wrought-iron chairs in the shade of the palm tree. 'They are building me a new house.' He laughs. 'But who knows when they will finish.'

Dr Mohammed Ben Abdallah is a renowned Ghanaian Pan-Africanist, and as we take our seats I tell him that it is his Pan Africanist 'beliefs' that I wish to ask him about. Not long after the first slave ships set sail from the West African coast, the idea that those of Africa, and those of African origin 'overseas' somehow constituted a family—albeit a family with a broken history—took hold. The idea was seized upon with a particular enthusiasm by those 'overseas' who, upon arriving in the Americas, were suddenly distressed to discover that they were black—or to put it more accurately, they were not white. There was engendered in their souls a romantic yearning to return 'home' to a family and a place where they could be free from the stigma of race. They would be 'home' again, albeit in a strange and forbidding region where the language, climate and culture were now alien to them, but at least they would be 'home'.

Clumsy experiments such as the founding of the countries of Sierra Leone and Liberia as places to which former British and American slaves might be returned, provided early models for those interested in this 'healing' process of reunification. Unfortunately, many 'returnees' often arrived with the impression that they were somehow superior to the natives of 'Darkest Africa' and the idealistic notion of family soon floundered against the rocks of reality. The nineteenth-century African-American writer and thinker Frederick Douglass was particularly dismissive of the virtues of Pan-African family 'reunification':

> . . . the savage chiefs on the western coast of Africa, who for ages have been accustomed to selling their captives into bondage, and pocketing the ready cash for them, will not more readily see and accept our moral and economical ideas, than the slave-traders of Maryland and Virginia.

While Douglass may have had little interest in returning to the 'dark' past, others such as Marcus Garvey, who in the early twentieth century enlisted the support of tens of thousands of diasporan Africans for his 'Back to Africa' movement, have been able successfully to stimulate 'family' members into thinking of Africa as 'home'. These days a great part of the responsibility for keeping the family flame burning is now being borne by those of Africa, who appear to be craving a new unity with their diasporan brothers; the same 'brothers' they helped to sell into slavery.

In a few days, Panafest will begin in Elmina and Cape Coast. The publicity material that was sent to me in London advertised it as 'the biggest gathering of the African family to celebrate our cultural unity. Artists and intellectuals of Africa and the diaspora are gathering together as a family in Mother Africa, in order that they might celebrate their values.' Naturally enough, Dr Mohammed Ben Abdallah is on the organizing committee of

Panafest. He adjusts his chair so that his back is to the sun. He is now totally in the shade. Overhead I hear the sudden breaking of leaves as a coconut plummets from a high branch. It thuds into the soil only a yard or two from where I am sitting. 'Is it safe, here?' I ask. Mansour and Dr Ben Abdallah laugh, but it seems to me a reasonable question. I soon realize that I am not going to be furnished with an answer.

Pan-Africanism, insists Dr Ben Abdallah, is a simple concept which involves the solidarity and cohesion of all Africans and people of African descent. 'We have to look after our own interests. We have to rescue the continuity of our values from the past, values such as our art, the wisdom of our elders and our ways of doing things, because with the coming of foreigners and imperialism many things were thrown away. The intrusion of Europe produced Eurocentric Africans who don't know who they are'. The good doctor finishes his opening volley in a quiet voice, but his jabbing accusatory finger suggests that all three of us know who he is talking about. Dr Ben Abdallah speaks like a man for whom even the slightest conversation is always a battle of wills.

How, I ask, does one 'go back' to the past in this Pan-Africanist model? Dr Ben Abdallah laughs out loud, and looks to Mansour for confirmation of the absurdity of my question. This, of course, places my employee in a difficult position, which he handles with admirable tact as he smiles and lowers his eyes. Dr Ben Abdallah snaps out a large handkerchief and mops his brow.

'One does not go back, it is all about moving forward. There are three questions.' He holds up three short fingers. 'One, what has been inflicted upon us, and is it good or is it bad? Two, what of our own culture have we managed to carry with us into the present? Three, what from the past can we lift into the future?'

But why, I ask, would one want to reach to the past? If it is past, then surely it is past for a reason.

'No, no, no.' Dr Ben Abdallah jumps from his chair, which causes it momentarily to rock back on to its hind legs. 'No,' he says again, for added emphasis. Dr Ben Abdallah mounts his imaginary lecture podium. He informs me that generally cultures have been allowed to evolve naturally and abandon that which is of no use to them as they borrow and adapt from other cultures. But with Africa we have been denied this process. We have, in fact, been cut off from much that is valuable and useful, such as our own system of democracy, our own medicines, our own languages, our own methods of conservation. Europe has grafted her ways on to ours but, as any doctor knows, a foreign limb cannot be grafted without considerable preparation and testing to see if the host body will take this limb. In this case Europe made no preparatory explorations, and Africa was unprepared. As a consequence we continue to witness the sad results of 'this tragic experimentation'. According to Dr Ben Abdallah, 'our' best way forward is to look to the past and see what we left back there, and then make sure that there is nothing there that we should have brought with us to the present.

Dr Ben Abdallah resumes his seat. He gestures all around. 'Timber. The western countries are now telling us that we should know how to conserve and preserve. They talk to us as though we are children. But it is these very people who came into Africa who were cutting down our trees. They knew that in every village there was a sacred grove where you were not allowed to cut a tree, but they laughed at this superstition. Perhaps today they would call it conservation.' Dr Ben Abdallah again gestures to the trees. 'Welcome to my sacred grove.' He laughs and Mansour laughs out loud with him.

'Or take for instance the boundaries between the countries. But these are ridiculous. The Europeans came and they drew these lines on their maps, but the Masai do not recognize Kenya or Tanzania. They wander as they please. The great Ashante empire cannot be contained by European lines, and now white men look at these same maps in the United Nations and other places and say that Africa can never move forward as long as she wraps herself within these boundaries. Well, who made the boundaries? Our problem is that we do not as yet know how to rule ourselves because we still think of a Westminster model or a Washington model as democracy. That is not democracy, that is Western democracy. But before Western democracy there was African democracy, but I believe we have forgotten that somewhere in the past.'

Are you sure, I ask, that there is virtue in going back to retrieve it? Dr Ben Abdallah is sure. 'The African past is the key to our future.'

I glance across at Mansour, who beams back. His hero is performing well, and he imagines that I am impressed by Dr Ben Abdallah. In fact, I admire Dr Ben Abdallah's passion, although much of what he says seems to me to be too deeply rooted in theory. I am, however, particularly interested in how Dr Ben Abdallah imagines that the family connection with the diaspora can help to facilitate Africa changing for the better. As I think about how to raise this subject, a young girl wanders down from the terrace of the house bearing a tray. When she reaches our 'seminar room' she silently visits each of us in turn, hands us a glass of water, and then turns on her heels and walks slowly back in the direction of the terrace.

Dr Ben Abdallah begins to explain the complex relationship with the diaspora by making reference to the United States. 'Every Ghanaian who goes to America will tell you of the same experience.' I know where the good doctor is going with this. It is not just every Ghanaian who has had this experience, it is every black person who is not African-American. The experience is that of listening to white Americans congratulating you for not being a black American. In other words, 'you are different' from the others, which generally means not as angry, or lazy or truculent. They praise you by racially insulting you, and then compound the treachery by assuming that this exchange can be your 'secret conversation'. Dr Ben Abdallah continues. 'They take you to one side and tell you how different you are from

146

their own blacks.' He sighs and shakes his head. Mansour also shakes his head.

Then Dr Ben Abdallah suddenly snaps to attention. 'The truth is for every African-American drug-pusher and pimp there is a shrewd, honest businessman out there. But the white man does not want us to get on. Nkrumah saw no difference. He treated everyone as family. C. L. R. James, Padmore, Du Bois, everybody. In business, in intellectual activities, in the arts, we must find strength in each other, but there remain some African-Americans who would prefer to have nothing to do with Africa, and there are also many Africans who would prefer to deal with a corrupt American white man than an honest black one. They think that by doing business with a white it somehow legitimizes their status, but they are wrong, my friend.' He pauses. 'But they are wrong.'

I look back towards the large covered terrace, and see the women continuing to do their work. They seem totally oblivious to the nature of the Pan-African discourse that is taking place in the shade of the palm tree. In the momentary silence I hear the mellow sounds of Choice FM. I take another sip of water and then, still feeling thirsty, I drain the glass. There is only a small amount of humidity, but I feel as though I could quite happily succumb to sleep. I look at Dr Ben Abdallah, who also looks about ready to put down his historical freight and drift off to sleep.

As we drive along in the car, Mansour appears to be anxious. The interview had ended with Dr Ben Abdallah receiving a phone call from the university which necessitated his having to go immediately and visit the campus. We shook hands and I thanked him for his time and insights. He knew I was going to be at Panafest, but there was no suggestion that we should meet. The last subject that I had discussed with Dr Ben Abdallah was the slave trade. I asked him how the subject was taught in Ghanaian schools, suggesting that the treatment of this historical topic would probably provide the key to understanding West Africa's relationship with the diaspora. What were Ghanaian children told about the one primal moment when mother, father, sister, brother were captured, subjugated, and then put in European ships and transported across the Atlantic Ocean where they were then set to work in the American world? Were Ghanaian children taught to understand slavery as a European crime? Or was slavery regarded as something that African people helped to perpetrate, something for which they had to take responsibility? I was not quite sure what to make of Dr Ben Abdallah's answer. In fact, such was my incredulity that he took some offence.

'It is taught', he said, 'with the understanding that those sold into slavery were not always that good, and that in some respects they got what they deserved. The people running the slave forts were people of God, for after all Cape Coast Castle was the site of the first missionary school.'

I could not be sure that I had heard correctly, so I asked Dr Ben Abdallah if he was saying that Cape Coast Castle was not only operating as a slave fort where Africans were held captive prior to being shipped across the Atlantic, but it was also functioning as a school for African children? Dr Ben Abdallah nodded his head. He went on. 'You must not be too romantic about slavery. It was a terrible thing, but I still maintain that many of the Africans who left here were not good people. Today we have a real problem, though. A serious problem. We have to decide what to do with these slave forts. They contain a lot of our history, but they are in ruins and Ghana does not have the means to restore all of them. There is some renovation, in the hope that they can be made presentable for tourism, but renovation is not restoration.'

I asked him if renovation might not be seen as a process of literally and metaphorically whitewashing history. He thought about this for some moments and then he spoke with deliberation. 'These are holocaust sites for those in the diaspora, but none of you are doing anything about these places. I have spoken on this topic many times in the United States.'

So it's our responsibility?

Dr Ben Abdallah stood and paced for a few moments. 'The Jews would never have let their holocaust shrines become places that can crumble to the ground. It is your history, and their decline is not the fault of the Ghanaians. Do you think we need to be reminded about slavery? We know.'

I wanted to get this right, so I spoke slowly and with as much deliberation as I could muster. So you think that the process of renovation is destroying the history, but this is not the fault of the Ghanaians?

Dr Ben Abdallah was quick. 'We do not have the money. The United Nations has given some money, but it is not enough. If we can install a gift shop and sell postcards and attract tourism, then we must do what is necessary. When I was active in politics I said that these places should be given to those in the diaspora to look after. I still believe that.' And Ghanaian responsibility? 'For us, they do not mean the same thing as they do for you people.' At this juncture the same girl who had brought the tray of drinks reappeared and announced that there was a phone call from the university. We stood and shook hands. So much for Pan-Africanism, I thought. 'You people'?

Again Mansour swerves to avoid a pot-hole. We seem to be driving in a part of Accra that appears to have been laid out according to some grand plan. The streets, although badly in need of repair, are broad and straight, and the houses which line them are large and spacious. We are going to visit Dr Robert Lee, an African-American who settled in Ghana in the fifties, and began to practise as a dentist in this very suburb where he still lives and practises. Some years ago, Dr Lee attempted to take out a lease on a slave fort, only to find his considerable efforts thwarted by the Ghanaian government. In fact, he was attempting to do precisely what Dr Ben Abdallah seemed to be suggesting. Mansour keeps glancing at a piece of paper on which

I presume he has written the address. I look out of the car window and observe that the whole neighbourhood seems somewhat somnambulant.

I wait in a small musty-smelling room that is the anteroom of Dr Lee's dental surgery. Before me a sheaf of magazines lies on a small brown table like a deck of colourful glossy cards. All of the magazines are helplessly out of date, and most of them are falling apart in the humidity. A London contact had told me that if I could get an appointment to see Dr Lee, he would prove to be a valuable source of information. I therefore took the trouble to write him a lengthy letter before leaving for Ghana. When I called from my Accra hotel, Dr Lee answered the phone with his booming American voice. No, he had not received my letter. No, he did not know who I was. He did, however, agree to see me at the end of his working day. Through a half-open door I can see an empty dentist's chair. Above me a fan turns lazily. A weak pool of afternoon light spills across the floor. Silence. The receptionist at the end of the corridor simply stares into mid-air, and still there is no sign of Dr Lee.

My contact in London had interviewed Dr Lee for a BBC programme, and he possessed a small biographical file on a man he described to me as 'remarkable'. Dr Robert Lee was born in South Carolina, and grew up in Charleston. He studied in Tennessee and at Lincoln University in Pennsylvania, where he met the future President of Ghana, Kwame Nkrumah, who was then training to be a Presbyterian minister. Thereafter, Dr Lee went on to study dentistry in New York. He first visited the Gold Coast, as it then was, in 1953, and returned to settle and establish a practice in 1956. Among the many people of the African diaspora who visited in his wake, and whom he knew, were W. E. B. Du Bois, C. L. R. James, George Padmore, Richard Wright, Maya Angelou, Frantz Fanon, and John Hendrick Clarke. In fact, any prominent non-white visitor was somebody who would have been known to Dr Lee.

Having set up his dental practice, for the first ten years Dr Lee seldom travelled to the United States. He had a family to raise, and a business to establish. It was also very difficult and expensive to travel back and forth, although in recent years Dr Lee has apparently become a frequent visitor to the United States. He has a son in New York who, according to my friend's file, Dr Lee likes to describe as an African learning how to be an American. When I first heard about Dr Lee, I could not help wondering if this was a man who had stayed on past his time. I had come across white colonials in Africa, in India, and in the Caribbean who seemed to have fossilized while the world about them swirled with change. I wondered if Dr Lee was not in some ways an African-American 'fossil', a man whom time has stealthily, and now cruelly, overtaken.

He takes me by surprise. I am busily engaged in reading an old copy of *Time* magazine, trying to work out for myself why these news magazines always convince me that events long past have only just occurred, and then Dr Lee is standing before me, his arm outstretched. I stand and note that he is slimmer and shorter than I imagined him to be. Dr Lee has a big man's voice. He urges me to sit, and then he takes the seat opposite and looks at me with the concern of a man who wants to be generous, but who is not at all sure of how he might help. Before I have a chance to once again explain my purpose to him (an explanation which would merely be a restatement of what I had told him on the telephone), he decides to seize the moment.

'You see, fundamentally the United States remains a racist society. Wherever the English settled you'll find the heaviest racism. I know, of course, the laws have changed in the States, but it's still a plantation system, although the system has to think twice before it will move against you. But once it's made its mind up, then it moves, law or no law. Me, I don't have that kind of trouble when I'm in the States. You see, I'm older now, but it's the younger ones I feel for. When I was a boy in the south, the older men could get away with drinking water at the white fountains, but younger guys would get beaten up or worse.'

We fall into a trough of silence. I imagine that it has just occurred to Dr Lee that perhaps I do not necessarily want to speak about the United States. I am going to say something along these lines, but Dr Lee suddenly regains energy and asks me if this is my first time in Ghana. I tell him, no. 'There are problems in this country. Power, money, social position; people craved all of this back then and they are still craving it now. Sadly there is a high degree of colonial mentality that still exists in Ghana. The colonial-minded classes are ruling the country.' Dr Lee lowers his voice. 'Be careful to whom you say "brother", because they might be a colonial administrator or a slave-trader.'

Through the open window I can see Mansour pacing warily by the car. Occasionally he looks at the clapped-out Mercedes with what I can only imagine to be a mixture of pride and embarrassment. The car has managed so far, but we are both worried about whether it will take us to Elmina and Cape Coast. Mansour opens the door and sits on the edge of the seat. He lets his feet rest on the dusty road, and then he begins to scratch lines into the dust with the edge of his sandal. On the way to Dr Lee's, he told me that many black Americans think of themselves as better than Africans, and they therefore have a bad reputation in Ghana. He was keen to stress that this is not the case with Dr Lee. 'Many talk about "family",' said Mansour, 'without realizing that in Africa the family is not your colour, or your nation, but your tribe.' As far as Mansour is concerned, all Africans overseas are simply a different tribe.

Dr Lee points a finger in my direction, and his eyes light up a little. 'You were asking about the slave forts, right?' In both my letter (that he never received) and in my telephone call, I had told Dr Lee that it was his attempt to purchase a slave fort called Abanze Castle that first brought his name to my notice. 'You see,' says Dr Lee, 'I wanted to draw the local people's attention to these places that they call "castles", because I've studied a little psychiatry and I know the effect of these places on African mentality, both here and abroad.'

'An adverse effect?' I ask.

'Hell, yes. These forts are the places where Africans were separated and the African sense of self was broken. If the Atlantic Ocean was to dry up there would be a double highway from the Cape to Jamaica paved with African bones.'

I suggest to Dr Lee, who seems to be sitting further and further on the edge of his seat, that by calling them 'castles' and equating them with kings and queens and the Eurocentric tradition, the African is not facing the reality of what these places really mean.

'The African doesn't really understand the slave trade,' says Dr Lee. 'To bring it up causes him embarrassment. If they can make money out of turning these places into shrines of tourism for Africans in the diaspora to come back and weep and wail and gnash their teeth, then so be it. They're businessmen. But to go deeper into the psychological and historical import of the slave trade is not what most Africans wish to do.'

I wonder about those, like himself, who have chosen to return 'home'. I mention a group of African-Americans at Elmina whom I intend to visit. Dr Lee laughs, at first quietly, and then with mounting hilarity. 'Man, romantics. They come over, but they're not real. They don't speak the language, and the villagers laugh at them because they're trying to learn how to feel like an African. But they're not African, they're like me, African-American. A lot of their behaviour, consciously or subconsciously, is a criticism of the people they've settled amongst. Me, I never pretended to be anything other than what I am. An American living here, but you know you can get tired of translating in your mind. But at least I can do the translating. I had something to offer this country back in the fifties. I have something to offer them now. I'm a dentist, with a skill. What do these people have to offer?'

Indeed, what do they have to offer? And what would make a group of African-Americans uproot their 'comfortable' first-world lives and settle on the west coast of Africa? Romance? Dr Lee seems dismissive of the motives of the people in Elmina, but surely something had to be wrong with their lives in the United States to make them leave. And surely something has to be right with their new lives in Elmina to make them want to stay. It is getting dark. Mansour is now sitting in the car with the doors closed and the windows down. He is reading, but occasionally he seems to nod off to sleep for a moment, and then his head will suddenly snap back to attention. I gather my papers and stand to face Dr Lee, who seems surprised that I am ready to leave. I make my apologies for I do not wish to abandon Mansour for any longer than is necessary. I look at Dr Lee. It is true, he is a man who has stayed on, and he certainly exhibits the chief characteristic of such people. He wishes to talk to somebody from the old world. The subject is almost irrelevant, he simply wishes to talk. However, although Dr Robert Lee may have stayed on, he has not stayed on past 'his time'. He seems remarkably attuned to contemporary events and ideas, and I realize that I have seldom met anybody less 'fossilized' than Dr Lee.

'You see, back in the States they can call me a nigger all they like, but nobody can insult me any more. I won't fight, I'm calm inside. I'm not caught in the net of misinformation of a historical kind. Here, it's difficult. But I have no romance. I know what it's like to live without a television or a toilet, but they don't. The States has let them down in some way and they expect Africa to solve their problems for them. Africa isn't ready to do that. And maybe they're not ready for Africa. The States has got problems but it's their home. Hell, they're Americans.'

Back at the hotel I lie full-length on my bed and watch images of 'home'. Everton versus Manchester United. Mansour deposited me at the door to the hotel, but he was somewhat reluctant to turn off the engine for fear that the car would not start again. I quickly jumped out, told him that we would leave at eleven o'clock in the morning, and thanked him for his day's work. An exhausted Mansour promised that he would be ready and waiting at eleven o'clock sharp, and he wished me good-night. I stood and watched as the car bucked and lurched in the general direction of the main road. I wondered if Mansour was having second thoughts about this assignment. As I entered the hotel lobby and made my way towards the elevators, I decided that at some point I would talk with Mansour about the quandary that his life was ensnared in, and see if there was some way in which I might help him.

We drive slowly past the 'Don't Mind Your Wife' Bar and the 'Lover Boy' Haircut Salon. A huge hoarding at the side of the road announces '24 hour cure for Malaria', but gives no product name, or phone number. We are approaching a junction so Mansour begins to slow to a halt. Mansour had been late, and eleven o'clock had metamorphosed into noon. 'I had some trouble with the car.' I had already surmised this, but we appear to be doing all right now. The hinterland of Accra seems to be a vast market that is reluctant to surrender its territory to the countryside. On my side of the car an elderly blind man stands with a boy, whom I presume to be his son. Mansour leans across me and throws a handful of coins out of the window. They bounce and the old man hears the sound. 'Thank you', he says. The boy dives for the coins before the lights can turn green.

We wind our slow way through yet another throng of vendors. The streets are a dizzying clash of first and third world. Flimsy cardboard shacks suddenly give way to brand-new five-storey buildings with ATMs and air-conditioning. And then more shacks. In a car compound I notice an eclectic array of second-hand cars, mainly British and American, the American cars with their steering-wheels on the 'wrong' side. However, the evidence of Ghanaian driving suggests that this detail will not concern anybody. The vendors continue to walk between the cars selling shoes, photographs, air fresheners, pharmaceuticals and puppies. In this vast kinetic market there is nothing that one cannot buy. In the wake of the traders, the polio victims drag their twisted limbs along the ground. The luckier ones are being pushed in wheelchairs, and it is soon apparent that everybody has their territory clearly staked out. They all have only the one sentence: 'I beg you, my brother.'

Mansour suddenly pulls over into a garage. He explains that he thinks it politic to check the tyre pressure. Mansour suggests that I might stretch my legs or buy some water, and then he scampers off to find a man to help him. I get out of the car and stare up at the Ghanaian equivalent of the Marlboro Man peering down at me from an advertising hoarding. He is black, but not too black, with high cheekbones, a pencil-thin moustache, a gleaming white smile, thin lips, and relaxed hair. He has a woman on one arm, and he encourages us to drink local beer. Macho, independent, sensitive, African. On the other hand, the man helping Mansour wears clothes that are so blackened with filth that they match the dirt beneath his feet. When he has finished his 'job', the man charges me the equivalent of a dime.

The dust rises around the bald tyres of a bus as it pulls away from the garage. And then I notice that as the bus rumbles down the road the dust appears to follow like a spirit. We follow the dust following the bus. I find myself fascinated by the signs. Clearly Ghanaians have a genius for naming. 'Professor Classic Baldhead' Barbers; 'Sober Spot' Bar; 'God's Will' Beauty Salon; 'A Great Outfit' Clothes Store; 'CBS' Current Beauty Salon; 'Oasis of Love Travel and Tours'; and my favourite, which is the 'Figure Correction Shop', the Ghanaian equivalent of a weight loss centre. I glance across at Mansour, who is gripping the steering-wheel with great intensity. He is determined to thrash some life into this Mercedes. I am equally determined to get some sleep before we arrive at Elmina.

ELMINA: THE ENCOUNTER

As long ago as the Middle Ages, articles from West Africa, including gold, pepper, slaves and ivory, were being exported across the Saharan desert to North Africa, and from there these goods made their way into Europe. With the onset of the age of sailing and discovery, Europeans began to voyage in all directions in the hope they might develop new trading routes. Naturally enough, they were particularly interested in West Africa.

By 1462, Portuguese navigators had already sailed as far south as the mouths of the Senegal and the Gambia rivers. They explored this region, and then pressed on past the highlands of the country that would one day become Sierra Leone. For a time they traded in the area they called the Grain Coast (present-day Liberia), where they were keen to acquire 'Guinea Grains', which they subsequently utilized as pepper. However, with the opening up of European trade to the East Indies, and the sudden availability of 'real' pepper, the Portuguese soon lost interest in trading on this difficult part of the African coast, and they continued south. Beyond the Grain Coast lay the Ivory Coast, whose shoreline was filled with swamps and lagoons that were treacherous to negotiate, and whose stagnant waters proved to be a breeding ground for mosquitoes.

In 1471, the Portuguese arrived on the part of the coast that would eventually come to be known as the Gold Coast. They were pleasantly surprised by the solid ground, easily navigable inlets and fishing villages of the region, which suggested to them that in this place they might be able to trade for ivory with considerably more ease than they had been accustomed to. However, it was the fabulous abundance of gold that captured the Europeans' attention, gold that was worn about the bodies of the local Africans in the form of ornaments of great intricacy and delicacy. Three years later, in 1474, the Portuguese king, having been informed of the arrival in his kingdom of a succession of ships laden with gold, declared trading on this part of the

African coast to be a royal monopoly. The area was named by the Portuguese 'A Mina', or The Mine.

The place that proved most attractive to the Portuguese was a promontory known locally as 'The Village of Two Parts', which was in fact a single village divided into two by the mouth of the River Benya. Constructed on hard rock, and surrounded on three sides by water, it provided a perfect vantage-point from which to view all ocean-going traffic. Eventually the village became known as El Mina, which was a corruption of the Portuguese name for the whole region, 'A Mina'. Some years later the village became simply known as Elmina. It was at this place on the coast that the Portuguese began to trade with most vigour, excited as they were by the overwhelming quantities of gold that appeared to be available.

However, the amount of gold on display was deceptive, for the African people of Elmina had been collecting gold for thousands of years prior to the arrival of the Portuguese. With restricted opportunity for trading, gold was worn in the form of decorations that the Africans valued, but, as they were soon to discover, not as highly as the Europeans. Soon after their initial contact, the Portuguese realized that a few days' walk from the coast there were places where the natives were simply washing gold nuggets from streams. Further inland, and beyond this alluvial gold, there were mines with both horizontal and vertical shafts where veins of the precious metal were being excavated. While the Portuguese were delighted at this new opportunity to swell their wealth, the people of the region were similarly excited by this unexpected opportunity to trade this metal in exchange for European goods, such as cotton, wool, hatchets, knives, wine and, most importantly, brass that could be melted down and recast for local purposes. In the wake of the arrival of the Portuguese, African traders began to flock to this coastal region in the hope of encountering European traders.

An African trader from the interior could, in theory, arrive at the coast with a small box of gold and an ivory tusk, both of which he could easily convey by himself, and begin to trade with the Portuguese. In exchange for his goods he would receive many bundles of cloth, a profusion of brass bracelets, and numerous other items which he could not hope to carry by himself. Such a trader could hire servants to assist him, but if his journey back into the interior was likely to last several weeks then he might choose instead to purchase some slaves. The Portuguese would often sell such slaves to the African traders, for part of their trading practice already involved some exploratory trading in human beings, many of whom they brought with them to Elmina.

This intensive form of Afro-European trade involved great risks for both parties, and precautions had to be taken. The Africans soon discovered methods by which they could mix gold with copper filings, or fill large ivory tusks with lead so as to increase their weight. As a result, the Portuguese learned to employ a brass rod to sound the ivory tusks, and most trading ships took the precaution of sailing with a professional goldsmith. The Portuguese practice of watering wine, or doctoring bolts of tightly wrapped cloth by cutting out sections from the middle, or substituting coloured glass for precious gems soon came to the attention of the Africans. They realized that, like the Portuguese, they too would have to remain vigilant if this trading intercourse was to proceed to everybody's satisfaction.

In 1481, in order to facilitate future trade at Elmina, and to secure the region from the incursion of other European powers, King John II of Portugal gave orders to begin the construction of a fortified castle of hitherto unimagined proportions in this isolated part of Africa. The King's advisers were outraged by this decision, arguing that it would be impossible to protect and defend such a place. The King, however, would brook no opposition, and he insisted that because this was the richest part of the West African coastline other European traders would soon attempt to undermine the Portuguese foothold in the area.

Traders' reports had suggested to King John II that the thick and solid foundation of rock at Elmina would provide the ideal site for the construction of the castle. There was ample rock to quarry, and the quarrying would create a solid platform for the actual castle. To the east there was a beach that offered a landing place for large ships, while to the south-west there was a river which could handle small craft but which also provided some form of defence. To approach the proposed castle from the land would mean squeezing along an exposed narrow strip of land, bounded by tidal flats and the Atlantic. However, the most secure line of defence for the castle lay to the west, where the treacherous breakers of the Atlantic rolled up hard against yet more rock.

The King chose as his envoy Diego de Azambuja, a man who had already served some time as a soldier in Africa. He took the title 'captain-General', and under his command he assembled a collection of the finest Portuguese seamen and pilots, including Bartolomeu Dias who, some few years later, would gain fame as the first man to navigate around the Cape of Good Hope. Prior to his departure, Azambuja dispatched two transport ships that were fully laden with ready-dressed stones for windows and gates, all neatly ordered and marked, which he imagined would facilitate the speedy construction of the castle. The cargo also included timber, nails, bricks, tools, ready-mixed lime, in fact all the materials that King John II and his captain-General thought might be necessary in the coming weeks. The utilization of local stone and African labour, which they both understood to be an essential part of the whole enterprise, would have to be dealt with upon arrival.

On 12 December 1481, six hundred men under Diego de Azambuja's command, one hundred stone masons, carpenters, and skilled workmen, together with five hundred soldiers and sailors, set sail for Elmina in a squadron of ten caravels. Azambuja had decided that once they arrived it would be diplomatic to obtain permission to begin construction from the local

African king. After all, their mission was not motivated by a desire for conquest, but by a desire 'to make no end of coin by trade'. On Friday, 19 January 1482, Diego de Azambuja finally arrived at the mouth of the River Benya, and having ridden at anchor all night, the following morning he led his men ashore. His historic meeting with the local 'king' was recorded by two Portuguese scribes, Rui de Pina and Joao de Barros, their accounts being particularly cognizant of the formality of this initial encounter:

> He [Azambuja] went on land, clothed in silk and brocade, and with his men in good order. And at the foot of a tree, under the shade, he commanded a mass to be said and heard, the first that was said; and henceforth that valley was, and always shall be, called the Vale of St Sebastian. There, after eating, he ordered a richly ornamented platform to be erected; and he sat thereupon, accompanied by very honorable men, and with his trumpets, tambourines and drums, and all in an act of peace (*auto de paz*), in order to receive there, by agreement, the lord of the locality, named Caramansa, whom the blacks called king, and to speak with him.

There has been much debate about the identity of this 'king' called Caramansa, and some historians have speculated that the name of this 'chief of Elmina' is probably a corruption of the name Kwamena Ansah. However, this is a Fante name, and at this point in history there were no members of the Fante tribe on the coast. A more recent idea is that the word 'mansa', which is an Arabic name for trader, holds the clue to this conundrum. It is possible that a 'mansa' of some outstanding wealth and authority named Kara could have been the person who greeted Diego de Azambuja, hence 'Caramansa'. Soon after Azambuja's landing, this 'king', Caramansa, arrived to greet the Portuguese nobleman. He arrived on the scene in the company of his warriors:

Caramansa, being also one who wished to demonstrate his standing, arrived with many men drawn up in battle order, in a great din from side-drums, horns, bells and other instruments, more deafening than pleasing to the ears. Their dress was the one native to their own flesh, oiled and very shining, which made their skins blacker, a practice they follow for its elegance. Only their shameful parts were covered, some with monkey skins, others with palm cloths, but the leading men had coloured cloths acquired by traffic with our ships that went there to trade for gold. All in general came armed after their fashion, some with assegais and shields, others with bows and quivers of arrows, with many, in place of a helmet, wearing a monkey skin, the head of which was entirely studded with teeth of beasts—all these their devices to demonstrate their ferocity as warriors being so unseemly that they moved one to laughter rather than to fear. Those who among them were considered nobles had, as a token of their nobility, two pages following them, one of whom carried a round wooden seat for them to sit on when they cared to rest, and the other carried a battle shield. And these nobles wore a number of rings and jewels of gold in their hair and beard.

Despite the Portuguese amusement at the dress of Caramansa's warriors, the sight of 'King' Caramansa himself seems to have instilled in them the appropriate sense of respect and awe.

Their king, Caramansa, arrived in the midst of all, covered on his legs and arms with bracelets and circlets of gold, on his neck a collar from which hung some small bells, and twined in his beard some pieces of gold which so weighed down its hairs that the curly ones had become straight. In keeping with the honour of his person, he moved with very loitering steps, one foot before the other, and without turning his face to either side. While he was thus approaching solemnly, Diego de Azambuja remained motionless on his platform, until, as Caramansa reached the middle of our men, he moved off towards him. And when they were close, Caramansa took the hand of Diego de Azambuja, and releasing it snapped his fingers, saying these words, 'Bere! Bere!', which means 'Peace! Peace!', the snapping being their sign of the greatest courtesy they can render. The King, moving away, stood aside so that his men could approach Diego de Azambuja to do the same. But the way in which they snapped their fingers differed from that of the king, for they touched him after wetting a finger in their mouth and cleaning it on their chest—a gesture a person of lower standing makes to one of higher—as a guarantee of safety made here to princes, since they say that poison can be carried in a finger unless it is cleaned this way.

There then followed speechmaking, with Azambuja declaring (through an interpreter that the Portuguese had brought with them, a man of the region who had been previously taken to Lisbon for 'training') that they wished to construct a strong building for the secure storage of merchandise, and some dwelling houses. Although the full size and nature of the proposed building was never explained to the Africans, it would be fair to conjecture that the Africans had never before seen a building of more than one storey in height. Having explained his desire to begin construction, Azambuja continued and offered excessive thanks to 'the Lord the creator, who was God', and then suggested that Caramansa might wish to consider baptism for thereafter he would be 'as a friend and brother in this Faith of Christ'.

The Portuguese scribes record that Caramansa listened in silence. Azambuja continued, and credited Caramansa with having facilitated profitable and honourable contact with Portuguese traders during the preceding ten years, and then praised him further for his superiority of status and outstanding abilities. Azambuja explained that among the many advantages to the local Akan population of helping in the construction of a 'strong building' would be a significant share in the profits from this improved method of trading. There would also be enhanced local prestige, and the Portuguese would be able to offer considerable support in fighting local enemies. Caramansa fixed his eyes upon the ground for a short space of time, and he thought long and hard before replying.

> The king, together with those leading men of his, then replied, saying that the people of the Christians who up to that time had come had been few, dirty and base, but that the ones who now came were much the opposite, especially himself [Azambuja], who by his clothes and appearance must be the son or brother of the king of Portugal. At this, before they could proceed further with their speech, the captain immediately rejoindered, that he was not the son or brother of the king, his lord, but was one of his very minor vassals. For the king was so powerful and such a lord that in his kingdoms, which he commanded and they obeyed him, that he had two hundred thousand men, greater and better and richer.

A somewhat sceptical Caramansa listened to this interruption. When it was again his turn to speak he made it plain to Azambuja that men who met from time to time generally accorded each other greater respect than those who were neighbours. Caramansa stressed that although he wished to see the traffic in trade maintain its present dimensions, he rejected allegiance in any form either to the King of Portugal, or to the Christian God. Azambuja quickly countered, pointing out that by choosing this land as a place where he might erect a building and store his property, the King of Portugal was investing considerable faith in the honesty and wisdom of the men of this coast, for should deceitful practices break out, the king's army

was too distant to defend his sovereign rights. Azambuja continued by once more restating the fact that he was one of the lesser
vassals of the kingdom, and that he would rather lose his life
than fail to carry out the orders of his king.

> At this utterance, the blacks, seeing that their king [Cara-
> mansa] was astonished at such obedience and that he now
> struck one hand on the other, as a sign of their being compli-
> ant they also clapped hands, which broke into the speech of
> Diego de Azambuja. And before he could proceed further,
> once the noise had stopped Caramansa cut in, stating as a
> conclusion that he was content that the building he [Azam-
> buja] sought should be erected, exhorting him that peace
> and true dealing be kept.

Upon completion of the castle in 1482, African internal
trade to the coast became increasingly focused upon Elmina, for
the traders knew that their goods could be comfortably accom-
modated in the huge storerooms of the castle. African traders
no longer had to linger at the coast waiting for the arrival of
ships laden with European merchandise. Similarly, European
ships no longer had to anchor for weeks and months (having first
negotiated with yet another hostile tribal chief) waiting for their
holds to be sufficiently stocked with African supplies. The existence of Elmina Castle meant that the goods had already been
purchased, stored, and simply needed to be transported aboard
ship. A permanent European station meant that it was also
possible to maintain constant commercial contact with the hinterland. Furthermore, this method of trading also significantly
reduced the risk of fatal disease, the most common cause of
death being malaria or yellow fever, both of which were borne
by mosquitoes. In the mosquito-free environment of the castle, a
small European society of sixty-three persons was established,
complete with a chapel, a small garrison of soldiers, a surgeon,

and those individuals whose specific task was to trade with the local population.

The local economy of Elmina soon became almost totally dependent upon the Portuguese presence, with African carpenters and craftsmen not only maintaining and improving facilities at the castle, but also frequently called upon to work on the ships whose gear regularly needed repairing. Others in the village supplied food for both the inhabitants of the castle and for those who arrived on the ships. Elmina changed in nature, and became independent of its Akan neighbours both economically and in terms of its character. It rapidly became a large, multi-ethnic, multi-lingual place of trade which included people of mixed descent. Not only were there those whose fathers were European, but there were those whose fathers and mothers were of different African ethnic origins. Unlike the pro-Fante Cape Coast, some twenty miles to the east, heterogeneous Elmina managed to be both pro-Fante and pro-Asante, so that when conflict eventually erupted between these two great inland empires, Elmina was the one place on the coast where relative peace reigned.

Among the many visitors to Elmina was Christopher Columbus, who undoubtedly modelled the construction of his new-world forts on the 'miracle' he had witnessed on the coast of Africa at Elmina. Organized along the lines of a feudal household, with the governor at the head, this community provided the model for other European trading outposts that were soon developed on the West African coast, although none were ever as large or as efficient as Elmina Castle. If one imagines the Gold Coast to be a large shopping street, then Elmina Castle was undoubtedly its Harrods or Saks Fifth Avenue. After two years, a triumphant Azambuja returned to Portugal in 1484, knowing that he had successfully overseen the construction of the most substantial European building in the whole of Africa.

For the first fifty years after the establishment of Elmina Castle, the Portuguese perfected an administrative machinery

which ensured a steady flow of treasure back into the royal cof-
fers in Lisbon. They forbade Africans in their 'sphere of influence' from trading with any other European power, but there
was little necessity to vigorously enforce this law. Although English, French, and Spanish ships were actively exploring West
African waters, few ever travelled as far south and east as
Elmina. Those that sought to rob the Portuguese Mina caravels
would lie in wait further north, particularly in the narrow
waters around the Azores, although even here they were often
unsuccessful, for the Mina caravels were remarkably swift and
agile. However, such was the wealth of the Elmina region that
the loss of even a single caraval often had a profound effect on
the Portuguese crown revenues. But things were rapidly changing. By the middle of the sixteenth century, gold was no longer
the most profitable cargo to trade for on the shores of West
Africa. It was fast becoming clear to all the European powers,
including the Portuguese, that the really important commodity
on the West African coast was now human beings.

PANAFEST (1)

According to the publicity material, Panafest is to be a time
when the diasporan family returns to Mother Africa to celebrate
the arts, creativity and intellectual achievements of the Pan
African world. I feel considerable relief as Mansour pulls into
the car park of the Elmina Beach Hotel and Conference Centre,
and I stuff the publicity material back into my bag. Above the
entrance to the hotel a huge banner welcomes delegates and
participants back to Mother Africa. Mansour seems somewhat
disappointed that his 'fun' behind the wheel of the Mercedes
has come to a temporary end, but I stride purposefully away
from the car in search of a shower and a long rest. Kate, the
young manageress, is working behind the reception desk. She is
painfully thin, with a very dark complexion, and hair that has
been straightened and cut into a bob. 'I am happy to see you,'

she says as she hands me my registration card and a pen. 'Welcome to Elmina.'

The afternoon sun streaks through my bungalow's inadequate curtains and wakes me up. Outside I can hear the distant roar of the surf pounding against Elmina Beach. I have already decided that tonight I will attend the first of the Panafest events. There is to be a 'performance' at Elmina Castle, and during the following few days there will be other events and 'performances' in both Elmina and Cape Coast, some of which I have already circled in my programme. Welcome to Panafest. Prepare to be swept away by the romance of home. I step from my bed and shield my eyes against the glare.

As I climb the short incline to Elmina Castle, I notice that a large open tent has been erected on the grass outside the gates to the castle. Beneath the tent, chairs have been arranged so as to create an enclosed arena. Mansour points and informs me that later tonight the Western Diamonds, one of Ghana's most popular bands, will be playing a free concert. This accounts for the throng of people already crowding the area. 'Maybe we can go too?' suggests Mansour. Although I have no desire to attend the concert I shrug my shoulders in a neutral manner, and then press on through the crowd toward the gate. Having paid the entrance fees of 1,000 cedis each (about fifty cents), we cross the drawbridge and pass into the main courtyard of Elmina Castle.

The performance is supposed to start at 7.30 p.m. It is 7.30 p.m. A stage has been erected, with a Panafest logo trim tacked around the base, while the surface of the stage is littered with professional-looking musical and sound equipment. There is sufficient seating for an audience of about two hundred and fifty people, but at present there are only twenty 'Panafesters'. Mansour and I sit towards the front, and I watch as an Austrian television crew, who are clearly trying to make some kind of a documentary, continue to struggle with their 'communication problems' with the Ghanaian stage crew. The issue appears to be lighting. Or rather, the lack of lighting.

An hour passes, and the audience has now swollen to maybe twenty-four, but still nothing appears to be happening on stage. I look at the 'guests', a large number of whom seem to be European men in black Panafest T-shirts. They have the painfully malnourished look of people who have discovered a cause that will save them from their own oblivion. As I scan the faces of the admirably patient 'masses', two women with tattoos, sandals, baggy pants, rucksacks emblazoned with the Australian flag, and hair cropped high at the nape in an institutional fashion, wander into the courtyard and then take up seats to my side. They are both carrying bottles of beer, and one carries a small bongo drum. We nod in silent acknowledgement of each other's presence. Mansour looks at me and rolls his eyes.

Soon after, two young Ghanaian men appear at the entrance to the courtyard. They look around, see the two women, and practically sprint to join them. Uninvited, they sit one to either side of them. I notice the men's badges, which distinguish them as official Panafest 'guides'. And now the smaller of the two men begins to 'act' as a guide. He gestures to the courtyard that we are sitting in, and announces that this is where his people held their market. 'The Governor used to live up there.' He points to the Governor's residence high above the stage. 'The British built it.' He points now to Fort St Jago on the hill in the distance. 'Then they built that other fort to protect this one. This castle was used for prisoners.' In the midst of this torrent of disinformation, the 'guide' omits to point out the two female dungeons, each of which could accommodate up to one hundred and fifty slaves, or the male dungeon which often held upwards of a thousand slaves. Mansour is barely able to contain his rage, so I touch his arm in an attempt to reassure him that it is all right.

Having rewritten history, and totally failed to notice the sexual orientation of their new Australian 'friends', the Panafest 'guides' listen enthusiastically as the woman with the bongo drum explains that she has come to Africa to study drumming for three and a half months. 'My first instrument is the congas, but I have to find a master to teach me.' Predictably the Panafest 'guides' know of many 'masters' and they promise that tomorrow they will take the Australians to meet some masters. In fact, if there is anybody else that they would like to meet then they will take them to meet them. Two policemen parade in front of the stage and the Ghanaians point at them. 'Do your policemen in Australia wear berets?' Strange question, I think. 'But they are soldiers aren't they?' suggests a genuinely puzzled bongo player. Our Panafest 'guides' still have a long road to tread in the wooing department.

One and a half hours after the advertised time of the 'performance', the master of ceremonies for the evening, who looks to me to be little more than a schoolboy, picks up the microphone and addresses the spartan crowd, initially in Fante and then in English. This will, he promises, be an evening of great drama, but first we will begin with music. A local Roman Catholic choir of a dozen women, all dressed in white, are quickly ushered on to the stage where they begin to perform hymns in Fante. The locals in the crowd, including the 'guides', sing along with huge vocal enthusiasm. At the conclusion of the music, the theatrical entertainment commences. The play is about the removal of a local king to Sierra Leone in 1873 because he would not obey the British colonial rules. I soon understand that in Ghana naturalism can hold for only the briefest interlude. The 'performance' is punctuated by speeches to the audience, musical numbers, and drumming and dancing. The all-women cast play the male roles, and the 'drama' is made all the more difficult, for me at least, by the fact that the play is in Fante with no translation. After twenty minutes the bongo player to my left clearly grasps the full complexity of the narrative. 'Ah,' she says to her new Ghanaian friends, 'it's like an African pantomime.' A restraining hand keeps Mansour in his seat.

The following morning, the 'Day of Memorial and Remembrance' is scheduled to begin with a ceremony on the frontage at Elmina Castle. Mansour drives the short distance from the hotel to the castle at a madcap pace, slamming the Mercedes into curve after curve as though we are late for an urgent appointment. I realize that this family reunion is making him distinctly uncomfortable, and that at some point we will probably have to talk about this. We arrive at the frontage an hour later than the advertised start time, but I am not surprised to discover that, as yet, nothing is happening. I want to ask Mansour, why the rush? Mansour, however, is looking wistfully around the space which yesterday evening had played host to his beloved Western Diamonds. I leave him to his thoughts, and wander further up the incline of the hill. I am surrounded by cattle which range purposelessly across parched grass. They endeavour to scavenge, but do so without any apparent enthusiasm.

Mansour and I take our seats beneath the shade of the tent. An official helper in a bright, rainbow-coloured Panafest T-shirt hands out red strips of cloth which she tells us are worn in Fante and Asante culture to symbolize respect for somebody who has died. Because atonement rites are to be performed for those who perished in slavery, we are encouraged to wear the cloth around our head, neck, or wrist, according to how much of a statement we wish to make. Mansour and I are clearly 'wrist' people. Behind me I overhear an African-American woman remarking loudly to her African female friend about her concern that she does not have the right currency with which to buy a can of Coca-Cola. Then she remembers herself, and in the spirit of family unity she states that 'In New York we don't take cedis so we gotta make the effort. You know, one blood, one family.'

On her batik dress are emblazoned the words, 'Africa. Our Aim Unity', but despite the dreadlocks, the African garb, and the statement on her dress, I cannot help feeling that this is obviously an American woman in dark glasses. The man to her side, again demonstrably an American, wears a bright yellow costume which is decorated with a drawing of human cargo that is laid out in the hold of a slave ship. Above it are written the words 'Never forgive, Never forget'.

Two hours after the advertised time for the beginning of the programme, nothing is happening. Then a clearly intoxicated youth lurches into the middle of the square of grass and begins to gyrate to hi-life music and wave a Ghanaian flag. Mansour shrinks in his seat. Panafest is becoming something of a national embarrassment for him, although as I look down I can see that he is stirring his toes inside his shoes in time with the beat of the music. Suddenly, to the chaotic sound of drums, whistles, cowbells and the random firing of rifles, the 'royal procession' arrives. They are led by the 'warriors', who appear to be badly dressed unemployed youth and old men. After the 'warriors' come the more formally dressed and dignified 'elders'. Suddenly every white person in the audience seems to own a video camera. The more bold among them are jumping and dancing. A lone African man blows a trumpet and cavorts wildly before the procession, and he is soon joined by the intoxicated youth. The younger Ghanaian men, many of them sporting caps made up of the colours of the South African flag, and shirts and shoes emblazoned with the ubiquitous Nike swoosh, encourage their diasporan sisters to get up and liberate their spirits. A few non-diasporan sisters from Germany and Sweden are also encouraged to liberate their spirits.

Before the official atonement ceremony begins, and while this dancing and noise continues, I suddenly notice that somebody has placed a six-foot long pole draped with cloth across my lap. Mansour tells me that this is the local flag of Elmina, which is apparently demanding to be shown respect in the form of an offering. Two middle-aged men daubed in white paint, one in a Mike Tyson T-shirt, the other in a T-shirt bearing the image of the deceased rapper Tupac Shakur, stand expectedly with their palms spread wide. Meanwhile, back in the square, another drama is unfolding, A healthy-looking white ram is about to be sacrificed. Not unsurprisingly, the ram is struggling to free itself from the rope around its neck. Through the over-amplified system, the announcer speaks in a dignified whisper. 'At this time we want to sacrifice a ram to the ancestors who shed their blood in the cause of slavery.' He pauses. 'So bear with us.' An anguished cry of 'Oh no!' rises from the animal-loving American cousins of the diaspora. There is little time for emotion. The ram is quickly dispatched to meet its maker, and the vultures overhead display a renewed interest in the proceedings. A wave of disgust crests in the crowd. I show respect to the flag of Elmina by pulling some crumpled cedis from my trouser pocket.

Back at the hotel, I walk across the compound for a third time in an attempt to convince somebody in the office that unless the air-conditioning in my room is repaired I am likely to expire with the heat and humidity. However, behind the desk a harassed-looking Kate, a telephone pressed up to the side of her head, is clearly having problems of her own with the Jamaican contingent who, according to an interview in the local paper with their leader, Sista Pee, are in Ghana 'to discover their African roots, history and heritage'. Kate covers the speaker, and tells me that the thirty-seven Caribbean 'pilgrims' seem intent upon cooking in their own rooms, which involves lighting fires on tiled floors. Kate is also unhappy about certain substances which they seem keen to ingest. Having already been threatened with ejection by Kate, they have persisted and suddenly a diasporan crisis is looming. My air-conditioning problems begin to look small by comparison. This being the case, I decide to go outside and take a seat while Kate continues her telephonic diplomacy.

I turn my mind back to the events of the morning. The 'Day of Memorial and Remembrance' had officially recognized five 'Africans': Malcolm X, Steve Biko, Marcus Garvey, Patrice Lumumba, and Martin Luther King, Jr. Also remembered were those tribes who suffered greatly through slavery. After the slaughtering of the ram, there was a wreath-laying ceremony in the courtyard of the castle. A Jamaican laid a wreath for all who died in the 'African holocaust'. A wreath was then laid 'For African-Americans and all victims of anti-colonial struggles'. It seemed curious to me that this wreath was in the form of a cross. As another wreath, this one for departed African leaders, was being laid, an African-American man shouted at a white American female film director. The director was bellowing instructions above the sacred din of cowbells, flutes and 'the firing of musketry'. 'Show some damn respect!' cried the man, and the woman immediately, and reverentially, shut her mouth. She thereafter adopted the posture of a statue, allowing her long hair to be idly fingered by the wind. As I left the castle I saw three men unceremoniously dumping the carcass of the slaughtered ram behind a wooden drinks booth.

A sad-looking Kate appears at the door to her office and wearily lifts both arms to push back her straightened bob. She confesses that the Jamaicans will, in all likelihood, have to be expelled. More importantly, I am assured that my air-conditioning will be immediately fixed, which means that tonight I might actually get some sleep. I thank her and wander down to the restaurant overlooking the sea, where I take a chair. I sit and look out at the rough Atlantic breaking over the rocks and then surging up the beach. Hawkers are selling their wares, principally coconuts and sculpture made from fallen branches. They are, however, careful not to trespass too far on to the hotel grounds. I order a Coca-Cola from one of the small army of waiters who seem to do little more than brush flies and mosquitoes from their faces and stare into the distance. And then I see a middle-aged European woman who, having emerged from a 'dip' in the sea, seems to be vigorously rubbing dead skin from her body with a coarse towel. Mansour is asleep in his room, but I decide that in an hour or so I will rouse him and ask him to drive me to Cape Coast Castle, where a floodlighting ceremony is scheduled to take place.

CAPE COAST: AN AFRICAN MISSIONARY

I first discovered the name of Cape Coast Castle through reading the letters of a man called Philip Quaque. An unusual name, I thought, for an Englishman stationed in an African slave fort, but I imagined that perhaps some intermarriage had occurred to result in this hybrid name. In a letter dated 13 October 1811, which turns out to be Quaque's last known letter, the situation is clarified. Speaking of his own family's attitude towards his wife, Quaque observes that they

> . . . have grossly assaulted and maltreated her so shamefully as to cast a disgrace and infamy upon my character. Thus you see the avaricious disposition of the blacks, who are all for themselves and wish not that the inferior people should ever rise in equality with themselves. It is no wonder and too true a saying of our blessed Lord, that a man's foes shall be they of his household and that a prophet has no honour in his own country. Thus is the case now with me and I am fully convinced that the more a man do to these kind of people, the more ungrateful and unthankful they seem to be; it is like casting so many pearls before swine.

The content and tone of this letter make sense when one realizes that not only is Quaque's second wife an African, but Quaque too is an African.

Cape Coast Castle, where Philip Quaque lived and worked for fifty years, was the principal British trade fort on the West African coast. Originally built by the Swedish in 1652, the British captured it from the Dutch in 1662. In common with its neighbours, including the Portuguese Elmina Castle, the fortress had originally been built to facilitate trade in goods in order that a European power might exploit the gold for which the region was famed. However, by the time the British took charge of the fort, black gold—human cargo—was rapidly replacing yellow gold as the principal material of export. Quaque held two positions within the world of Cape Coast Castle. 'The Society for the Propagation of the Gospel in Foreign Parts' (SPG) paid him to live in the castle and act as 'Missionary, School Master, and Catechist to the Negroes on the Gold Coast'. Meanwhile, 'The Company of Merchants Trading to Africa', the association of British merchants who were engaged in the slave trade and who managed the British slave forts along the West African coast, recognized and rewarded Philip Quaque as the 'Chaplain' of Cape Coast Castle. This African man lived with the British slavers as their chaplain, and literally resided above the dungeons in which were held thousands of his fellow Africans awaiting transportation to the Americas.

Quaque is an anglicized version of Kweku, a Fante name given to a boy born on a Wednesday. Kweku was born in 1741, in the town of Cape Coast. In 1754, aged thirteen, Kweku was sponsored by the SPG so that he might visit England to complete his education. It was not uncommon for English religious organizations to identify African 'prodigies' and arrange for their education in England, the understanding being that they would eventually return to the African coast to help 'civilize' the natives. Quaque was dispatched together with two fellow Africans, Thomas Coboro and William Cudjo, and the SPG hoped that these three boys would eventually become Anglican missionaries. Sadly, soon after his arrival in England, Thomas Coboro died of tuberculosis, and William Cudjo was later to die after a nervous breakdown.

Quaque received instruction in religious education and the classics, and five years after his arrival, in 1759, he was baptized at St Mary's Church, Islington, where he received the Christian name, Philip. The eighteen-year-old Philip Quaque continued to live and study in London, and six years later, on 25 March 1765, he was ordained as a deacon by the Bishop of Exeter. Five weeks later, on 1 May of the same year, he was ordained a Priest by the Bishop of London, each distinction being bestowed in the Chapel Royal of St James's Palace. On 2 May, the day after his ordination as a priest, Philip Quaque married an Englishwoman, Catherine Blunt. With his education complete, and his personal life in order, the twenty-four-year-old African began to make plans for his return to the homeland that he had not seen for eleven years. He would be returning as a missionary to his own people.

In February 1766, Reverend Philip Quaque arrived back in Cape Coast with his joint appointment, a generous salary of £60 a year, plus an allowance for Mrs Quaque of £13 a year—an allowance which was traditionally offered as a way to induce white women to reside on the coast. In keeping with the practice of the time, Quaque was paid in goods that he was thereafter able to barter. He joined the English staff of an active slave fort, and he was allotted accommodation by the Governor.

Philip Quaque now took his place in the remarkable twilight world of inter-dependence and fusion which characterized the relationship between the native and the European in this period before the concrete formality and racial separation of the colonial period. Reverend Quaque was also accorded the honorary status of an English officer, and during the fifty years that he worked and resided on the coast he occasionally took temporary command of the lesser forts of Dixcove, Sekondi and Komenda. These secular duties caused him few problems, but his appointment as a chaplain who was expected to minister to the spiritual health of the British men was a difficult one. Philip Quaque's letters bear testimony to the fact that he found it almost impossible to interest the men in Christianity, for their attention was primarily focused on their twin passions of staying alive and making money.

In theory, all European men at Cape Coast were expected to attend service at 11.30 a.m on a Sunday morning or they were liable to be fined seven shillings and sixpence. However, most governors found ways to circumvent this ruling. A governor's diary entry from 1778 admits to the regular flaunting of this rule: 'No Divine Service this day, the Hall and other apartments being just freshly painted.' Other excuses included colds, rough winds, Dutch visitors, or just about anything that came to mind. Generally, the governor and his officers welcomed the presence of a chaplain who might bury them, or baptize their mulatto children, but they had little interest in listening to sermons about the immorality of their polygamous behaviour, or being subjected to homilies about putting God before profit. Given this climate of indifference, Philip Quaque turned most of his attention toward the task of spiritually administering to the indigenous population, but much to his dismay, his efforts failed to bear much fruit. Widespread ancestor worship, and the investing of natural objects, such as the sun, moon, rocks and sea, with deistic qualities formed the basis of the deeply en-trenched traditional belief system, which was integral to the Akan social and political structure.

Philip Quaque's greatest 'success' was the establishment of a school in his own rooms. Here he taught boys and girls religious knowledge, reading, writing and arithmetic:

> I established a seminary . . . in my own bed chamber for the instruction of mulatto children only of both sexes, the num-ber of which at present is but ten, who seem to take their learning surprisingly well and some have very good progress, considering the very short space of time they have been with me. And do intend shortly, God willing, to take a few of the rougher kind to see what can be really made out of them.

The number of students never grew to more than sixteen and on more than one occasion fell to one or even none. Quaque, however, never received the separate school building that he always hoped for, and his school merely limped along in a precarious fashion so that in the end it was difficult for him to regard the experience as anything other than a failure.

In fact, towards the end of his life Philip Quaque came to regard his time on the coast as little more than fifty years of failure and disappointment. His English wife, Catherine, had died in November 1766, nine months after their arrival, succumbing to the strain of living under a tropical climate. Although he married twice more, both times to African women, the unions were not successful. In 1769 he married his late wife's maid, but she died the following year giving birth to a daughter. His final marriage was to an 'adult black girl' whom he had baptized, but the evidence of his letters suggest that this marriage ended in disappointment and bitterness. His three children, a son James, and two daughters, were sent to England for their education, Quaque having decided that this was the best place for them, but little is known of their subsequent lives.

Philip Quaque had to endure much in the way of conflict between the SPG, with their religiously inspired ambitions, and 'The Company of Merchants Trading to Africa', who expected Quaque to place their commercial and military interests above all others. When he refused to do so, he was on more than one occasion suspended and expelled from the castle. Saddened and thoroughly fatigued, Philip Quaque died on 17 October 1816, a man in his mid-seventies who had survived much personal and political turmoil. Appropriately enough, he was laid to rest in the courtyard of Cape Coast Castle.

On rereading the letters of Philip Quaque, which are dated 1766 to 1811, it is remarkable to consider that although he lived and worked through the height of the slave trade, the first rumblings of the anti-slavery movement, and the eventual abolition of the trade, nowhere does he make reference to his feelings about his 'brothers and sisters' in the dungeons beneath his feet. His many conflicts with European authority, and his impatience with African forms of worship and the 'uncivil' social ways of the local people, are all documented, as is his gradual abandonment of any African 'costume'. (Soon after his return to the West African coast, Philip Quaque 'discovered' that he could no longer communicate with the people amongst whom he was born, and he went so far as to call 'their' language a 'vile jargon'.) However, Philip Quaque never once expressed moral outrage at the indignities that were being visited upon fellow Africans.

Clearly, at some point Philip Quaque made peace with a version of himself that was radically different from Kweku. Perhaps on the day of his baptism? The day of his marriage? Or on the ship as he sailed back to the Gold Coast? The ambivalence, pain, and pathos of his letters signify loss. Loss of home, loss of language, loss of self, but never loss of dignity. In his final dispatch, he recognizes the failure of his mission. However, Philip Quaque never abandoned hope. Even as a seventy-year-old ailing man writing to England in 1811, and doing so from the heart of a human factory, his tone still betrayed a glimmer of optimism and the courage of restraint.

The state of this unsuccessful mission, I had formerly had some hopes of its growth, but at present on the face of things bears but an indifferent aspect. I have my doubt of its increase unless a new change should take place for the better. I could wish to say more on this topic, but I write much in pain and time fails me as His Majesty's ship the Thais, captain Scobell, goes away from hence tomorrow morning without fail, and therefore hope your goodness will excuse this scrawl as I have no time to lose. But beg leave to inform the Society that within these few years, I have buried two and fifty persons and baptized eleven children. Prayer regularly every day in my room and on Sundays some of the gentlemen do attend. I hope to be more explicit in my next, should God permit me my health. Accept of my sincere and hearty wishes and prayers for your health and continuance.

PANAFEST (2)

I am awakened by a loud commotion. I open my eyes and discover that I am still sitting in the chair overlooking the Atlantic Ocean. I glance over to the restaurant behind me where I can now see that Kate is being confronted by a large, dreadlocked Jamaican woman who I assume to be the 'leader', Sista Pee. 'Listen,' she shouts, 'the one thing we can tell you Africans about is tourism. We're from Jamaica and we know how to do tourism, you hear me?'

Kate nods. I look across and see that the restaurant is full of slightly overweight Jamaicans, with shorts that are positively voluminous and T-shirts that are both a little too small and somewhat unconvincing in the stridency of their message, 'Jesus is a Black Man'. I am particularly taken by a T-shirt which features a picture of Alex Haley's Kunte Kinte clutching the trunks of two trees as though they are prison bars, and peering through the undergrowth. Presumably keeping a wary eye out for incompetent hotel managers.

'I tired of telling you that every room must have a bathroom, in the same room but through a door, you hear? These days people don't go out into the fresh air to do their business, you understanding me?' With this said, the woman beats a triumphant retreat and rejoins her party.

Kate walks over to where I am sitting. She slumps down into the chair next to mine and simply stares at the ocean. The wind is causing the waves to rise and cap, then burst into foam before they fall away. I listen to the whispering of the palms overhead, and try to imagine what she is suffering. Sweat begins to dampen the inside of my cap. I have already witnessed the barefoot Jamaican posse wandering the coconut-speckled compound, giving the clenched fist salute every time they see an African, and bellowing 'Jah Rastafari' to each other. For some reason they seem to have decided that 'Yeah man' will be 'my' greeting. Kate slowly shakes her head. 'They're still cooking in their rooms. And the lemon grass that we plant outside each bungalow to keep the mosquitoes away, they're plucking it out and making tea from it.' Clearly this family reunion is not working for Kate or her staff. An almost imperceptible shudder rattles through her thin body. 'They keep buying sugar cane and instructing the cooks how to prepare it. And soup. Why do they need so much soup?'

I knock loudly on Mansour's door. After a short while a barefoot Mansour gingerly opens the door and rubs sleep from his eyes. Then he shields his eyes from the glare of sunset. I remind him that tonight he has to drop me at Cape Coast Castle for the floodlighting ceremony. 'That's tomorrow,' he says drily. 'Tonight you're going to Elmina Castle.' He is right. There is to be an evening of 'musical presentations'. I had already agreed that Mansour could visit some family in the town of Elmina, and then come back to collect me at the conclusion of the 'presentations'. I ask Mansour how much time he will need with his family. He simply shrugs one shoulder and smiles. I understand. It does not matter. I suggest that we meet by the car in half an hour, and Mansour glances at his watch and nods. OK then, I say. 'OK' replies Mansour, and he then closes his door.

As we speed along the now familiar route from the hotel to Elmina Castle, I sense that Mansour would be happy for me to say 'Let's just keep driving and go back to Accra.' In fact, the prospect of visiting his family seems to be depressing him almost as much as the events of Panafest. I realize that we will have to talk, and soon. The conversation about his desire to leave Ghana once again has been left unresolved, and Mansour is looking to me to negotiate the awkwardness of his 'request' for help. In the meantime, Mansour's driving is becoming increasingly frightening. I have banned music in the car in the hope that he might concentrate on the road, but music or no music, Mansour is helplessly 'African' when it comes to driving. In common with 'his people', he seldom indicates when turning, the horn blares continually, he enjoys overtaking on the inside or on a blind corner, and he thinks nothing of stopping in the middle of the road simply to chat to another driver. The overwhelming evidence of the rusting hulks by the side of the highway appear to be invisible to Mansour's eyes.

Mansour releases me at the gates to the castle. My nerves are shot. I am able to gather myself and wish him a pleasant evening with his family; he disappears in a cloud of dust and spinning wheels. I shield my eyes from the debris and walk the few yards to the ticket counter. I am over an hour and a half late, but the woman selling tickets barely looks up at me. 'Come back in two minutes.' Incredibly enough, I am early. 'Two minutes?' I ask, unable to believe that she is serious. 'Two, ten, just come back.' She laughs now.

I walk down the main street of Elmina, which is flanked on either side by stone buildings of either one or two stories. I have time to kill and as I walk I listen, both to Fante and English. Elmina, this small fishing and salt-making township of twenty thousand people, has been an international outpost for over five hundred years. Pedestrians flow in both directions, unafraid, claiming the road, seemingly oblivious to the occasional car that surges past with its horn blowing. I watch as a bicycle tremors into view kicking up dust, its owner peddling furiously. By far the liveliest buildings are the gaudily painted bars with loud music blasting from inside. The favoured tunes appear to be slow American soul music, particularly Luther Vandross or Toni Braxton, but the occasional bar dares to play the more dynamic West African hi-life or Caribbean calypso.

The most ubiquitous people are the street vendors, whose goods sit atop single pieces of wood that are supported on concrete block pillars. Bread and batteries; eggs and air fresheners; candles and packets of kenke. Incongruous goods neatly arranged under the glare of kerosene lamps. A woman stirs a huge pot of cornmeal with a large stick, and a crowd of eager-looking boys gaze at the pot, the leader of the group sporting a T-shirt with the three proud letters, USA. I notice that the only solitary people are the vendors, for everyone else sits, stands, or moves in a group. The fusion of candles and electricity throws long eccentric shadows, and creates a curiously illuminated pallor on the faces of passers-by. I walk on and realize that the pungent odour that stings my nose is a combination of smoked fish from the vendors' tables and excrement from the gutters. At precisely the point where the main street dog-legs to the right there is a church from whose vantage point one can see the full length of the street.

Back at Elmina Castle the performance is now two hours overdue. I take my seat and watch as a young man performs a sound check by singing a whimsical Michael Jackson tune. He laughs as he does so, clearly amused by his own cleverness. Above the stage the wind gently unfolds a Panafest banner, so that it swings in the evening breeze. Behind me two drunk white South Africans open yet another tin of beer and shout 'Go Apartheid'. Above the Panafest banner, I stare at a sky that is literally choked with stars. There is no pollution and I possess a clear and uninterrupted view to the heavens. The South Africans are now shouting for 'dancing girls', but the forty or so locals, mainly middle-aged couples and their families, refuse to acknowledge the two drunks.

Twenty-five minutes later, a large black South African woman, dressed from head to foot in red, comes onstage and announces, 'the "Family Singers" from Durban, South Africa, who, because of the changes in South Africa, "are able to reunite the African family".' The drunk South Africans now begin to barrack the woman in Afrikaans, until they realize that there are rather a lot of black familial eyes upon them. The bald one of the pair leans forward, taps me on the shoulder, and asks where I am from. His lips have cracked like paint under the sun. In a gesture of diasporan solidarity I ignore him. One of the 'Family Singers' then invites the audience to stand and raise their right hands in a clenched fist salute. The 'singer' cries, 'Long live the Spirit of Africa!' Various Presidents are invoked, beginning with

Nkrumah, but mercifully not including Amin or Bokassa, or any of the more obvious 'suspects'. And then the sound system packs up and I realize that it is time to leave my now subdued South African 'friends' and find Mansour.

The following evening, at a Panafest venue in a field near Cape Coast, I arrive as a Ghanaian poet is 'uniting' Harlem to Ghana, and Ghana to Guyana. He speaks of 'people kneeling together in a sea of blood in the eye of the hurricane'. He implores us to 'come home'. He reminds us, 'We have pain, but we hold the world record for survival against the most unreasonable odds. We smell of mists of powdered memories. Those who took our voice are surprised that they couldn't take away our song or our dance.' At the conclusion of his performance the Danish Ambassador, resplendent in an African print dress, is presented to the crowd. She walks to the microphone with a carefully corseted 'freedom'. Apparently she sponsored this event, and she makes a short, gracious speech, although the smile that decorates her face looks like a mask that she occasionally wears. The decidedly unsweet 'Chocolate Voices' from Tema are next onstage, but having listened to their first few 'songs' I decide that it is time to call it a day. I am 'Panafested'.

As I make my way back to the car (where Mansour has secreted himself with a book), I run a gauntlet of young children. They hold out scraps of paper with their addresses hastily scribbled on them. They are looking for a 'pen-pal', the idea being that once they have developed a 'relationship' with a 'foreigner', they hope that this unsuspecting 'pen-pal' might one day ask them to visit. The 'pen-pal' is to be their passport out of Africa. This is a long-term investment. As a silent, sulking Mansour thrashes the car back in the direction of the hotel, I wonder if he is not a little jealous of these children. At least they still have hopes of leaving Ghana. Mansour, on the other hand, may well have used up his only chance and he has returned with nothing. When I reach the hotel I see a gloomy-looking Kate sitting by herself in the bar. She tells me that earlier in the day the

Jamaicans demanded to make a telephone call to the offices of Air Jamaica. In London. Eventually she had to turn over her office to them, where they then spent four hours on the telephone and tied up all the international lines. Kate sighs and beckons a waiter. She asks me if I would like a beer.

Back in my room I turn on the television and lie full length on my bed. Predictably enough, the lead story on the Ghanaian television news channel is about Panafest, and it features decidedly shaky footage of ministerial speeches. Each speech makes continual reference to the building of bridges between the mother continent and the people of the diaspora. Not only in the arts but in the fields of tourism and economics too. Then an African-American man named Sonny, who is dressed in the requisite African gear, makes a speech in which he asks that 'those of our ancestors who are still enslaved in the Americas should not be forgotten'. Who on earth is he talking about? This continual rush to overstatement is causing me to suffer from diasporan fatigue. I crawl into my African bed and pull the cover over my head.

MANSOUR

Mohammed Mansour Nassirudeen was born in 1961 in Kumasi, the capital city of the Asante empire. He attended primary school in Kumasi and then moved to live in northern Ghana, in the town of Tamoli. From there, the family moved to the Apa region, to a town called Tumu where he undertook his secondary schooling and achieved four 'A' level passes in Islamic Studies, Government, Economics and the General Paper. In 1975, while Mansour was still at school, his father died, leaving four wives and twenty-six children. Suddenly life was difficult, and Mansour realized that he would have to start earning money to help out his mother and siblings.

In 1978, during the school holidays, Mansour left Ghana for the first time and visited a brother in Nigeria in the hope that he might earn cash and buy provisions for the family. There was an

2 of the

oil boom in Nigeria and for five years his eldest brother had been based in Lagos as an assistant to a Ghanaian man who operated a fleet of lorries which transported kola nuts and plywood from Ghana to Nigeria. A seventeen-year-old Mansour was terrified by this first visit to Lagos. Within hours of his arrival he saw a human body that had been cut in two at the torso, and later in his visit he saw a woman who had been raped and then placed on railway lines. Her tongue had been cut out, and her private parts mutilated. For a month, young Mansour observed the world that was Nigeria, and then, much to his relief, he went home to Ghana.

Four years later, a nervous Mansour returned again to Lagos in the hope of finding some work and eventually bribing a 'visa conductor' who might arrange for him to travel to the United States, or anywhere that was 'first world'. During his school-days, Mansour had aspired to be a journalist, or something in international relations, but because of financial strictures at home it was abundantly clear that he would be unable to go to university in Ghana. Mansour had long understood that his best hope would be to go abroad, find work so that he could remit some foreign currency to help his family, and attempt to gain his education in a foreign university.

After seven months in Nigeria, Mansour had still not found any work. Then his brother discovered that Libya was recruiting West Africans to come and work on short-term contracts, so he scraped together enough money from friends in Nigeria so that he could buy his young brother a one-way ticket on Aeroflot from Lagos to Tripoli. Although Mansour was relieved that he would finally be earning money and achieving some form of independence, he had no idea that he would be spending the next two and a half years of his life in North Africa.

Mansour was surprised to discover that Libya, whose economy was bolstered by the oil boom, boasted many 'luxury' goods and supplies that were almost unheard of in Ghana. However, he was soon dispirited when he realized the banality of the job he was given to perform. Mansour was simply expected to 'dress beds' for the British, Canadian, American, Irish and Spanish expatriate oil workers of the Oasis Oil Company at their desert oil terminal in Sidra. It did not take long for his Libyan employees to realize that Mansour was fully fluent in Arabic and once they had discovered his linguistic skills, Mansour was redeployed and assigned to work for the Arab Catering and Construction Company. This company was responsible for providing food and supplies to the oil terminal, and Mansour's new responsibilities included opening up the doors to the food supply cupboards in order that the cooks might take what they wanted, and being in charge of the general distribution of food, soap, and insecticides. In fact, Mansour soon found himself shouldering total responsibility for the distribution of supplies throughout the community.

Although the other Ghanaian workers were paid more than Mansour for continuing to 'dress beds', Mansour's assumed 'privileges' soon brought him into conflict with his countrymen. He argued with them that his job was more stressful than theirs, for he was always subject to being awoken in the middle of the night if the expatriates wanted their rations or some extra food for emergencies. Mansour also had to do office work, for his nominal boss was illiterate. However, all of this made no difference to the other Ghanaians and, burdened by the strain of the situation, after a year and a half Mansour decided to take a holiday and visit an older brother who was studying medicine at a university in Cairo. He spent a month in Cairo with his brother, and on his return to Libya, Mansour decided to focus purposefully upon the task of migrating to the United States, where he felt he could both better himself and make some money.

Mansour began now to make friends with the American expatriates, hoping that they might eventually be able to help him enter the United States. He became close to a man named Richard White, who was based in Florida, and through him Mansour began a correspondence course in Business Law at the

University of Oklahoma which he pursued for almost a year. However, having passed his first set of examinations, Mansour learned that his forty-one-year-old brother in Cairo had suddenly died of smoking-related bronchial problems, and Mansour was rearranged by grief. In the middle of 1985, he had little choice but to leave Libya and travel to Cairo to sort out the affairs of his brother, and make sure that any outstanding debts that his brother had incurred were properly reimbursed. Once he arrived in Cairo, Mansour settled in his brother's old room and arranged for a new Ghanaian passport to be brought into Egypt through a contact in the Ghanaian embassy. Mansour's present passport had many Libyan stamps in it, and Mansour imagined that this might cause him problems with his potential migration to the 'first world'.

Between the summer of 1985 and the middle of 1987, Mansour lived in Cairo where he studied Arabic at the Azhar Institute and lived on his savings from Libya. He was, of course, still hoping to get somebody in the United States to sponsor him with a letter of invitation so that he might obtain a tourist visa. By this time his friend, Richard White, had returned to the United States and was enrolled in Florida State University. He remitted prospectuses, books, and papers to Mansour in Cairo, but until Mansour received a formal letter of invitation from somebody, he thought it best not to apply for a visa and risk being rejected. Unfortunately, by now Mansour's money was running out. Returning to Libya and his old job was out of the question, for when he left the country the authorities had stamped his visa with the words, 'Final Exit'. Mansour also felt that he could not go back to Ghana because of his pride. He had not yet obtained an education, and before he returned he wanted to have at least earned a degree.

During a holiday break from his studies at the Azhar Institute, Mansour sailed across the Red Sea and found work on a Saudi Arabian building site, where he was led to believe that his job would be to mix and haul concrete. However, soon after his arrival his bosses decided to put him to work high up on some wooden scaffolding with a jackhammer, but without a harness or any other type of safety support. When Mansour complained that this was far too dangerous, they dismissed him. He found work on another building site, but he was treated with similar disdain. They put him to work carrying long steel rods, but the ground was littered with nails and sharp objects. Eventually Mansour stepped on a large nail and injured himself seriously. With blood pouring from a badly infected wound, he was rushed to hospital where he spent most of his savings receiving treatment. Thereafter, having sufficiently recuperated, Mansour undertook the haj to Mecca, and in early 1987 he returned to Cairo with hopes of now studying in Britain as opposed to the United States.

Mansour's only joy upon returning to Cairo was his discovery that a group of his Ghanaian friends were now studying at the American University in Cairo on an exchange program from the University of Ghana. One of them 'gave' Mansour $400, which Mansour had calculated would enable him to purchase a return ticket to London on Yugoslavian Airlines via Belgrade. However, before Mansour could buy the ticket, he would have to obtain a visa. He wrote to a holiday farm near Peterborough, and applied for a summer job as a fruit-picker. Within a matter of weeks they wrote back and offered him a job. At the British Embassy in Cairo, Mansour produced the letter and his passport, plus evidence that he was studying in Cairo, but they told him to go away and come back with more documentation. Mansour returned again, this time with an official letter from his Egyptian Institute explaining that in order to finish his studies and achieve accreditation he would have to return to Cairo. Having re-examined his papers, the British Embassy gave Mansour a three-month student working visa, and Mansour made ready to leave Egypt for London, by way of Yugoslavia. Mansour's passport was taken from him in Belgrade, which caused him great anxiety, but once Mansour arrived at Heathrow Airport the immigration officials handed it back to him when they saw that he had $600 to support himself, a job on a holiday farm, and a letter announcing that he would have to return to Cairo in order to complete his studies.

Before arriving in Britain, Mansour had telephoned a Ghanaian friend who had advised him to take the underground train to Leytonstone in east London. Mansour followed his friend's instructions and was soon reunited with him. However, shortly after Mansour's arrival, his friend had to return to Ghana to complete the final year of his degree. A reluctant Mansour also had to leave London in order that he might take up his job. He travelled from St Pancras Station to Peterborough, where he was contracted to spend three weeks picking strawberries and spring onions with people of all nationalities. The 'pickers' were provided with dormitory-style accommodation, free food and £30 a week. Mansour's best friend on the farm was a Danish girl, a student who, like Mansour and everybody else, had to leave the farm after their three-week working holiday. She returned to Denmark, while Mansour returned to London and moved in with a Ghanaian man he had met while working in Saudi Arabia.

Mansour spent his nights riding the tubes and buses, going from hotel to hotel looking for cleaning jobs so that he could make a little money. Eventually Mansour's friend locked him out, having decided that Mansour was little more than an unnecessary burden. Suddenly homeless, a panic-stricken Mansour searched for and eventually found his only other contact in London, a man who was the great-great-grandson of the instructor who had taught his father Arabic. It transpired that this man owned a semi-detached house in Harlesden, and he offered Mansour a room at the top of the house so long as he looked after the property. Mansour was obliged to pay only for the electricity he used and nothing else.

Having now decided that he would stay on in London, Mansour found work at a supermarket where he was quickly made supervisor. His job was to place the orders, rotate the stock, and check the till totals. When Mansour realized that his visa was about to expire, he enrolled in a local 'business school' whose principal purpose was to enable students to obtain visas to stay on in Britain. Students were, however, not allowed to work. In March 1988, while Mansour's passport was being processed at the Home Office, Mansour fell out with his boss. A Ghanaian like himself, Mansour's boss had given his girlfriend's sister a job at the supermarket. Mansour was in charge of her duties, but on the first day she told him that she did not know how to sweep a floor and she asked him to demonstrate. Mansour became angry with her attitude and sent her home in frustration.

Mansour's boss then called the police and said that he knew of an illegal immigrant who was working without permission. Mansour was cataloguing stock in the video section of the supermarket when the police arrived and asked him to accompany them to the police station. Once there, they noted his National Insurance card and his letter from the Home Office saying that his passport was being 'processed', but they still fingerprinted him and locked him up overnight. The following day an immigration officer interviewed Mansour, and then the police took him back to his room in Harlesden where they gathered up all of his pay slips and again reminded him that while he was in Britain he was not allowed to work. Eventually, Mansour attended Magistrate's court in Harlesden, where he was fined £50 and instructed that during his time in Britain he was allowed to study, but under no circumstances could he work. For the next six months Mansour made a little money by undertaking private teaching of Arabic in the Wembley area. Mansour accepted whatever people could afford to give him, but regarded his teaching as little more than voluntary work for the financial return was so meagre.

By October 1988, Mansour was struggling for money and he was depressed. Although he knew it to be illegal, he decided to apply for a job at a newly opened Sainsbury's supermarket, where he told them that he was a part-time student. By this deception he obtained work and remained at Sainsbury's for nearly two years, until August 1990. During this time, Mansour enrolled in a Rapid Results College to study 'A' level Government and Politics, and Economics, but he was not serious about the enterprise, especially given the fact that he had already studied and passed these subjects while at secondary school in Ghana. He craved the discipline of regular assignments, but Mansour was essentially working full-time. In the summer of 1990, Mansour changed jobs and went to work at a Tesco supermarket in Neasden which provided him with more flexible hours. He stacked shelves at night, which meant that in theory he could begin to study in the daytime.

In the autumn of 1990, after three years in Britain, Mansour enrolled at Birkbeck College, London University to study on a two-year diploma course in economics and sociology. He worked from 7 p.m. to 7 a.m. at the Tesco's supermarket, and thereafter he would return home and sleep. From 2 p.m. to 5 p.m. Mansour would study, but he soon found the routine punishing. He could not afford to work shorter hours because his family in Ghana had become increasingly dependent upon him. As if this were not enough pressure, he was now forced to move out of the house in Harlesden, for the owner had decided to sell up and return to Ghana. Mansour moved to Stonebridge, where he was able to arrange to sublet a one-bedroom flat from a Ghanaian friend, but the price was a hefty £55 a week.

Almost inevitably, the two-year diploma began to stretch over three, then four years. In the spring of 1994, Mansour relocated to Ladbroke Grove, where a Pakistani friend rented him a two-bedroom flat at £40 a week. Mansour had so far obtained a merit pass in economics and sociology, and a credit pass in economics and public policy, but these were merely two of the four sections of the diploma. He bought a car in order to help him travel between his night job at the Tesco's supermarket, his studying at the college and the private teaching which he continued to undertake, but life was difficult for him.

Almost inevitably, in August 1994, Mansour was arrested while working at the supermarket. Having been tipped off by the Greek night manager, the police turned up at 4 a.m. looking for 'illegals'. The 'illegals', mainly Nigerians, Gambians and Ghanaians, were all handcuffed and taken to Wembley police station where they were subjected to much racist abuse and then locked up. The following evening, at 8 p.m., Mansour was finally interviewed by an immigration officer in the presence of a solicitor's assistant. Before being released he was once again reminded that he was not allowed to work, and while his case was being investigated he was ordered to report to the police station once a week to 'sign in'.

To begin with Mansour assiduously 'signed in' every week, but he was frustrated by the fact that there seemed to be no progress with his 'case'. On taking advice from friends, Mansour went to see a new solicitor, a Ghanaian named Terry Ackah, who Mansour had been led to believe had a good record of arranging for people to stay on in Britain. Mr Ackah told Mansour that his particular case was 'very complex' and that he should stop 'signing in' and simply go 'underground'. Therefore, in September 1994, Mansour went 'underground'. Because Mr Ackah had also advised him that he might be traced through Birkbeck, Mansour stopped attending college.

These were particularly bleak and poverty-stricken times for Mansour, but as his Pakistani friend understood the situation he was at least able to keep a roof over his head. When he was not teaching his Arabic classes, Mansour spent all of his time reading, but his shortage of money continued to be a serious problem. Fully cognizant of the risk that he was taking, Mansour decided to take a job as a delivery driver for Pizza Hut. He had rearranged his personal priorities, and Mansour was now only interested in making some money and leaving Britain. He had calculated that around £15,000 would be a 'respectable' sum for him to go back to Ghana with, but his first week at work proved to be his last.

Mansour did not know where he was driving most of the time, and Pizza Hut received an avalanche of complaints about the cold and soggy food that he was delivering. After a bitter argument with his employers, Mansour left without bothering to collect any money for his week's work. He took on more Arabic teaching in Wembley and Harrow, and he was forced to move yet again, this time to North Wembley, because his Pakistani friend was selling his property. Eventually, Mansour managed to find a private two-bedroom flat where he was fortunate enough to be able to come to an arrangement where he paid only for the utility bills. Mansour had no job, no income, and he felt that he had lost focus in his life. Although the police had seriously cautioned him against doing so, Mansour scoured bakeries, supermarkets, hotels, in fact everywhere in a futile effort to find work.

In November 1994, after an Islamic gathering in Wembley, Mansour was asked if he would drive two Bosnian girls home to Hendon. He dropped them off, but on the way home he was pulled over by a police van and breathalyzed. Mansour had not been drinking, and he passed the Breathalyzer test without any problem. However, one question led to another until the subject of his legal residence status came up. At this point Mansour admitted that his situation was 'irregular', and he was immediately taken to Kilburn police station for the night.

Learning of his plight, a Ghanaian friend contacted yet another solicitor, who told the police that Mansour was a 'student' who was trying to regulate his affairs. Mansour was thereafter released, and told to report back in three days' time. Upon re-presenting himself, Mansour was held in custody under an order from the Home Office. After five days he was taken from Kilburn police station and transferred to Harmondsworth Detention Centre, near Heathrow airport, where he was interviewed. Three weeks later, Mansour was transferred to the Haslar Detention Centre, near Gosport, which is effectively run along the lines of a prison.

Mansour was to eventually spend seven and a half months at Haslar. His new lawyer, a Dr Alim, told the police that Mansour was running from persecution in Ghana and that his life would be in danger should he ever return there. He then informed his client that when he was questioned at his formal hearing he should repeat the lie that the government of Ghana was persecuting him. After three frustrating months in Haslar, Mansour was finally scheduled to appear before the immigration tribunal at Heathrow for his formal hearing. However, unfortunately for Mansour, his lawyer did not turn up so the police had no option but to take him back to Haslar. Three months later, Mansour appeared again before the tribunal, and although his lawyer once more failed to turn up, Mansour had this time arranged to defend himself. He claimed that back home in Ghana he belonged to the wrong political party, and should he be deported he feared for his life. A few weeks later, on 28 June 1995, Mansour was presented with a one-way airline ticket and escorted on board a British Airways plane bound for Accra.

When Mansour arrived at Accra airport it was his younger brother who met him, the same younger brother who had been there at the airport when I had arrived. After eight years in the 'first world', Mansour was arriving home with just £300 and a chaos of luggage slung over one shoulder in a bag. He was sad to have left Britain, for he had not obtained the education that he had dreamed of. He also knew that he would miss the bookshops of London, his friends and the lifestyle. He also, if truth be told, felt somewhat ashamed of his 'failure' in the world beyond Ghana. However, like it or not, he was now home.

Since his return, Mansour has been unemployed. I hand him a bottle of Coca-Cola and pull up a chair next to his on the patio outside my Elmina hotel room. Mansour tells me that he lives on money that friends send to him. He has 'survived' two and a half years of this dependency upon people in London, or in one case, Japan. He confesses that he seems to have lost both purpose and energy. I ask him how he fills his Ghanaian days. These days, he says, he simply watches a friend who fixes computers. He says that he is hoping to 'pick up something', but it is unclear to me, and presumably to him, just what that 'something' might be.

Mansour tells me that here in Ghana he considers cleaning jobs, or making beds, or stacking shelves, or delivering food to be beneath him. Yet, I say, it appears that he is happy to go to London or Libya and do such work there. I try to explain to Mansour that he must find some way to put his pride to one side. Mansour takes the bottle of Coca-Cola from his mouth and looks at me in mock astonishment. The truth is that Mansour has no real faith in Ghana. He considers my suggestion of getting on the bottom rung of the ladder and working his way up within Ghanaian society as simply laughable. 'The only way up in Ghana is out,' he exclaims. 'And then you come back with money and a degree. That is how you progress in Ghana. You leave.'

These days, Mansour's country of choice is once again the United States, the land of opportunity where anybody can make it. He considers American blacks to be hampered by racism in a way in which he is sure he will never be. 'Why can't they get a job?' His aim is to go there and get a degree, and then come back and serve his country in government or civil service. He has a three-stage plan. In five years' time he would like to have first a degree, then a house and finally a family. Again, I ask him what he is doing to make this dream come true, but he cannot point to anything. He mentions to me that with $5000 he can get a false visa for the USA and a new passport. I look at him. Is he really asking me for money? Mansour, who has not even bothered to apply for a job since returning to Ghana. His country. A democratic country of eighteen million people with a diversified economy. Mansour who has spent all of his time looking for a way to leave. Mansour, African supplicant, who lives off money remitted from abroad by friends. Able-bodied, smart Mansour, presenting himself as 'third world' victim.

HASHUVAH: THE RETURN

... the African movement means to us what the Zionist movement must mean to the Jews, the centralization of the race effort and the recognition of a racial fount.

W. E. B. DU BOIS (1919)

I know that as an African there is nothing I can not do than embrace my fellow Africans who through no fault of theirs had to leave home to stay among foreigners. I feel for you and like Joseph who was sold to Egypt, he prepared a place for his people to stay and at long last his people returned to their fatherland, and with this assurance, I believe that all Africans in foreign lands will return to inherit the land their fathers fought for.

NANA OSABARIMBA KODWO MBRA V

'Mabel's Table' is a small cluster of wooden tables and chairs that are arranged under thatched roofs shaped like top hats. Down the grassy, coconut-strewn slope there is a narrow strip of beach which quickly gives way to the pounding surf of the Atlantic Ocean. In the distance one can clearly see the unmistakable outline of Elmina Castle. Mabel, a Ghanaian woman in her early thirties, serves food at her own unique pace. Her customers are diasporan returnees who busy themselves taking photographs and making video recordings of this historic encounter with Africa. Two minibuses, with bored Ghanaian drivers, are parked outside the rickety bamboo fence which encircles the compound. The compound belongs to Kohain Halevi, an African-American who, together with a small group of fellow Americans, has returned 'home' to settle in the motherland. The local people call these Americans, 'the rich people who have come late'.

Kohain Halevi is a dapper and handsome man of about 5 foot 8 inches. As he walks towards me I can see that he looks considerably younger than his forty-five years. He has a nicely sculpted beard and bright, committed eyes. He retakes his seat, and then he gestures to his wife, Mabel, telling her that she should bring drinks. He lowers his eyes. 'I'm sorry to be so long on the telephone, my brother.'

In fact, it matters little to me that he has been absent for nearly half an hour, for this has given me the opportunity to watch the returnees. When he wants to make a point, Kohain's voice drops a note and then slowly climbs towards higher registers. He likes to be definite and clear about things, but all the while he maintains impeccable manners. Kohain has spoken to me of 'servicing' such groups, often as many as seventy people. If they come to Ghana under his sponsorship their two- to three-day stay in the Cape Coast/Elmina area includes a visit to a local village, a trek in the Kakum National Park, a lecture by Kohain, and the opportunity of participating in the 'thru the door of no return' ceremony, which is conducted by Kohain and his two African-American colleagues, Nana and Imakhus, who operate One Africa Productions Tours and Speciality Services Ltd. Cultural tourism is, according to Kohain, a 'potential goldmine'.

Kohain Halevi was born Wayne Boykin in Mount Vernon, a small commuter city in Westchester County to the north of New York City. His father was a presser in a dry-cleaning business who, in the early 1930s, migrated north from North Carolina. Every Sunday his father would take his young son into Harlem, where Wayne was exposed to the Harlem street-corner preachers and the Garveyites. Thereafter, father and son would go to the Apollo Theatre where Wayne would see the many musical acts that subsequently became world-famous. Wayne's father lectured him on the personalities, the sights, and the history of Harlem, and encouraged him to read books, principally the 'holy trinity' of Baldwin, Wright and Ellison. However, Kohain remembers that as a young boy *The Autobiography of Malcolm X* was the most powerful and important book in his life.

In high school, Wayne was an art major, and he chose to study art education at college so that he could always fall back on being a teacher if his imagined life as an 'artist' failed to materialize. He attended Savannah State College in Georgia, where, much to his disappointment, he found the values of the old south still intact. It was a sleepy campus, not known for militancy or agitation, and the student body was not allied to SNCC or any radical organization. Wayne was largely instrumental in eventually getting African Studies on to the college curriculum, but it was the life off-campus that helped him to keep his radical edge. Kohain shakes his head and sighs as he recounts stopping at a gas station where a group of whites, who were supposed to be pumping gas, seemed intent upon ignoring him. He yelled out of the car, 'Hey, aren't you going to help?' They shouted back, 'Get out of the car and get it yourself, nigger!' As far as Wayne's friends were concerned, this was the end of the episode. Wayne, however, insisted on shouting back at the whites and he had to be held down in his seat.

Kohain looks up as an old man with a walking stick slowly approaches us. He stops, and in an overly dramatic manner, he points to Kohain. He speaks Fante, and the open palm suggests that he is begging. Kohain waves his hand dismissively. The old man touches the brim of his hat and, with shoulders hunched and head down, he leans into the slight breeze and begins to move off. As the old man withdraws, Kohain tells me that this is a daily occurrence and that he has to be careful that he only gives coins to one beggar a day. Kohain stands and excuses himself. I follow him with my eyes as he goes to the small hut that serves as a kitchen. Presumably he wants to make sure that Mabel is coping with the rush of orders from the returnees. I look down the slope and become mesmerized by the breaking waves, which constitute a bizarrely noisy intrusion into an otherwise peaceful world. I remember the words that a Zimbabwean writer once shared with me; the sea, he said, carries Africa on her back like an island.

I watch now as Kohain fusses around the returnees. They are a group of Canadian-Jamaican youngsters from Toronto who have won a nationwide essay competition to write about Africa, the prize being a fully paid trip to Ghana. They are all smartly turned out in a cross-cultural fusion of dress; Nike T-shirts, Kente scarves and belts, baggy jeans, backpacks, and the occasional Panafest T-shirt. For them this is a summer vacation with cultural overtones. I watch as they tease the lizards, fill their water bottles, then crank up the reggae and rap as they prepare to reboard their minibuses. Their Canadian group leader attempts to marshal them into order, but they begin now to dance. Kohain returns with a fistful of cedis, and I realize that he has been making sure that they have paid their bill in full before leaving.

In 1975, Wayne graduated from Savannah State College and returned north to New York, where he felt ready to embrace a spiritual life. Despite the fact that his mother attended a traditional church, and his father had little time for spirituality in any form, Wayne decided that he wished to be trained in Hebrew customs and culture. His understanding of the Bible had led him to believe that God would eventually lead black people in America out of their bondage. Remembering his father's Garveyite affiliations, Wayne understood this to mean out of the United States and back to Africa, the promised land, the land of the ancestors. The idea of 'the chosen people' greatly appealed to Wayne, and in 1975 he enrolled in the Hasadbah Yisrael Congregation in Brooklyn, New York, where he intended to pursue Hebraic Studies, learn the rituals, study the Torah, and familiarize himself with the traditions of Judaic life.

After one year at the Hasadbah Yisrael Congregation, Wayne

enrolled in the 'House of David House of Study' in Brooklyn where he spent a further seven years studying for the priesthood in a class that was comprised of twenty-five African-American students. They were all from the New York area, and they all possessed a powerful sense that one day they would leave the United States, and return to the Hebrew traditions that they believe were practised in Africa before the onset of the Atlantic slave trade. Describing themselves as 'Hebrew Israelites' they saw themselves in the 'Back to Africa' tradition of Rabbi Josiah Ford, who was the Musical captain for Marcus Garvey, and who in 1930 led a group of African-Americans to Ethiopia. In recent years 'Hebrew Israelite' congregations have left the United States for Liberia and the Ivory Coast. Kohain informs me that in 1969 a group established themselves in the Negev desert in Israel where they now constitute a community of over 2,000 people.

In 1983, Kohain completed his training at the 'House of David House of Study' and he formed his own congregation in Mount Vernon. He also established himself as the cultural director of the Bereshith Cultural Institute, Inc., of Mount Vernon, where he presented himself as 'historian, educator, artist'. Kohain pressed the local government authorities for better schools, and he often gave lectures on subjects such as 'The Impact of Identity and Culture on Education for Blacks'. In 1986, Kohain led a group of twenty-six African-Americans on a proposed eight-day, seven-night trip to Israel. However, at the airport in Tel Aviv they were detained and denied entry into the State of Israel, for the Israelis feared that they might settle with the African-Americans in the Negev desert. Kohain's group were held for thirty-six hours, their passports seized and, although they were in possession of return air tickets and had paid for their accommodation and board in advance, they were deported. There was neither a refund nor an apology from the State of Israel.

On his return home, an angry and embittered Kohain looked around at his present situation. He decided that life in the

United States was not that much of an improvement over the cold shoulder that they had just received in Israel. Kohain laughs and shakes his head as he tells me this. In actual fact, Kohain traces his loss of faith in the United States 'system' back to his attendance of the 1984 Democratic convention in San Francisco where the presidential candidate Walter Mondale, having made it clear that he did not want Jesse Jackson, chose Geraldine Ferraro as a running mate. Kohain organized the fateful trip to Israel as something of a response to the disappointment of the convention, but upon reaching the Holy Land the international face of racism became strikingly clear.

In April 1987, Kohain began planning an inaugural trip to Ghana, the idea being that he wished to discover if there was land available for purchase, and if the atmosphere was amenable for Africans in the diaspora to consider resettling there. The previous year Kohain's niece had married a Ghanaian named Isaac Simmonds, but shortly after the wedding the bridegroom had learned that he would have to return home for there was a distinct possibility that he would be elected as a chief by the elders of the Fante people. Simmonds told Kohain that 'his' Passover ceremony was similar to traditional ceremonies in Ghana, so Kohain had already begun to imagine that there might be a particular histo-cultural link to Ghana. In August 1987, Kohain led a group of sixteen African-Americans, a dozen of whom were members of his Hebrew congregation, on a two-week trip to the place they hoped might be 'the promised land'. For all of them, this would be their first time in Africa.

After spending the first night in Accra, the group travelled to Elmina, where they witnessed the installation of Isaac Simmonds as Nana Gyepi III. At the ceremony they were introduced to the King of the Cape Coast Fante, Nana Osabarimba Kodwo Mbra V, whose very first greeting to the African-American 'pilgrims' was to encourage them to return home. 'Welcome home,' he said, and promised them that should they return then he would make land available so they could build houses and factories. During the trip, the eighty-six-year-old Hebrew Queen of the congregation, Balkis Makeda, died. As Kohain remembers it, 'her spirit was released in Elmina', which seemed to the group to be a powerful sign that Elmina was indeed their rightful place.

Another sign of the appropriate nature of this 'homecoming' was the fact that during this visit four members of the group were 'snatched' and 'blessed' with the honorary positions of 'Asafo', or chief. Kohain explains that an individual has no way of knowing that he is a candidate, and then suddenly he is 'seized' and carried around on people's shoulders and it is announced to him that he is a chief. Thereafter, there are rituals of purification and washing under the supervision of a priest. Kohain, being a holy man, could not be 'snatched' and made into an 'Asafo Nana', but he was delighted for the four members of his party who were fortunate enough to have this honour bestowed upon them. As their sojourn came to an end, Kohain and everybody else in the group were astonished by how perfect this 'homecoming' felt. Their expectations were daily exceeded, and before they left Ghana they pledged that they would return and make this country their home. They revisited Nana Osabarimba Kodwo Mbra V and formally accepted his invitation to return and settle, which pleased him greatly.

Before leaving Ghana, Kohain was able to offer the king some spiritual advice and guidance, urging him to accept the fact that despite his own Christian beliefs he should not view traditional African worship as being incompatible with Christianity, or any other form of religion. Nana Osabarimba Kodwo Mbra V was grateful for Kohain's instruction, and his gratitude increased when Kohain invited the king to officially visit with them in the United States, where Kohain hoped that the king might issue a formal invitation to all Africans in the diaspora to return home. The following year, in the company of eight chiefs and one wife, the king made an official visit to the United States, and Kohain's home city of Mount Vernon hosted him. The king then went on to the 1988 Black Mayor's conference in

New York City where he did indeed issue a formal invitation to all Africans in the diaspora to return home. According to Kohain, this historic declaration was the first of its type from an African to his 'relatives' overseas.

While the king was in the United States, Kohain was able to discuss further with him his plans for coming 'home'. Kohain's research had led him to understand that of the forty-seven forts on the west coast of Africa, twenty-nine of them were in Ghana. It seemed clear to Kohain that most people had arrived in the Americas through the gateway of Ghana, and it therefore seemed appropriate that this should be the gateway of return. Kohain decided to call his movement 'Hashuvah', or the return. He established a committee to draw up a programme and it was decided that the one contribution that the returnees could immediately make would be to organize a nursery and primary school facility in the Elmina/Cape Coast area. This would, they felt, indicate the serious nature of their intent.

In 1991, Kohain travelled to Ghana and was able to purchase his first plot of land; the land on which 'Mabel's Table' is situated. He paid $1,000 to a family, but negotiated the deal through a middleman who took a 50 per cent commission. In 1992, Kohain paid $1,500 for a second piece of land, and in 1993 he began to build a house. Finally, in 1994, Kohain settled permanently in Elmina with his new wife, Mabel, and their son, Kwame. Kohain is divorced from his first wife in the United States, but by her he has two children, a boy and a girl, who are now grown-up, and for whom Kohain has bought plots of land in Elmina so that they too might eventually permanently resettle in West Africa.

Kohain takes a drink of beer and looks around. He has finished narrating his story. At least for the present. He turns now to current events and tells me that he has established a whole infrastructure so that African-Americans can return 'home' and buy land without somebody 'chopping their money'. He points to a house and tells me that his African-American 'business partner', Nana, and his African-American wife, Imahkus, live there. Apparently, there are half a dozen plots in the area that have been purchased by African-Americans who are 'seriously considering' Africa as a place to which they might resettle. Kohain sees himself as a man who can help blacks remake themselves in the land of their forefathers. To this end he is assisting Leonard Jeffries, an outspoken afrocentric teacher from New York, who wishes to buy a house that is presently owned by white evangelists. I have seen the house. It is difficult to miss. The front of the house is emblazoned with the painted slogan, 'At the Name of Jesus/ Every knee shall bow'.

Kohain tells me that he is advising the Ghanaian government by sitting on a committee which is seeking to formulate a policy by which all Africans in the diaspora might be able to acquire dual citizenship with Ghana. This idea surprises me, and clearly Kohain detects my scepticism. He snaps the tops from two more bottles of beer, and passes one to me. He impresses upon me the fact that he does not consider Ghana to be a romantic retreat away from the battleground of the United States. In fact, he believes that until Africa is free there will be no strong base from which to wage the battle in the United States. Kohain takes a sip of beer. 'I have been chosen to come to Africa as a relatively young man with my strength and purpose still intact.'

On the local front, Kohain and his 'partner' Nana have been attempting to convince the authorities that there should be a 'sensitization programme' at both Elmina and Cape Coast Castles, similar to the ones at Pearl Harbour and Auschwitz. In this way, before visitors even enter the physical premises they are prepared for the significance of what they are being exposed to. Kohain's failure to convince the authorities of the need for such a programme has led him to attempt to purchase Abanze Castle, the same castle that Dr Lee attempted to purchase. Kohain's idea is to turn it into a place of pilgrimage, 'like Muslims go to Mecca, or the Wailing Wall for the Jews'. Abanze Castle would be a place to which all African-Americans in the diaspora could return and 'cleanse their spirits'.

I listen to Kohain, but I remain somewhat unconvinced. As he tells me that slavery happened because the Almighty ordained it for those who disobeyed his commandments, I bite my tongue. In the future he imagines a mixed community of believers and non-believers, but is there really ever going to be a viable community of diasporan blacks in Elmina? Most Ghanaians simply do not understand why an African-American would willingly leave the United States to come and live in Ghana. Kohain explains to me that he is using his talents to make Africa strong; that he is not a temporary visitor; that he is not thinking of leaving. 'Why', he asks, 'do you think white people are here? They can see that Africa has virtues, that it is worth developing. I tell the Africans, why don't you people develop this country? We can help.'

I look at Kohain as he convinces himself. Suddenly he seems a long way from home. Wayne Boykin from Mount Vernon. Already it has been a long journey. He must be tired. His speech falls flat. We both watch in silence as yet another Fante-speaking beggar slowly approaches Mabel's Table.

Mansour sits on a plastic chair on the small concrete terrace outside of his room. He sees me walking towards him and he looks up from his newspaper. Without saying a word he hands me the newspaper which is neatly folded at the item that he wishes me to look at. The headline reads, 'Donation for Oguaa Omanhene's Burial'. Beneath the headline there is a colour picture of Kohain handing some drinks and a boxful of provisions to an African man in traditional dress. Two other Ghanaian men, and a Ghanaian woman, are standing in the background and observing this exchange. The words beneath the picture read: 'Rabbi Kohain Halevi makes the donation on behalf of Bereshith Hashuvah Ghana Limited, the African-Hebrew Community and Asafo of Ghana, Mount Vernon, New York, USA and the Returning African Descendants Community of the Central Region'. I look at Mansour, who slowly shakes his head.

In the early evening, one of Kate's assistants offers to give me a ride into Elmina. Mansour is still depressed and I have told him to take the evening off, watch television and then get some sleep. Besides, I want to spend some time by myself. The young man stops the hotel minibus by the church, which stands at the mid-point of the main street. I thank him and step out and into the moving sea of vendors, who are walking back and forth with a casual tramp. They sell toilet paper, chewing gum, ties, hand-kerchiefs, in fact anything that one might conceivably want. Behind the 'I Jah Man' reggae stall, which is piled high with shoes, necklaces and Bob Marley T-shirts, I see a man who stands beside an ancient wheelbarrow which is brimming with coconuts. Behind him a sign that has been hastily painted on to a stone wall: 'Don't urinate here. Fine 5,000 cedis.' I start to walk off and notice that a stray dog is shadowing my progress.

A young boy lopes towards me in a Chicago Bulls vest. He carries himself with the clumsy grace of a basketball player, and he has already cultivated the athlete's glazed look of indifference. I stop the boy and ask him if he has ever seen the Bulls play. The startled boy says 'Yes', and then tells me that on Saturday afternoons Ghanaian television shows the highlights of American basketball games. 'I like them all, especially that black man.' They're nearly all black, I say. 'No, the black man.' Michael Jordan? 'Yes, him.' I look at the young boy, his top lip quivering, eager to wear a moustache, and then we both start to laugh. He breaks into a broad, winning smile.

The wooden floor of the 'Candlelight Bar' is thickly padded with dirt. It is the music that has drawn me in; soul, rap, calypso, reggae; Babyface, Coolio, Sparrow, Inner Circle. The music of the diaspora emanating from the high-tech 'loot' of voyages to the west. Heavy bass, heavy rhythm. I order a beer from Tony, a slim man whose eyes dart in every direction. He tells me that he lived in London for five years, and before this he lived for five years in Germany. As though keen to announce the sophistication of his international credentials, Tony changes the music to the light jazz of Grover Washington, Jr. And then he presents me with a Star beer in a tall glass that is sweating rivulets of ice water. We both clink glasses, and take a drink. I glance at the three women in kente at the next table, all of whom are drinking pints of beer. Women who earn money with their lips and hips? For a few seconds Tony concentrates on his dying cigarette before tossing it to the floor, getting out another, and immediately lighting it. He blows smoke spinning out in a flurry of spirals, and then he remembers that he must stub out the old cigarette so he twists his foot into it. Through the doorway I see Ghanaian families taking their evening paseo together, the men walking with a particularly dignified calm, like Romans in their African 'togas'. The moving sea of vendors continues to flow. Tony pulls up a stool and settles at my table. He begins. 'I miss London.'

PANAFEST (3)

I had read in the Panafest programme that at the Cultural Centre in Cape Coast, there would be a wall-mounted exhibition dedicated to the achievement of Africans, and those of African origin in the diaspora. When I arrive at the Cultural Centre I discover it to be a cluttered and confusing place. True enough, the purpose of the exhibition, in keeping with the larger Panafest manifesto, is to stimulate afrocentric pride, but the roster of historical 'achievers' is a familiar one ranging from Cleopatra to Maya Angelou, from Hadrian to Colin Powell. I turn my attentions to the art exhibition, but the 'exhibits' are atrocious and feature infantile drawings and unspeakable oil paintings. And then I notice a neatly presented, uncharacteristically organized corner of the Cultural Centre. A carefully stencilled banner announces 'The African Hebrew Israelite Community: The Kingdom of God on Earth'. I read on:

Black Hebrew members maintain that their pilgrimage to the Holy land in 1969 was actually a return to their land of origin, that they are the descendants of Hebrew Israelites driven into African exile from Jerusalem in AD 70.

By 1980, between fifteen hundred and two thousand members had moved to Israel . . . Political and public pressure from the African-American community led to negotiations with government officials, which paved the way for a normalization of relations and the permanent residence status now enjoyed by community members.

An integral part of the mosaic which is modern-day Israel, the Hebrew Israelite Community is making outstanding contributions to the country in the areas of natural food products and organic agriculture, music, fashion design and manufacturing, holistic healthcare and education. Theirs is a story of faith, perseverance and a shining example of what can be accomplished through cooperation between diverse communities.

Perhaps I am reading with my mouth open, for when I look up I see a tall, well-dressed man, with a briefcase in one hand, staring at me.

'Brother, where are you from?'

I recognize the American accent, and the 'intrusive' nature of the question. I offer him no choice. 'The Caribbean.'

'Do you know of our people?' He takes a step towards me, a step that I know is meant to be comforting, but his height and demeanour render this movement somewhat threatening.

'What people?'

He gestures with his head towards the information neatly tacked to the boards. Does he, I wonder, simply stand here and wait for unsuspecting victims like myself so that he can engage them in conversation? Or is he about to try to press 'membership' upon me?

'You seem interested, but I do not wish to interrupt. If you have any questions then just ask, my brother. I will be here.' He smiles and takes a step backwards. I turn back towards the boards.

The Hebrew Israelite Community, the largest organized settlement of African-Americans outside the United States . . . is known for the absence of violence, drug abuse and other social ills . . . Ben-Ammi's Israeli community is free of drugs and violence. Education is a priority . . . In five years, none of the members has had cancer, diabetes, venereal disease, or AIDS.

After three decades of living outside the United States the African Hebrew Israelites can point to a record of . . .

> No Black-on-Black Crime
> No Drive-By Shootings
> No Drug Addicts
> No Crack Houses
> No Gangs
> No Cancer
> No AIDS
> No Smoking
> No Prostitution
> No Burglar Alarms
> No Profanity
> No Child Molestation
> No Welfare
> No Inferiority Complex
> No Murders
> No Guns
> No Drug Dealers
> No Rapes
> No Traffic Fatalities
> No High Blood Pressure
> No Homosexuality

No Alcoholism
No Battered Women
No Locked Doors
No Obscene Music
No Child Neglect
No Homelessness
No Racism

For more than two decades the Black Hebrews of Dimona have been paying their heavy dues down in the Negev. They have displayed an admirable capacity to survive—an amalgam of persistence, vision, and adaptability . . .

I am particularly taken with the colloquialism of the phrase, 'paying their heavy dues'. It brings a wry smile to my face. And then my friend rematerializes. 'My brother, can we mail you some literature?' I shake my head. No thanks. 'Do you need more information?'

'I'll just finish reading.'

'I understand.' He bows slightly. 'Peace be with you, my brother.' Once again my friend disappears into the ether.

The truth is, I have no idea of what to make of these Black Hebrews. 'No AIDS'? 'No Cancer'? Their world is packaged and presented as though it were a celestial compound of heaven here on earth. Are they serious? I decide to read the final board.

A group of 93 colourful dark-skinned people, mostly women and children, landed unexpectedly in 1969 and stunned government officials with their demand to be absorbed into the country as Jews . . . their settling was the first mark in the making of a unique community on the Israeli scene . . . When others arrived the authorities hardened their position. Their Judaism was not recognized and the proposal to be converted was rejected by members of the community who indeed stuck to their Judaism . . . the community views the land of Israel as the spiritual center of the world and its self as a messenger of her holistic way of life based on love for the creation in all aspects.

Are they serious? Have these African-Americans truly found their 'home'? I look around, but just when I need him there is no sign of the 'recruiter'. It is time to go back to car and Mansour.

The University of Cape Coast had posted flyers throughout Elmina and Cape Coast which announced that, in conjunction with the other cultural events that were happening during this Panafest celebration, there would be a book launch on their campus to which everyone was invited. The university itself is a somewhat run-down campus university whose grey concrete buildings have become mildewed by a couple of decades of exposure to excessive sun and rain. Mansour guides the once more ailing Mercedes into a parking space under the spreading shade of an ancient tree and as he does so I read a poster which hangs limply from the wall of a university building. The headline is clear, 'The African Diaspora', but beneath this heading the words are tightly packed and, from this distance, indecipherable. I have to get out of the car and walk right up to the poster in order to read the work of a Ghanaian poet.

> . . . a people fired a deep bronze in the crucible, swept snarling through burning oceans and heated marshlands to the edge where cotton was king and cane sap sweetened the soil. Even bent under foreign skies the African in them came out, like dark spots on the sun. A weak people never build a world power, and we know today it was their sweat that made fertile the soil of the new world. They gave us the gift of song and humanized the world they founded by vesting the meaning of freedom with a new destiny.

More overstatement. I turn to say something to Mansour, but realize that he is standing stubbornly by the car.

The book launch is scheduled to take place in a lecture theatre whose seats are steeply raked. The seats are equipped with small intrusive wooden flaps for 'desktops', which means that it is almost impossible to sit without one's knees resting up against one's chest. Many among the stern-looking scholars are dressed in a dazzling array of colours which nicely offset the supposed seriousness of the occasion. Then a young man, with the corded forearms of a junior lecturer, leaps suddenly to his feet and shouts to a man on the other side of the hall. 'Eh, what do you mean what am I doing here? I am Panafesting, of course.' People burst out laughing, and one or two applaud. His brief performance over, the smiling man resumes his seat. An hour later the festive atmosphere has significantly subsided. I look helplessly at my watch, and then glance over at Mansour, who is nodding off in the heat. The anticipatory glee has now been replaced by a resigned hum of indifference that is occasionally cut with a noticeable hubbub of annoyance.

The double doors to the auditorium swing dramatically open and in march three men in dashikis and sunglasses who tote boxes of books as though they are full of explosives. A group of highly anxious men, who purposefully carry briefcases and small tape machines, enter in their wake and now take up their seats alongside their fellow scholars. A heavy-breasted, wide-hipped Ghanaian female academic takes the microphone and proudly announces that she has a post in the United States as a professor. She then welcomes us to the 'colloquium'. She encourages us to think about Du Bois's 'Talented Tenth'; she implores us to consider who we are writing for, 'if not the readers who are the community, then who?' I am unable to decipher just what she is talking about, so I look to Mansour for help, but Mansour has clearly succumbed to some kind of peaceful coma. Through the window I can see that the impatient evening has already hurried the afternoon out of the sky. The professor continues and an-

nounces that before the commencement of the main programme she wishes to remind us that tonight there will be a performance of a play by the National Players of Ghana. The play is
intriguingly entitled *A Nightingale for Dr DuBois*.

Before the play begins, the master of ceremonies informs his
audience that he would like everybody to turn to the person
next to them and say, 'I love you'. I announce to Mansour that it
is time to quit Panafesting. We immediately leave, and we do so
without declaring our love for each other.

Back at the hotel, I pass by the reception area to pick up my
faxes. A distraught-looking Kate whispers to me that I should
meet her in the bar. She needs to talk. Five minutes later, Kate
is sipping an orange juice and explaining to me that she was
reluctantly left with no choice but to ask the Jamaicans to leave.
Kate sighs. Clearly this has been a painful decision, and to some
degree an admission of failure on her part. Despite her pleas,
the Jamaicans had not only continued to cook and smoke dope
in their rooms, some had even taken to inviting Ghanaians from
the village back to their rooms to stay with them. 'Dirty, barefoot people', says Kate. Clearly Kate has had enough. She waves
to the waiter and signals for him to bring me another bottle of
beer.

'They think that if they dress down and filthy then they are
being African.'

I stare blankly at Kate, for only now do I realize just how
angry she is. I sympathize. How can I not, for I have seen it day
in and day out during this Panafest. People of the diaspora who
expect the continent to solve whatever psychological problems
they possess. People of the diaspora who dress the part, have
their hair done, buy beads, and fill their spiritual 'fuel tank' in
preparation for the return journey to 'Babylon'. They have deep

wounds that need to be healed, but if 'their' Africa fails them in any way, if 'their' Africa disappoints, then they will immediately accuse 'these Africans' of catering to the white man. The same white man that they work for in New York, or Toronto, or even Jamaica. Do they not understand? Africa cannot cure. Africa cannot make anybody feel whole. Africa is not a psychiatrist. I look at poor Kate. She is no longer sipping her orange juice. Kate is simply staring at the moonlit breakers that pound against the shore with a regular beat. The look on her pained face is eloquent. What on earth do these people want?

> *Subdued and time-lost*
> *Are the drums—and yet*
> *Through some vast mist of race*
> *There comes this song*
> *I do not understand,*
> *This song of atavistic land,*
> *Of bitter yearnings lost*
> *Without a place—*
> *So long,*
> *So far away*
> *Is Africa's*
>
> *Darkface.*
>
> LANGSTON HUGHES

THRU THE DOOR OF NO RETURN

'Tomorrow you must come to the "Thru the Door of No Return" ceremony,' says Kohain. 'It is our contribution to Panafest, and you will meet Nana and Imahkus.' Kohain and I are sitting together at an otherwise deserted Mabel's Table. Kohain has already told me about his 'partners' Nana and Imahkus, two African-American 'elders' who, like Kohain, are from the New York area. Nana used to be a fireman, and his wife, Imahkus, used to manage a travel agency in Brooklyn. They are veterans of the inaugural visit to Ghana in 1987, and like Kohain they too knew immediately that they wished to settle in the mother country. For both Nana and Imahkus, the United States is a place of the past. They are now 'home'.

I see Nana sitting on the outer wall of Cape Coast Castle, high above the sea. I recognize him from the description that Kohain has given me. A tall man in his early seventies, with long grey dreadlocks, he has the enviable appearance of a man who has found inner spiritual peace in the autumnal years of his life. I introduce myself to Nana, and then ask him what time the ceremony will begin. 'What time? My brother, time is irrelevant in Africa.' I have actually noticed this fact, but I deem it impolitic to say anything. Nana continues. 'In Africa, I don't wear a watch. You see the sun does rise at six-fifteen in the morning, and the sun does go down at six-fifteen at night. Same thing, every day. No difference. Never a difference. If a man can discipline himself within this framework then all you have to do is look to the sky and time will appear.' I look at a serene Nana, and mention to him that only yesterday a man at the Cape Coast Cultural Centre tried to sell me a wooden clock that was carved in the shape of Africa. Nana rises to the occasion. 'Africa has no use for clocks. It does have no time for such useless things.'

We are joined by a worried-looking Kohain. Even though Africa has no use for time, there are clusters of 'guests' in the courtyard of the castle who look as though their patience is beginning to wear a little thin. Some even have the temerity to glance at their wristwatches. Kohain tells me that he asked the Panafest committee to supply one hundred and fifty chairs, and to suspend the regular guided tours of the castle so that he could have privacy for the ceremony. He speaks quickly, like a man who has only just come to the realization that he has been cheated. He had also asked that on this day nobody should be charged for admission. This is the only one of his requests that has been met. Originally Kohain's programme was scheduled to be held on a special 'reverential' night, but what he terms 'heavy politics' behind the scenes has resulted in Kohain and his group being effectively marginalized by the Panafest authorities. A sympathetic Nana rolls his eyes and looks helplessly to the sky. Presumably to check the time.

In keeping with tradition, about one and a half hours after the scheduled commencement of the ceremony there is movement. We are encouraged, by an American woman in traditional Ghanaian dress, to take a candle. There are thirty of us gathered in the courtyard, a mixture of diasporan refugees, European tourists, and one or two puzzled Ghanaians. All around us, the 'regular' tourists are being ushered through the castle on their 'official' guided tours. Our group, the participants in the 'Thru the Door of No Return' ceremony, represent a strange anomaly in the middle of the courtyard. I begin to feel self-conscious. Clearly this chaos is not what Kohain had in mind. I look to my feet and realize that by my left foot there is a marble plaque. It marks the burial place of Philip Quaque.

The American woman finishes handing out the candles, and it would appear that the proceedings are about to commence. A small wooden podium, boldly painted with the slogans 'One Love' and 'One Africa', is trundled out before us. A clutter of chairs are arranged on the podium, which soon bear the weight of Kohain, Nana, and a dreadlocked woman I imagine to be Imahkus. They are joined by a small sixty-year-old man, who I decide must be the 'Jamaican brother' Kohain has mentioned. Leon Morrison is apparently better known as 'Bongo Shorty', although Kohain seems unable to pinpoint the etymology of his name. To the side of the podium there are a half-dozen chairs for the 'elders' among the returnees. Having handed out all the candles, the African-American woman now pours a libation to the spirit of the ancestors. We all watch in silence. Having sufficiently 'wet the soil', she now lights some incense that she holds in a brass container and she swings it about her so that we are all soon breathing the pungent fumes.

Imahkus begins the proceedings. She is a frail-looking woman in her late sixties, and she wears a dress with the words 'One Africa' printed upon it. As she stands, the sun livens her grey locks. First of all, she introduces her 'kingman' to the small gathering. Nana—her kingman—smiles. Both he and Bongo Shorty have drums which they now beat as Imahkus continues with her 'presentation'. She first welcomes the 'family' back home to the dungeons. 'Giving all Honour to God and the spirit of the ancestors.' Imahkus claims victory and triumph for us as a people, because we are returning to the scene of the crime strong, ever-ready and vigorous to take part in the struggle. 'Though we were carried far away to strange lands, we return home.' I notice that the proceedings are being videotaped by many of the onlookers, including a Ghanaian man and his blonde wife. The woman clutches the hand of their five-year-old son with increasing determination as Imahkus's oratory rises and falls, and Nana and Bongo Shorty's drumming begins to achieve an insistent tempo that clearly terrifies her.

And then suddenly, and with dramatic authority, Imahkus stops and lowers her voice. She wishes to achieve a particular significance. She announces to the small group that although it had previously been agreed that the dungeons, and the castle itself, would be closed to the public in order to preserve the sanctity of the upcoming ceremony, the Ghanaian Panafest officials have callously violated this agreement. The crowd mutter in sympathetic agreement, as though thoroughly familiar with the treachery of what has occurred. Imahkus has made her point, and she now presses on. 'The water that divides us is not as strong as the blood that binds us. We know you're with us, God, because no people on the face of the earth have ever gone through this. Give thanks to those who crossed the water during the middle passage, and those whose bones are at the bottom of the Atlantic.' Imahkus is now feeling the spirit, and shaking her castanets, and to my immediate left I can see that the 'libatress' is pouring new libations and preparing to burn fresh incense.

'This is a dungeon, not a castle,' proclaims Imahkus. 'Let us remember those who were eaten by sharks, and those who reached America and survived and raised families.' As the new libations are poured Imahkus encourages us to shout 'Amen' or 'Yow' (the choice is ours) as the water hits the ground. 'The ancestors are receiving us! They are receiving us!' Having established contact, she confirms that she has returned to the land of her ancestors. Having crossed the Atlantic, 'the watery grave of our ancestors', she is now home. 'I am home! I am home! There are six families here now, and more coming.' She stops and raises her voice; 'More coming!'

It is clear that, for Imahkus, this introduction to the ceremony of 'Thru the Door of No Return' is in part a public relations exercise. Bongo Shorty is now introduced as 'a one-man contractor'; a man who since he arrived 'home' with his Jamaican queen, has built two fishing boats by himself, one thirty feet in length, one fifteen feet in length, and all without the aid of any electrical tools. Bongo Shorty raps out a powerful flourish on his drums and acknowledges the diasporan round of applause. 'This ceremony is for African people, not tourists,' declares Imahkus. A few guilty glances are exchanged. 'It was developed for African descendants. The African holocaust of one hundred million merits a ceremony on at least the same level, and with the same degree of seriousness with which our Semitic brothers celebrate the loss of their six million.'

Having made this 'Semitic' connection, Imahkus is ready now to welcome the representatives from Israel, a group of three women and four men, all African-Americans, who sing together under the name of 'Prophetic Destiny'. The representatives from Israel open their 'set' by asking the now shrinking group, 'How's everybody doing?' Having received a positive answer they launch into their 'hit', 'We ain't gonna be no slave no more'. This, they say, is a song about 'breaking away from the system'. The pourer of libations and swinger of the incense now passes among the 'survivors', encouraging us to chant 'No more!

No more!' and somewhat violently punch the air with our fists. I look up to the ramparts where a group of European tourists, and their Ghanaian guide, are looking down in astonishment.

Kohain does not punch the air. He seems to be finding it hard to hide his obvious disappointment with the whole proceedings. The actual ceremony is clearly still some way off, but unless somebody ejects the tourists it will not be possible for Kohain to privately escort his 'guests' into the dungeons and call 'to the spirit of the ancestors'. There is another problem. Kohain's group of maybe two dozen or so includes white people. Kohain has made it clear to me that only those who are obviously of African origin are permitted to take part in the ceremony. What to do with those not of African origin? Nana and Imahkus seem oblivious to this crisis, while Bongo Shorty simply pounds away on his drum in a frenzied manner which suggests that, as far as he is concerned, this is not his problem.

I realize that if I am to meet Mansour and make it back to Accra in time for my night flight, I will have to leave. Just as I am preparing to signal my imminent departure to Kohain, Imahkus stands and introduces a Jamaican 'poet' from the 'carry-be-yon'. He is dressed in a hooded black robe, and he is happy to bring us all greetings from the late Haile Selassie. Just in case the white people in the audience are not feeling alienated enough he states the 'fact' that this is not a place for white people. The blonde woman flushes red and slowly leads her confused Ghanaian husband and even more confused son away from the scene. The Jamaican 'poet' looks at them as they depart, as though pleased with the practical evidence of the power of his words.

I try to catch Kohain's eyes, but he is looking at the space between his sandalled feet. Then I feel a tap on my shoulder and I turn and see Mansour pointing to the western instrument on his wrist. The 'poet' continues. As he speaks he waves his hands which are buckled and misshapen, like wind-blown trees. 'I man cannot bathe in the sea any more for it be a graveyard for my own flesh and blood.' The crowd applaud. 'I come from Jamaica, which is one hundred and forty four miles by fifty-two miles, but this is goat space, not man space. I don't want to give up no continent for no island.' The poet smiles a gap-toothed smile; some teeth are missing, some just crooked. The African-American 'elders' seated to the side of the platform appear to be particularly happy. Like everybody else, they seem relieved to have been offered the opportunity to view history through the narrow prism of their own pigmentation. Bongo Shorty, recognizing one of his own countrymen, releases his locks and shakes his head so that his hair dances wildly. Bongo Shorty begins to sing. Imahkus stands and reminds us that this is Psalm 137 ('By the rivers of Babylon, there we sat down, yea, we wept, when we remembered Zion'). Kohain, naked without dreadlocks, looks up. His face is a Guernica of distress. A brief meeting of our eyes suggests farewell, and then he looks down again at the space between his sandalled feet. Mansour and I turn to take our leave. As we do so, I take care to step over, and not on, the tomb of Philip Quaque.

III

HOME

Home is the place where, when you have to go there, they
have to take you in.

ROBERT FROST

On a hot southern afternoon I pull the car over to the kerb.
Broad Street is aptly named. It is wide, handsome and marks
the social line of acceptability in Charleston, South Carolina.
The upper classes are known as SOBs—they reside South of
Broad. Perhaps it is just nervous habit, but in the south I am
always careful to obey the rules. Not to jaywalk, not to double-
park, not to 'forget' to put money into the parking meter. I
scramble through the ashtray for coins, and then step out of the
car and into the sweltering humidity. I glance at my watch, and
then look across the street to number 18. Lloyd Wilcox's office
is on the third floor. It is nearly 3.30 p.m. Time to go.

I had imagined that the elevator would be an old-fashioned
type that would necessitate my manually sliding a door to, and
caging myself in. I could not be further from the truth. Although
the outside of the building suggests an earlier century, the inside
has been thoroughly renovated and is modern in design. How-

ever, as I step from the elevator and into Mr Wilcox's office, it is clear that modernity has bypassed the Wilcox chambers. The Dickensian atmosphere is buzzing with activity as assistants and interns rush from one room to the other, laden with boxes and papers. Mercifully, there is air-conditioning. Mr Wilcox's secretary, an elderly lady who is clearly the dominant figure in the office, turns to face me as I walk in.

'Now, you must be Mr Phillips.'

Before I can reply, she speaks again.

'Mr Wilcox is expecting you.' She looks at her watch. 'Right about now, I'd say.'

The panelled door is ajar, and Mr Wilcox's secretary pushes gingerly at it. I wait for the hinges to squeal but there is no noise. She pops her head around the corner, but she speaks in a low voice so I cannot hear what she is saying. A few whispered moments later her head reappears. 'Mr Lloyd Wilcox will see you now.'

She opens the door a little wider, but she does not move. I carefully negotiate my way around her, and squeeze into the office where I discover Mr Lloyd Wilcox sitting regally behind his desk. He neither gets up, nor does he look up. With a movement of his hand Mr Lloyd Wilcox gestures me to sit on the wooden chair on the other side of his desk, which I do.

Lloyd Wilcox arrived in Charleston, South Carolina, on 19 August 1929. He worked initially for Mitchell and Holbeck at 31 Broad Street, where he practised as a young lawyer. Next door to Mitchell and Holbeck at 33 Broad Street were the offices of J. Waties Waring, a more senior lawyer, and a man who had long been recognized as one of the leading citizens of Charleston. I have come to talk to the ninety-four-year-old Lloyd Wilcox in the hope that he might be willing to rekindle some old memories of J. Waties Waring. I have been led to believe that while they could not be described as good friends, there was certainly a professional and personal relationship between the two men which went beyond courtesy.

'He was a very good lawyer,' says Mr Wilcox. He looks up now. 'Meticulous. I tried cases in court before him when he became a judge and he was always prepared. As a corporation lawyer he had substantial clients. He represented the city for one thing. And West Virginia Pulp and Paper. But later, as a judge, he ran a tight court and was fair to attorneys.'

'So you knew him as a friend, as a fellow lawyer and eventually as a judge.'

'I did. He had the windows up in his courtroom in winter, though. He didn't like to get too warm. Always had those windows up.'

Mr Lloyd Wilcox's eyes are focused, and he does not blink. He is dressed smartly in collar and tie and, despite the heat, a jacket. I cannot help noticing that his shirt collar seems a little too large for his wrinkled neck, which emerges like that of a tortoise.

'Now then, I'd be correct in thinking that you'd be too young to have ever met the judge, am I right?'

I nod and smile at the same time. How, I wonder, can I steer Mr Wilcox on to the controversial subject of Judge Waring's 'reputation' in Charleston? I have no desire to cause offence, but this is the territory that I wish to cover. But I am forgetting. Mr Lloyd Wilcox is a lawyer. Despite his advanced years, he is thinking one step ahead of me.

'You see the only time he raised people's ire was when he decided to change the system and let anybody vote.'

'Anybody?' I ask.

'Sure, anybody. Nobody in the south agreed with him, although I suppose people in the north were probably in favour. But letting anybody vote was not the way we did things down here. That particular legal decision caused more problems for him than the second marriage ever did.'

Mr Wilcox covers his mouth with the back of his bony hand and coughs gently. His hand is shaking slightly, and then suddenly, and without warning, this one cough swells into a violent, unexpected storm of coughing, and his body begins to shake.

His secretary rushes in without knocking and hands Mr Wilcox a beaker of water. He drinks quickly and gratefully. Although we have only spoken for a few moments, I wonder if I have not already overstayed my time. But then his secretary retrieves the beaker and once more leaves us alone. Mr Wilcox dabs at his mouth with a folded white handkerchief, and then he carefully tucks it away into his breast pocket. He focuses his eyes upon me.

'But people also didn't approve of how he treated his wife. The first one, that is. She was real popular around here. They turned against him because of that too. The new wife, she was never socially accepted. But I expect you know that.'

Mr Wilcox continues to stare directly at me, not in an unfriendly manner, but with a gaze that I nevertheless find disconcerting.

I am fascinated by Mr Wilcox's choice of words. According to him, the judge changed a 'system' so that just 'anybody' could vote. I fully understand who the 'anybodys' are, but I wonder if Mr Wilcox will spell out whatever it was that he objected to in this new 'system'. In fact, whatever it is that I suspect he still objects to.

'Would you,' I ask, 'with hindsight, now approve of what the judge did?'

Mr Wilcox does not miss a beat. He places both of his hands on the top of his desk, and he pushes himself up in his seat.

'I wouldn't have done what he did, but that's his business. I'm a reconstructed southerner. I only want to belong to institutions that want me.'

The 'institution', in this case, being democracy. I choose not to say this.

'He was a very lonely man after that decision. A lone wolf. I didn't know anybody in town who agreed with him on anything. They all sided with the first wife.'

I realize that Mr Wilcox's secretary is now standing at my

shoulder. Somehow she has managed silently to re-enter the office. I turn to look at her, and immediately I understand. I stand and offer my hand to Mr Wilcox, which he shakes with a firm grip. His hand is warm. I look at Mr Lloyd Wilcox, whose experience spans nearly a full century. Has he truly managed to file his memories successfully, and, one must presume, his feelings? What does Mr Lloyd Wilcox see when he leaves his office and walks out into the streets of Charleston? After all, the evidence of life in the south no longer supports his view of the world. There is dissonance in his world. As Mr Lloyd Wilcox releases my hand I think of Judge Waring. Mr Wilcox knows full well that a great deal of the responsibility for disrupting the 'natural order' of life in the south lies with his 'friend' the judge. He knows full well that his 'friend' the judge is considered by many, including Mr Wilcox, to be a 'traitor'. I look at Mr Wilcox and know that the honest, heartfelt words are forever tied up in the knot of his tongue. I almost feel sorry for Mr Lloyd Wilcox.

The man who had suggested that I speak with Mr Wilcox is himself a lawyer, and a relative of the judge. Tom Waring entered the profession late, having served in the military. He remembers that one day as a thirty-one-year-old 'young' lawyer, he was dispatched to renew his law professor's car tax, but there was a long line. He returned to the office and decided to telephone the tax department and pretend to be the law professor, in the hope that he might be offered preferential treatment. When he told the black clerk that 'he' would be sending over a young man named Tom Waring, the clerk asked if this Tom Waring was in any way related to 'the judge'. When Tom Waring assured him that he was, the black clerk told him to have this Tom Waring bypass the line, come around to the back door, and knock three times. The black clerk would take care of him.

Mr Lloyd Wilcox restlessly shuffles some papers on his desk. 'I once more thank you for your time,' he says.

And then it strikes me. They may dislike Judge Waring

because of his legal pronouncements. They may even dislike Judge Waring for dispensing with his first wife, a South Carolina belle, and marrying a northern divorcee. But they dislike him most of all because they can never totally dismiss him. Judge J. Waties Waring's pedigree is such that he represents the mould out of which the élite of Charleston have been, and continue to be, fashioned. To dismiss him out of hand would be akin to dismissing themselves, so they can only disapprove, which means that they must entertain inquiries and curiosity, even from people such as myself. Over thirty years after his death, Judge Waring continues to disturb the SOBs. He continues to disrupt their ability to file their memories neatly, and their feelings. Mr Lloyd Wilcox's eyes are no longer upon me.

I decide to walk the short distance to the crossroads where Broad Street intersects with Meeting Street. This junction marks the centre of the old city, and it is the place that the horse-and-carriage drivers of a previous era used to call the 'four corners of the law'. According to their stories, the four buildings on each corner represented a different 'law': St Michael's Church, the Charleston County Courthouse, Charleston City Hall, and the Federal Post Office, which also houses the small Federal Courthouse. Charlestonians love to tell stories, particularly of the past. The story of the stubborn and vengeful old man and his scandalous divorce is a Charleston story. However, to the SOBs, this is not a narrative about morality and conscience, it is simply a tale of bad social manners. This, of course, makes the story easier to 'file' and to recall. I look slowly from one corner of the law to the next. It is late afternoon and the sun is beginning to set. Outside St Michael's Church, three black women sit in the shade selling sweetgrass baskets. They look at me, as though curious to know my story, but they would recognize my story; it is a story of the past. As they sit in the shadow of the 'four corners of the law', and attempt to sell their sweetgrass baskets to the passing tourists, I hope they have not forgotten their story.

Home

·   ·   ·

From the *New York Post*, Wednesday, 11 October 1950:

CHARLESTON, SC

The stoning of Federal Judge J. Waties Waring's home here on Monday climaxed a week of terror and intimidation during which Mrs Waring was jostled on the streets and jeeringly called a 'witch', the *Post* learned today.

Mrs Elizabeth Waring, the Detroit-born wife of the Southern champion of equal rights for Negroes, said today that the hurling of bricks through a window and screen door of their home was accompanied by the firing of three shots.

'I don't know if they were blank shells as later suggested by one of the FBI agents,' she said, 'or whether they were fired into the air, since no bullet marks were found on the house.

'But both the Judge and I distinctly heard the three shots just before a brick crashed through the window under which we were sitting playing canasta.

'It was because of the firing that we both ran into the dining room and crouched behind the wall there while I tried vainly to get the FBI on the phone. We were not sure then that the shots hadn't been fired directly into the house.'

Mrs Waring said the attacks were carried out by the white supremacy advocates who resented Judge Waring's 1947 action in opening white Democratic primaries to Negro voters.

'This latest series of incidents started last week, as soon as we returned from our summer vacation in New York and other Northern centers,' she said.

'Twice last week, I was rudely and insultingly jostled on the street by grown men. The first time, I was on my way to the post office and one man broke away from three others who had been blocking the sidewalk and deliberately bumped roughly into me.

'I was almost knocked into the gutter, but I stood my ground and looked him straight in the eyes. He glared back for a minute and then stood aside sneeringly so I could pass. The same thing happened a couple of days later.'

The telephone calls had started earlier in the week, she said, and 'every time I went into the streets, several young drugstore cowboys would yell "witch" and even worse terms as I passed.'

Mrs Waring believes that the original attack had been planned for last Saturday and was thwarted only by a visit of two FBI men to the house that day.

'After the anonymous callers kept asking if we were going to be at home over the weekend, Judge Waring called the FBI and told them about it. So, after the agents came, everything was quiet until Monday night and we thought it was all over.'

Mrs Waring said that a stranger had come to the house Thursday and 'insisted on coming inside although he knew the judge was sitting in court.' When she wouldn't let him in, she said, he loitered about the neighbourhood and later followed her down the street.

And, on Saturday afternoon, Judge Waring had reprimanded a group of youths—'they were around 19 or in their early 20s'—for yelling 'witch' and obscene epithets at his wife as the couple walked down the street.

During the Monday night incident, Mrs Waring said she called the FBI, but 'they were closed for the night. I then called the local police, and while waiting for them, I called Walter White [executive director of the NAACP] in New York.

'If you've lived under what we have been forced to live under down here since 1947, you'd realize why I wanted some contact with the outside world—with civilization.'

Statement given to the United Press, 10 October, 1950 by Judge J. Waties Waring:

Evidently the attack last night upon my wife and myself was done in protest against the position I had taken in regard to the equality of citizens and Civil Rights to all Americans. It was evidently a protest and an attempt to intimidate and impede. It was an evidence of the stubborn, savage sentiment of this State and particularly of this community in fighting the American creed and the creed of true Religion. The Dixiecrat movement, camouflaged under the name of States Rights, is the dying gasp of White Supremacy and SLAVE-OCRACY. It is an attack upon the UNION which I represent. It is well that the eyes of the Nation be turned upon this great evil and that the people of America awake to the necessity to stamp it out by taking active measures to make these people recognize and obey the tenets of the Constitution of the United States. I shall continue to fight for Freedom and Democracy.

Charles Town was established in 1670 by the British as a peninsular port with the Ashley River to the west and the Cooper River to the east. The original settlers had to overcome many difficulties, including hostile Indians, Spanish pirates, storms, disease, much flooding and blisteringly hot summers. However, they persisted, and under the leadership of Baron Ashley, later the first Earl of Shaftesbury, they eventually named their settlement after their king. A large number of the arrivants were religious refugees, primarily Quakers, French Huguenots, Baptists and Presbyterians, and they were determined to succeed despite the inhospitable nature of their environment. The town's first exports were deerskins, furs and maritime supplies such as tar, timber and turpentine, all of which were easily available in the nearby pine forests. These products were shipped back to England, where they were sold at a profit and thereafter utilized in the country's naval and merchant fleets. The first planters arrived from the British Caribbean colony of Barbados, and they were joined by others from Europe. These planters found themselves in a busy harbour town whose dirt streets were densely populated with mariners, fur traders, African slaves and prosti-tutes, but they soon settled down to their task and established large plantations along the banks of the rivers.

By the end of the 1730s, Charles Town boasted a population of 6,000 people, which made it the fourth largest town in British North America after New York, Philadelphia and Bos-ton. Hundreds of ships a year were arriving from England and the Caribbean, bringing consumer items such as wine, sugar and rum. These same ships left laden with local produce, although by now the rice that was cultivated on the huge river plantations was by far the most profitable of the locally produced exports. The labour employed on these plantations was slave labour, and the 'industry' of the slave trade was greatly adding to the wealth of both the town and the royal colony of South Carolina. In the single year between 1772 and 1773, the records reveal that more than sixty-five vessels carrying in excess of 10,000 African slaves entered the port of Charles Town.

Standard practice was for the slaves to be first quarantined, in enormous pens known as 'pest houses'. Once they were 'sea-soned', the Africans were then transferred to the mainland to be sold in the town's slave marts. Almost one third of all the Africans who entered the North American world in captivity passed through the gateway of Charleston, South Carolina. In 1783, at the end of the Revolutionary War, the newly 'liberated' young city changed its name from Charles Town to Charleston, and continued to enjoy its status as the most important port between Philadelphia and the Caribbean. The city was located at the centre of a vast network of commerce that reached across the Atlantic to Africa and Europe, and which penetrated the American continent as far west as the Mississippi River. By 1820, about 58 per cent of the city's population was black, which increased the ever-present threat of slave rebellion, although even the occasional uprising could not dampen the confidence of the Charlestonian aristocracy. However, all of this civic enthusiasm was soon quelled with the advent of the Civil War.

At 4 a.m. on 12 April 1861, cadets from the military academy, The Citadel, fired a cannon at Fort Sumter, which was situated on a small island which overlooked the entrance to Charleston Harbour. During the course of the next few years, the Union repeatedly tried and failed to take Charleston by both land and sea, but on the morning of 18 February 1865, Union troops finally landed at the foot of Broad Street. Thereafter began the decline of the 'kingdom by the sea', which for two hundred years had controlled the politics and the economy of the southern states. Thousands of newly freed slaves deserted the plantations, and the city, humiliated by defeat, ravaged by the physical scars of war and depressed by the realities of 'Reconstruction', slid rapidly into decline. However, the mercantile and planter families who lived south of Broad still retained a tight grip on the social life of Charleston. In other 'fallen' cities such as Nashville and Atlanta, responsibility for civic leadership passed to those who were invested in the future, as opposed to the past. In Charleston, the 'aristocracy' simply refused to acknowledge these new circumstances.

In 1683, Benjamin Waring, the founder of the Waring family in South Carolina, settled 700 acres which bordered the Ashley River. Eleven years later, in 1694, William Waties, the eldest of the Waties line, migrated to South Carolina from Wales, and he settled 250 acres of coastal land. For two hundred years the fortunes of these two families rose and fell, but the families were always respected as pillars of the society. Julius Waties Waring was born in Charleston on 27 July 1880, but in spite of the fact that both his parents possessed distinguished names, in common with the post-bellum times, the family finances were in a precarious position. Edward Waring, Julius's father, had left school early and run away to join the confederate army. After the Civil War he managed to obtain a senior clerical position with the South Carolina Railroad Company, where he remained an employee until the company was declared bankrupt. After this calamity, Edward Waring was elected county superintendent of education, a position he held until his death in 1916. Despite his financial difficulties, Edward Waring was not only a part of the SOB set, he remained a thoroughgoing confederate, a steward of the South Carolina Society, and a member of Charleston's exclusive St George's Society. Julius Waties Waring's 'roots' on both sides of his family stretched back across eight generations of Charlestonian privilege, and in later years an ironic Judge Waring often described his family as 'fine, decent slaveholders'.

On 12 February 1946, Isaac Woodward, a twenty-seven-year-old black soldier was discharged from the army at Camp Gordon, a base near Augusta, Georgia. He was tired, hungry and keen to get back to his wife who lived in Winnsboro, South Carolina. In the afternoon he boarded a bus and settled in for the long ride north. After winding through miles of southern countryside the bus eventually stopped by the side of the road in a sleepy South Carolina town called Batesburg. A puzzled Isaac created a visor with his forearm, and peered through the window into the darkness. Then he felt a hand drop hard onto his shoulder, and he heard a white man's voice ordering him off the bus. Isaac stood and followed the man, and the other passengers scrutinized him as he squeezed down the aisle. Once he had stepped into the chilly night, Isaac Woodward was confronted by two policemen who told him that he was under arrest. They ordered him to come along to the police station.

The following morning, Isaac Woodward appeared in the court of the mayor of Batesburg. Isaac looked dishevelled and in need of sleep, but the one aspect of his person that was most transformed were his eyes, which were red and swollen. He blinked ferociously, unable to look into the light for any length of time, and although he wanted to raise his hands to rub his eyes he refrained, fearful that he would be breaking decorum. Mayor H. E. Quarles accused Isaac of public drunkenness and disorderly conduct, and a somewhat bemused Isaac pleaded guilty. A fine of $50 was levied, but Isaac had only $44 on his person which the judge decided to accept, suspending the outstanding $6. Isaac was dismissed and ordered to leave Batesburg. However, later that same day, and in much distress, he checked himself into the veteran's hospital in Columbia. Three agonising months later, Isaac Woodward was finally released and allowed to go home. He was totally blind.

By the late summer of 1946, the case of Isaac Woodward had become a national issue. Woodward claimed that the Batesburg chief of police, Lynwood Shull, had gouged his eyes with a blackjack. For his part, Shull, admitted that he had hit the 'unruly' veteran across the face after Woodward had lunged at his blackjack. Isaac's parents, who lived in the Bronx in New York City, organized a rally in mid-August 1946 which was attended by 20,000 people, including many celebrities. The guest speaker was the honorary chairman of the Isaac Woodward Benefit Committee, Mayor O'Dwyer of New York. Mayor O'Dwyer vociferously denounced the southern brutality that had been visited upon the young veteran and called for justice.

As a result of public pressure, Isaac Woodward was invited to come before the Department of Justice and tell his side of the story. Such federal intervention in what would otherwise be regarded as a matter for the state authorities, was greatly resented by white South Carolinians. On 26 September 1946, the U.S. attorney in Columbia decided to charge Police Chief Shull with violating Woodward's rights 'to be secure in his person and to be immune from illegal assault and battery'. If convicted, Lynwood Shull faced either a year in prison or a $1,000 fine, or both. His bail was posted by three prominent citizens of Batesburg, including Mayor Quarles, and the trial date was set for 5 November, to be heard before Judge Waring. Although Judge Waring was concerned that there appeared to be an unseemly haste about the manner in which the Department of Justice was bringing the case to trial, a haste perhaps not unconnected with the forthcoming election year, he was none the less relieved that they were at least taking up the case.

The chief witness for the government was Isaac Woodward himself, who appeared in a neat brown suit and wearing dark glasses. A thin, nervous man, he was led to the dock where he swore on the Bible. Woodward claimed that a few miles outside of Augusta the bus stopped to pick up some passengers, and he asked the driver to wait while he went to use the restroom. The driver began to curse Woodward, and told him in no uncertain terms to return to his seat. Woodward refused and told him that he expected to be treated like a man, and that he also expected to be spoken to with the same courtesy with which he was speaking to the driver. With this said, he left the bus and went to the restroom. When the bus reached Batesburg the driver instructed Woodward to leave the bus where he said there was 'someone I want you to see'. Police Chief Lynwood Shull and another policeman were standing at the bus stop, and when Isaac started to explain his difficulty with the driver, Shull hit him on the head with his blackjack and told him to 'shut up'. The two policemen then physically forced Isaac around the corner and out of sight of the bus. Shull asked Isaac if he had been discharged from the army, and Isaac replied 'Yes', which seemed to inflame Shull who wished to be addressed, 'Yes, sir'. Isaac complied but Shull began to beat him, and there followed a struggle in which Isaac admitted grabbing Shull's billy club to prevent any further physical injury. When the other policeman drew his pistol, Isaac released the billy club. He was then taken to prison and charged.

Two of the passengers on the bus were called as defence witnesses. A white veteran and a University of South Carolina student, both of whom testified that although there had been some fun and jollification among some army vets, nobody was drunk and no complaint had been made against Isaac Woodward. The bus driver, however, was adamant that Woodward was out of control. He claimed that Isaac had offered a white soldier a drink, and that his language was so offensive a white couple had asked that Woodward be put off the bus. Lynwood Shull 'confirmed' that Woodward was drunk and abusive, and conceded that he may have accidentally 'bumped' him lightly in the eyes in self-defence. Mayor Quarles reported that Woodward had admitted, in his court, to being drunk and disorderly, and a Batesburg physician, who claimed to have examined Isaac, said that the damage to his eyes might well have been caused by a single 'perfectly timed' blow. Character witnesses for Police Chief Shull included a black minister, and the county sheriff.

Judge Waring watched the proceedings with a growing sense of despair. He knew that the all-white jury were not only aware of the national significance of the case, but that they would almost certainly acquit. In his charge to them he reminded them that, 'You are trying only one police officer', not the south's racial customs. However, Police Chief Shull's attorneys were not so circumspect in their approach. One of them claimed that Isaac belonged to 'an inferior race', and that his vulgarity was 'not the talk of a sober South Carolina Negro'. Another attorney finished his address to the jury by asserting that if delivering a verdict which flies in the face of the federal government 'means that South Carolina'll have to secede again, then let's secede!' The verdict was, as Waring knew it would be, for acquittal.

The case of Isaac Woodward had a profound effect on Judge J. Waties Waring. He openly declared that he had no quarrel with the verdict delivered by the jury, for he knew the real villains to be the Department of Justice, who had improperly prepared the case and presented it in a shabby manner. Judge Waring broke with custom and made public his disapproval of the Department of Justice's failure to treat the case with the dignity he felt it deserved:

I have no comment or criticism of them [the jury] now. I couldn't ask them to find [Shull] guilty on the slimness of

that case, but I was shocked at the hypocrisy of my government and your government in submitting that disgraceful
case before a jury. I was also hurt that I was made a party to
it, because I had to be a party to it, however unwilling I was.

Tom Waring looks suspiciously at me. We are seated in the
magazine-filled lobby of his Charleston law firm, Holmes and
Thomson. 'Now you're gonna be fair now, right? We've had a lot
of northern fellars down here over the years.'

I look closely at Tom Waring. He is obviously caught between
a loyalty to his father, a newspaperman who loathed Judge J.
Waties Waring, and his fascination with the great-uncle he
clearly respects. 'I'm interested in the judge,' I say.

Tom Waring thinks for a moment. He never met his great-
uncle. I am sure that had he met him, the judge would have had
a profound effect on Tom Waring's life. I also imagine that fifty-
four-year-old Tom Waring knows this. He rubs his palm across
his clean-shaven chin.

'I see. So you're interested in the judge. Well, that's good. I
reckon that's good.'

Julius Waties Waring enrolled at the College of Charleston,
where he worked hard and, in 1900, graduated with honours,
second in his class. He decided upon a career in law, although
there was no immediate connection with the profession on
either side of his family. Having made his decision, Waring realized that he would be unable to attend law school as the family
did not possess the resources to support him. He therefore got
himself articled (without fees) to a Charleston law firm, and he
studied law by reading assiduously at nights and helping around
the office in the day. Two years later he travelled to Columbia
and passed the bar exam, after which he was accepted as a
young lawyer into the Charleston firm of J. P. Kennedy Bryan.
In 1913, Waring married one of the most eligible young

women in Charleston, Annie Gammell. She was a year older than him and also an eighth-generation Charlestonian, and together they moved into a two-storey, relatively modest home at 61 Meeting Street. Originally a carriage house for a much larger adjacent property, its size was far outweighed by the splendour of its location in Charleston's élite district to the south of Broad. In 1914, Waring was appointed to the position of assistant U.S. attorney for South Carolina's eastern district, where he further honed his legal skills and extended his circle of useful contacts. The election of 1920 swept the Republicans into power in Washington, and sensing that Democrats such as himself might now be subject to suspicion, Waring decided to resign his office. He hoped that the federal experience he had gained might enable him to expand his private practice rapidly, having re-established it on Broad Street in partnership with a younger lawyer named David A. Brockinton.

Throughout the 1920s Waring's practice flourished, attracting a number of large private clients, including the city's newspapers. However, in common with the rest of the country, Waring and Brockinton had to acknowledge that the national climate was one of economic depression and they were soon looking for ways to bolster their income. In 1931, through his close association with the Mayor of Charleston, Burnet Rhett Maybank, Waring was appointed City Attorney for Charleston, a position he would hold for over ten years. As City Attorney (or Corporation Counsel), he was responsible for offering legal advice on a number of issues, from the safety of drainage covers on the sidewalks to how best to protect the city's money in the face of banks collapsing and individuals being unable, or unwilling, to pay their taxes. On issues to do with race, Waring embraced the prejudices of his birth and status. As a child he had a black nurse called Hannah, but Waring never knew whether she possessed a surname. In his private practice he preferred Brockinton, who had grown up on a plantation, to deal with black clients, and although he remained respectful he was never comfortable around black people. When, at the outbreak of war, the army leased Charleston's Stoney Field to be used as a recreation area, Waring, in his capacity as City Attorney, insisted that it be clearly stipulated in the lease that the field 'shall be strictly limited to soldiers of the White or Caucasian Race'. When the army officials informed him that this would inevitably be the case, and there was therefore no need to spell it out, Julius Waties Waring would have none of this.

On 26 January 1942, in the Federal courtroom at the corner of Broad and Meeting Street, only a short distance from where Waring and his wife Annie had lived for over twenty-five years, the oath of office was administered whereby President Franklin D. Roosevelt appointed J. Waties Waring as a federal judge in South Carolina, for the eastern district, with a seat at Charleston. Many considered this a long overdue appointment, but others were actively surprised that the position should have gone to a sixty-one-year-old man. However, as Waring took the oath as a federal judge, in the presence of his wife, his daughter Anne, his business partner D. A. Brockinton, and numerous members of his family, one could have been forgiven for assuming that he had now reached the apotheosis of his successful career. He had long been one of the most prominent of Charleston's citizens, a member of the prestigious St George's and St Cecilia Societies, a captain in the Charleston Light Dragoons, and a member of the Charleston Club. Waring and his wife regularly entertained at their Meeting Street home, and at their summer cottage on Sullivan's Island, and to anybody in Charleston society looking on, the judgeship was merely further evidence of his status in the city as a respected man of great influence and importance. However, all of this was about to change radically.

Judge Waring's relationship with his wife, Miss Annie, was outwardly warm, but behind closed doors things were cold and somewhat aloof. In common with the practice of many men of his class and station, the judge had been a long-time private philanderer. As the years passed he not only found it increasingly difficult to share his passions with his wife, he came to regard her as intellectually inferior. For her part, Annie was proud of her somewhat distant husband, and increasingly so after he was appointed to the federal bench. Judge Waring, however, soon after taking his seat, found himself being stirred by his attraction to another woman, and in the tight-knit world of Charleston society the rumours began to fly.

Elizabeth Avery was born in Michigan in 1895. She had a privileged upbringing with well-to-do parents who enjoyed a great social status in the Detroit community. At the age of twenty she married a successful lawyer and businessman, by whom she had two sons and a daughter. After nearly two decades of marriage she met a wealthy Connecticut art dealer named Henry Hoffman, and she swiftly divorced her husband and married Hoffman, who was twenty-five years her senior. Although Hoffman lived principally in Connecticut, he also owned one of the large houses south of Broad where he chose to spend the winter. Soon after their marriage, the lively, outgoing Elizabeth Avery was introduced to the Charleston set and her connection to this new social world was further solidified by the marriage, in 1942, of her daughter Anne to a man whose parents were from Charleston.

It was not long before Henry and Elizabeth Hoffman became frequent bridge partners of the Warings. Soon after this, Elizabeth and Judge Waring became secret lovers. In late February 1945, Judge Waring felt he could no longer conceal his love for Elizabeth from his long-suffering wife, and so he confessed his feelings and asked Miss Annie for a divorce. This was unlikely to be a comfortable procedure for a man with the high public profile of Judge Waring, a task made doubly difficult by the fact that in the state of South Carolina there was no legal provision for divorce. Judge Waring suggested that his traumatized wife establish legal residence in Florida, where divorce was permitted, and so Miss Annie temporarily left town. In May 1945, a generous divorce settlement was drawn up, which by no means alleviated the mental anguish that Miss Annie was suffering, a result of this separation from the husband to whom she was devoted.

On 7 June 1945, a Florida judge issued a decree dissolving Judge Waring's marriage to the former Annie Gammell. The sixty-six-year-old Annie returned to Charleston, but she was devastated and seemed incapable of fully grasping what had happened to her. A little over a week later, on 15 June, in Greenwich, Connecticut, a newly divorced Elizabeth married her beloved Judge Waring. The house at 61 Meeting Street, which had originally belonged to Annie, was now the judge's as part of the Florida divorce settlement. Shortly after the Connecticut wedding, the judge returned to live at 'Annie's house' with his new bride, a move which scandalized Charleston society. Elizabeth's Yankee background, and her history of broken marriages, did not endear her to the SOB set. Furthermore, Elizabeth was an attractive, self-confident, fifty-year-old woman who would brook no nonsense from anybody; she was, in many ways, the antithesis of the flexible, accommodating southern belle who knew her place.

Judge Waring's new marriage marked the end of his life in Charleston society as he had known it before. There were those who decided to leave a room whenever Judge Waring and his wife entered; there were those who refused to extend invitations to the most straightforward of events to Judge Waring and his new wife; and whenever Judge Waring and his new wife threw a party at 61 Meeting Street, an embarrassing number of guests simply refused to attend. Although, in later years, the judge and Elizabeth always maintained that they were socially ostracized by Charleston society for the 'crime' of falling in love, there is probably some truth to the claims of those in Charleston society who insist that the judge and Elizabeth, highly sensitive to people's ambivalence towards them, chose to cut themselves off as much as they were actively cut off. In other words, they managed to do a fair amount of the snubbing themselves, which would seem to be in tune with the strong nature of their characters. Judge Waring's subsequent Civil Rights decisions and his loud pronouncements with regard to codes of racial behaviour as practised in the south merely exacerbated what was an already deteriorating situation at home in Charleston.

I look around her room and can see that it represents a tidy, probably happy life. Everything is in its place. Every photograph is nicely dusted, the books are shelved in alphabetical order, the magazines are all current issues and neatly arranged on the coffee table, the flowers in the jar are fresh, and the floor is brightly polished so that it seems almost sinful to walk upon it. She lives alone in the upstairs apartment of this two-storey building, serene, graceful and surrounded by her memories. These days, few people beyond friends and family seek her out. Strangers, like myself, generally come to ask her about the past. For most of the 1950s, Elizabeth Waring considered Ruby Cornwell to be her best friend, which would hardly be remarkable except for the fact that Ruby Cornwell is black. And we are talking about Charleston, South Carolina.

Mrs Cornwell hands me a cup of coffee in a delicate china cup and saucer, and then she sits in a chair opposite me. She points to the plate of biscuits. 'Help yourself.'

I notice that she has not made a cup of coffee for herself, but I decide not to mention this omission. This wafer-thin woman clearly knows her own mind. I take a sip of coffee and wonder if I should begin to ask my questions. Mrs Cornwell readjusts her position on her chair, and then she begins to speak as though we have been talking for hours.

'It was after he became a judge that he developed this passion for justice. You see, he was faced with so much reality that he could not ignore it. My theory is that the type of law he was practising before he became a judge did not really give him much of an opportunity for moral posturing. But Elizabeth read to him. She converted him in a sense. From Saul, he became Paul. He was always a decent man, but these things had never been set before him until he became a judge.'

Beyond Mrs Cornwell, I look through an uncurtained window. It is beginning to get dark. Night is falling quickly. Ruby Pendergrass Cornwell was born in 1903 in Forestaw, South Carolina. She completed her high-school diploma at the Daytona Institute in Daytona, Florida, and thereafter she spent four years at Talladega College, Alabama, where in 1925 she earned a Bachelor of Arts degree. Having graduated, she married Dr. A. T. Cornwell, a practising dentist, and the two of them made their home in Charleston, South Carolina. Dr A. T. and Mrs Ruby Cornwell first met the Warings socially at a cocktail party on New Year's Day, 1950. Then, after Elizabeth Waring's infamous YWCA speech, Mrs Cornwell sent her flowers, and Elizabeth Waring responded by inviting her to tea at 61 Meeting Street. This gesture scandalised Charleston society, for this was the first time that black people had ever been entertained south of Broad.

Elizabeth Waring soon came to regard Ruby Cornwell as her closest friend, but the fact that blacks were now being encouraged to visit the Waring household put an end to any possibility of the Warings ever being reaccepted by white Charleston society.

However, it was not only the whites who were critical of the Warings' 'open door' policy. One of Charleston's most prominent black citizens told Mrs Cornwell that, 'just because the whites don't want them, I won't let them have me'. In fact, not every black person regarded the Warings as 'decent', or the judge's decisions as necessarily in the best interests of 'progress'. Mrs Cornwell remembers an exasperated Judge Waring declaring to her that 'he often felt like a general who said "let's take the hill", and he'd charge off and then look back from the top of the hill and there would be nobody there'. Mrs Cornwell sighs.

'He didn't understand, but a lot of black people viewed him as the friendless man who suddenly wanted to be friends with them. Many black people were also worried for their jobs, or simply frightened. I remember, at a reception, Mrs Waring asked me to pour the coffee, which seemed to offend some of the black people present. But I just saw it as an honour that she was extending to me, for she was acknowledging me as the assistant hostess.'

In the fading light, Mrs Cornwell stands and pours me another cup of coffee. And then she sits, and I notice that her mind seems to have momentarily spun off into a dreamworld. Clearly there was more than just plain friendship between the Cornwells and the Warings. There was a dependency of sorts. Again, Mrs Cornwell focuses on me.

'You know,' she begins, 'the judge's "baptism of fire" was the case of the soldier who was blinded. He had never really known us, except as labourers, and he had just gone along with the system. He'd never known us as responsible citizens.'

She pauses and thinks for a moment.

'He very much treated them decently, but as long as they stayed in their place.' Again she pauses, but this time I sense that Mrs Cornwell has momentarily lost the thread of whatever it was she was going to say. 'Us' or 'them'? It is all too confusing. She looks across at me and smiles.

Shortly after the Isaac Woodward trial, Judge Waring sought to change some of the discriminatory practices in his courtroom. Juror lists were traditionally colour-coded, with the letter 'C' placed beside the names of the prospective black jurors. Judge Waring ended this. He also made it standard practice to address black people by their titles, as Mr or Mrs, as opposed to simply using their first names. He had also noticed that juries tended to arrange themselves 'naturally' with the white jurors seated to the front and the black jurors to the rear, so he introduced mandatory integrated seating. During the recess periods, when black jurors were generally asked to eat in the kitchen of a restaurant while white jurors ate in the front, he now ensured that everybody sat and ate together, even though this practice regularly offended the 'morals' of the white clientele in the various restaurants near to the courthouse. Finally, in 1948, Judge Waring appointed John Fleming, the son of a black shoemaker, to be the court bailiff, a highly visible position of great ceremonial significance.

The judge's first real judicial volley against the system was fired soon after the Isaac Woodward case. In August 1946 the South Carolina Democratic party held its primary, and a black voter, George Elmore, attempted and failed to cast a vote. Elmore, with the aid of his lawyer, Thurgood Marshall of the NAACP, filed a class action suit against the Clarendon County Democratic committee. Their argument was that the refusal to let blacks take part in the primary, in a one-party Democratic state, was a clear violation of the Fifteenth Amendment's ban on racial discrimination in voting. In July 1947, Judge Waring made a decision which backed the NAACP's reading of the situation, and he confirmed that it was discriminatory to exclude blacks from the Democratic state primary given the direct correlation between this vote and the subsequent general election. In their defence the white South Carolina Democrats had argued that their party operated along the lines of a private club and they should therefore be allowed to determine who was eligible to be a member and thus to vote, but Judge Waring reminded them that private clubs do not elect the president of the United States. National attention for Judge Waring's decision was already expected, but it became a certainty when, in his concluding remarks, the judge offered the following advice. 'It is time', he said, 'for South Carolina to rejoin the Union. It is time to fall in step with the other states and to adopt the Amer-

ican way of conducting elections.' White South Carolinians
were incensed, but blacks throughout the nation recognized the
significance of the ruling. On appeal, Judge Waring's ruling was
upheld, and the Supreme Court refused to review the case. As a
result 35,000 blacks were among the 800,000 South Carolinians
enrolled and therefore eligible to vote in the 1948 Democratic
primaries, and the vast majority of the blacks found their way to
the polls and voted without incident.

After the 1948 elections, the southern white community's
resentment towards the Warings increased. Congressman L.
Mendel Rivers of South Carolina, an unapologetic segregationist, called Waring a 'monster' and sought to institute impeach-
ment proceedings against him. Back in Charleston the telephone
at 61 Meeting Street rang nearly all day long, and when the
callers heard Elizabeth's voice they would shout 'Nigger lover',
or whisper 'prostitute', or engage in deep breathing, or simply
hang up. Elizabeth sometimes tried to goad the callers into the
open, but most of the time these cowardly intruders not only
chose to remain anonymous, they were also happy with the
knowledge that they were most likely rendering it difficult for
the Warings to make outside calls. Eventually a second line, with
an unlisted number, was installed and at nights the main line
was always disconnected so that the Warings could get some
sleep. On 11 October 1948, while in New York City escaping
what he described as Charleston's 'narrow provincialism', Judge
Waring further alienated his fellow southerners by declaring, at
a lunch given in his honour by the New York Chapter of the
National Lawyers Guild, that

My people have one outstanding fault, the terrible fault of
prejudice. They have been born and educated to feel that a
Negro is some kind of an animal that ought to be well-
treated and given kindness, but as a matter of favour, not
right. That's not the kind of conception that we should show
to the world.

In quick succession, Judge Waring resigned from the St Cecilia Society, the Charleston Club, and the South Carolina Society. He also resigned his captaincy in the élite Charleston Light Dragoons and ended his affiliation with the local Episcopal church.

As a result of their shrinking social circle, and perhaps as a natural outgrowth of their new concerns, Judge Waring and Elizabeth now found themselves mixing almost exclusively with blacks. However, the type of black people they mixed with were generally professional people, doctors, insurance men, and pastors whose income and standing were independent of the white power structure. To many whites, the Warings' entertaining of blacks in their Meeting Street house, and the Warings' reciprocal visiting of blacks in their homes, was vaguely amusing, suggesting as it did the degree of isolation which had been foisted upon them. However, to others, the Warings' social behaviour was a more serious transgression of the decent white values of Charleston than anything the judge had ever decreed from the federal bench.

The most frequent of the black visitors to 61 Meeting Street was Mrs Ruby Cornwell. Mrs Cornwell was adamant about propriety, and she refused to answer or engage with anyone who would not pay her the compliment, or simple courtesy, of addressing her by her title, 'Mrs'. When Mrs Cornwell first met the Warings, there quickly developed a particular fondness between Elizabeth and Ruby Cornwell, with the judge's wife lamenting that her 'lovely Ruby' had been in Charleston all this time and Elizabeth was so 'unaware'. Although it is easy to be cynical about the motives for this friendship, there is little doubt that Elizabeth was relieved to find a female companion with whom she could be intimate, and Ruby was equally relieved to have her notions of white bigotry so severely challenged. However, it is probably Elizabeth who was the more in need of companionship, for her status in Charleston had been that of *persona non grata* since she 'stole' the judge away from

Miss Annie. The judge was at least 'one of them', albeit one who had strayed, but his 'wife' was regarded as a thoroughly unacceptable 'low class Yankee woman'. However, Elizabeth Waring, the woman they now referred to as 'the Witch of Meeting Street', was about to descend even further down the ladder of social regard.

On the evening of Monday, 16 January 1950, at Charleston's all-black Coming Street branch of the YWCA, Elizabeth Waring gave a speech which catapulted her into the national limelight. There were many, both black and white, who, learning of Elizabeth Waring's invitation to speak, urged her not to accept, arguing that nothing good could come of it. However, Elizabeth was adamant that she should speak, and she enjoyed a great deal of publicity in the days leading up to January 16th. Judge Waring was aware that there might be some attempt to sabotage the meeting, and he therefore asked that guards be stationed by the light switches in the auditorium to prevent any attempts at disruption. However, he in no way tried to dissuade his wife from making her speech. Far from it. He was, as ever, supportive of whatever she wished to do, and her potential outspokenness on issues of race would have come as no surprise to him.

On the evening of the speech, one hundred and fifty people crowded into the auditorium, including a number of white reporters, and they listened to Elizabeth Waring speak out on the injustices of race relations as they currently existed. She extravagantly praised black people as having 'spiritually . . . long surpassed whites' and having lived 'Christ's teaching by the Golden Rule'. However, she was careful to state that some of this obedience had perhaps taken the edge off action, which is what she declared to be necessary if black people were to throw off the yoke of white southern tyranny. It was a startling speech, for many of the blacks had never before heard a white woman blaze with fury on their behalf. However, the portion of Elizabeth's speech which made state, and national, headlines, and caused looks of astonishment in the hall, was her characterization of southern whites. She described them as 'a sick, confused and decadent people . . . full of pride and complacency, introverted, morally weak, and low . . . so self-centred that they have not considered themselves as part of the country since the Civil War'.

The next day, and for weeks afterwards, the newspapers were full of stories about Elizabeth Waring. Coverage in *Time* magazine, the *New York Times*, and numerous national publications, suggested that this was a courageous woman speaking out on a subject that most were content to remain silent about. On 11 February 1950, Elizabeth Waring appeared on NBC's *Meet the Press*, and during her appearance she chose to speak out in favour of racial intermarriage. Her detractors were apoplectic with rage. The abusive phone calls became incessant, and a mountain of hate mail piled up at both 61 Meeting Street and the judge's chambers. A New York correspondent hoped that she might be 'raped by a diseased nigger', while a woman from Columbia hoped to be equally devastating by suggesting that her speech had seriously undermined all the 'good work' that her husband had done. For his part, Judge Waring was proud of his wife's speech and ready and willing to deal with the avalanche of hostile commentary. Most Charlestonians believed that the primary motive for the behaviour of both the Warings was social revenge, and that Elizabeth was acting like a child who had not been invited to the party and who now wanted to spoil it for everybody. Far from shrinking under this barrage of attack, Elizabeth Waring seemed reinvigorated. As she told *Time* magazine, 'If one has a cause, one has to be willing to suffer for it.'

A few weeks after the YWCA speech, a small cross with the initials KKK on it was burned in front of 61 Meeting Street. The police, and the Charleston press, regarded it as nothing more than high pranks, but the Warings—who were away in New York at the time—took it as another opportunity to lambast the south. Judge Waring told an audience in New York, 'We don't have a Negro problem in the South: we have a white problem.' The hostility towards Elizabeth and Judge Waring was mounting in direct proportion to the growth in their national fame. If Judge Waring was known as 'the traitor who let the niggers vote', then his wife was 'the woman who let the niggers into her house'. Either way, most Charlestonians felt that they ought to be 'run out of town'. The reproaches, both overt and covert, eventually resulted in a brick being thrown through the window of 61 Meeting Street and shots being fired. In the wake of this attack the judge berated the police, the FBI and the press for the lack of protection accorded to himself and his wife. Both privately and publicly, they made it clear that they would not be intimidated, and Elizabeth was quoted as declaring, 'If they think they can frighten us, they're greatly mistaken. We both believe in the dignity and equality of all people and no attacks by race supremacists—even a fatal one—will ever alter that belief or our determination to defend it to the end.'

But things were no longer that simple. The Warings were being physically threatened, and the United States Attorney General, J. Howard McGrath, arranged for U.S. Deputy Marshalls to be stationed outside 61 Meeting Street and to follow the Warings wherever they went. When they went to the Cornwells' house to play bridge, the marshals assigned to them would wait outside in an unmarked car. The Warings no longer had any privacy and their social lives were utterly broken. White Charlestonians were either too frightened or too disgusted to be seen in their presence, and when the Warings walked the streets people turned and looked the other way. Judge Waring was born and raised as an eighth-generation Charlestonian and the city, with all her traditions, was deeply ingrained in his blood. Charleston was his home, but this proud man had offended his peers and chosen to act against their traditions. They had made clear their disappointment and outrage and, unused to having anything other than his own way, Judge Waring had spurned them.

Now he had only the company of his vilified wife and that of the 'contemptible' negroes. The situation was somewhat easier for Elizabeth, for this was not her home, but for J. Waties Waring, no amount of anger, passion and pride could hide the fact that, in all but name, he was now homeless.

> . . . *simple change of place is seldom exile*
> . . . *there's a truer banishment*
> *'Tis to be*
> *An exile on the spot where you were born;*
> *A stranger on the hearth which saw your youth,*
> *Banished from the hearts to which your heart is turned.*
> Extract from nineteenth-century Charleston writer
> WILLIAM GILMORE SIMS,
> quoted in a letter to Judge Waring, 1952

Mrs Ruby Cornwell stands up and holds out her hand. I shake it and thank her for being so generous with her time. It is dark now, but she does not seem to notice. A lamp would shine like a beacon in this gloom.

'It was a great punishment for her to live without a social life. When she first came to Charleston with her second husband, the affluent whites told her that she was "good party material".'

I quickly gather up my notes and begin to follow Mrs Cornwell towards the door. She stops, and looks me full in the face. 'But eventually she found a social life among us blacks.'

I feel as if Mrs Cornwell is testing me, ready to pounce on any response that she does not approve of. And then she relents and touches my arm.

'I'm so happy that you came to find me. He was a prophet without honour in his own land. And she always said that he was so much warmer with the blacks than with the other social set. The whites.'

She opens the door. The humid air rushes in and almost overpowers me.

'But he was disappointed. He thought we could have done more. But we didn't have the same choices that he had. He could go away, but this was our home. We had to stay here. People had to be brave, but they had to be careful.'

As I get into my car, I look back and see ninety-six-year-old Mrs Ruby Cornwell standing at the top of the steps looking down at me. I turn back the clock. She was a mature woman in her late forties, with a well-founded suspicion of southern whites. And then the Warings entered her life. Just what did they offer her beyond friendship? Hope? A feeling of being accepted? There were those in the black community who scorned Mrs Ruby Cornwell for 'rushing' to mix with the spurned white people. Was it simply a shared love of bridge and justice? I look at Mrs Ruby Cornwell, whose house is crammed with the evidence of a rich life, and I know that one corner of her heart is clearly reserved for the few years that she spent as Elizabeth Waring's best friend. If she offered the Warings the possibility of friendship at a time when they desperately needed it, the Warings offered her the opportunity to see herself reflected in a different, an unexpected mirror. And the pride in what she saw still infuses her soul today.

On 22 December 1950, Henry Briggs, a thirty-four-year-old black Navy veteran and father of five children, filed a complaint in Clarendon County against the chairman of the district's board of education, Roderick Elliot, and other members of the board of trustees. He did so with the backing of the NAACP, and the complaint was soon known as *Briggs v. Elliot*. The issue was the legitimacy of offering 'separate but equal' education, and if it was possible for this practice to exist without it being detrimental to the welfare of black students. This was a direct challenge to South Carolina's state laws, which held the notion of 'separate but equal' to be the foundation stone upon which the society was built, including its educational system. It was soon clear that a special three-judge panel of federal judges would have to be convened to hear the complaint, of which Judge Waring would be but one voice. Thurgood Marshall, the chief prosecutor for the plaintiff, realized that the other two judges, Parker and Timmerman, were likely to oppose his argument that it was unconstitutional to insist on 'separate but equal' in any U.S. school, for segregation could never help to promote equal opportunities. However, he pressed the case in the hope that he might be able to persuade Parker, at least, into seeing things his way.

Predictably, Thurgood Marshall's suit failed, with Parker and Timmerman voting to uphold the notion of 'separate but equal' and Judge Waring writing a dissenting opinion which was immediately recognized as a landmark document in the Civil Rights struggle. The two-day trial was itself something of a *cause célèbre*, with crowds of poor blacks from all over the county and surrounding areas vying to get into the small second-floor federal courtroom in Charleston. The events were widely covered and reported nationally, but although the black spectators had hoped for a 'breakthrough' in Civil Rights legislation, the depressing reality of the situation was all too clear to Judge Waring. Privately, he felt that Thurgood Marshall might have prepared a stronger and more forceful case, but his greatest contempt was for his fellow judge, Parker. While he did not expect any 'help' from the die-hard segregationist Timmerman, he knew Parker to be a man of conscience, or so he thought. Sadly, by the end of the case, Judge Waring had come to the conclusion that Parker was no more a man of conscience than the next segregationist, and that in all likelihood he had one eye on a potential seat in the Supreme Court.

The only court of appeal beyond a three-judge district court was the Supreme Court itself and, with some secret urging from Judge Waring, the NAACP and Thurgood Marshall decided to take this step. Unfortunately, the challenge to what Judge Waring insisted was 'the false doctrine' of 'separate but equal' looked just as likely to fail before the Supreme Court, and so a weary Judge Waring decided that he would take this opportunity to retire from the federal bench. 26 January 1952, would mark the tenth anniversary of his tenure as a federal judge and he would be eligible for retirement at full salary. Accordingly he informed President Truman and Judge Parker of his decision. On 28 January, the Supreme Court made their decision, remanding *Briggs v. Elliot* back to South Carolina for the three-judge panel to review the situation further. Sadly, for Judge Waring it was all now academic. He had reached the sad conclusion that the white people of South Carolina might feel better disposed to weigh issues relating to race and Civil Rights, and perhaps even come down on the side of justice, if their 'hate object' was removed.

Privately, of course, Judge Waring was disappointed that his career on the bench should be ending in this manner. However, he was proud that his dissenting opinion in this case would be his final act as a judge, and he hoped that his dissent might pave the way for a permanent Supreme Court ruling against segregation that he felt sure must be just around the corner. Judge J. Waties Waring was to be proved right. Two years later, *Brown v. Board of Education*, the case that eventually brought an end to legalized segregation, was argued by Thurgood Marshall along the lines of Judge Waring's learned dissent in *Briggs v. Elliot*. But *Brown v. Board of Education* lay in the future. In 1952 Judge Waring was a seventy-two-year-old man who was unhappy with the insults, the ostracization, and the mental anguish of being a pariah in the land that he loved. He was painfully out of tune with his home, and he decided that he had no choice but to leave. It was simply too burdensome to be among those who openly hated you in a place you called 'home'.

> From their testimony [witnesses], it was clearly apparent, as it should be to any thoughtful person, irrespective of having such expert testimony, that segregation in education can

never produce equality and that it is an evil that must be eradicated. This case presents the matter clearly for adjudication and I am of the opinion that all of the legal guideposts, expert testimony, common sense and reason point unerringly to the conclusion that the system of segregation in education adopted and practiced in the State of South Carolina must go and must go now.

Segregation is per se *inequality.*

> from BRIGGS V. ELLIOT, in the District Court
> of the United States for the Eastern District
> of South Carolina Charleston Division,
> Civil Action No. 2657. Dissenting Opinion,
> J. Waties Waring, United States District Judge.
> 23 June 1951

Does the Queen Bee soar to heights in Heaven above?
As does our Ruby
Does she descend to earth with dignity and grace?
As does our Ruby
Is the Bee as ethereal, as versatile, as radiant with love?
As is our Queen Bee
As Noble of nature, as pure of soul, as beauteous of face?
As is our Ruby.

ELIZABETH WARING

Sullivan's Island is a four-mile-long sandbar where the élite of Charleston society regularly spend their summers in large, airy houses by the sea. I drive past these houses, and the bars and restaurants which enjoy a seasonal trade, and park my car by the Stella Maris Catholic Church. Built between 1869 and 1873, it is a small, modest stone building with spectacularly coloured stained-glass windows. I tug at the heavy wooden door and pass into the dark interior. The benches are arranged in obedient rows, and the air is heavy with a dank, almost musty smell. A journalist named Robert Stockton had told me that Father

McInnerney was the person who might have the best idea of where the old pest houses were. Apparently, Father McInnerney has done some research into Sullivan's Island and its history, and according to Robert Stockton, if anybody knew where they used to be then he would. But there is no sign of Father McInnerney. The church is empty.

I wander out of the Stella Maris Catholic Church and tramp along the ill-defined paths that are flanked on either side by tall grass. Of the many people that I have asked, nobody seems to know exactly where the pest houses were located, and of course nobody has thought it necessary at least to speculate and mark a place with a monument or plaque. Apparently there are plans to do so, but as yet there is nothing. It should, after all, be one of the most significant sites in the United States: the place where over 30 per cent of the African population first landed in the North American world. The black Ellis Island. Robert Stockton's best guess was that the pest houses were situated somewhere between the Stella Maris Catholic Church and a wooden jetty on the north shore. I am wandering this ground now. Behind the church there are private houses with long wooden jetties which protrude into the creek. The jetties are marked 'Private Dock'. 'Private'. Private. Private summer houses with manicured lawns and securely moored fishing boats. Private.

I look out from this grassy marshland and can see the low-lying mainland. This is a secluded cove, and a perfect place for 'seasoning' slaves. Private. The day is hazy and Charleston is out of sight. A solitary cloud undresses the sun, which sheds another shell of heat. I watch a fishing boat, its nets hoisted high above its head, kicking up a playful surf as it slowly purrs its way home. Sullivan's Island is an eerie and troubled place. Flat, marsh, grassland. An arrival in America. Having crossed the Atlantic in the belly of a ship. An arrival. Here, in America. Step ashore, out of sight of Charleston. To be fed, watered, scrubbed, prepared. To be sold. Back home, a similar climate. Different vegetation. Different birds. Family. An arrival. Low, low land. Water. The mainland lying low in the hazy distance. Charleston. Farewell Africa. Welcome to America.

You, ladies and gentlemen, have come here from various countries. You have brought to us ideas that must help us. The different countries of this globe can all contribute and help us in these United States. We speak of ourselves and of our country as a melting pot, where all nations, and races, and creeds can assemble and become one called America. And that is something that we should always work for. But let us not forget that merely calling ourselves Americans means that we are better than everybody else. Because what we have that is good has come to us from other lands. We have acquired from the Northern European countries systems of law and order, forms of government. We have acquired from the Southern countries of Europe literature, and architecture, and beauty. We have acquired from the people of Africa the Egyptian culture, music, rhythm, softness and beauty. We have acquired from the Asiatic countries most of our systems of philosophy, and all of our leading religious ideas. The great pervading religious groups have come out of Asia. And so let us not say, as so many small minds in this country say, that those people are benighted Europeans, or Africans, or Asians, but remember that the people of India and China, and many other parts of this globe, are just as worthy of having freedom as we are. Many of them are striving to be freed from the shackles that have been imposed upon them by Western civilization. And as we would be free, so they must be free, and the duty of this great land of ours is not to enslave anybody, but to do its part in freeing everybody, in becoming the great leader of the world, not as the most powerful, not as the greatest Army, or Navy, or Air Force, not as the richest, but as the great leader of democracy and freedom, the great leader in providing for the peoples of this world a decent living in a decent land, where free people may enjoy the freedom of governing themselves and using their systems without interference with us, or interference by us.

And now ladies and gentlemen, I have talked perhaps too long, but I am so glad to see you and have you here. We are not only glad to have you, but we need you. As I have said, and I say again, this country is not a finished product. It has plenty of defects. It has plenty of troubles. It has plenty of worries. And we want good minds, clean minds, energetic and interested minds, to come in and join in and help us solve the problems, many of which are the result of our own errors in the past. We want your help. We want you as American citizens to take your burden, your part, and I believe that we are going to make this country worthy of our forefather's intentions when it was formed, and when they signed that great Declaration in which they declared all men are equal.

Ladies and gentlemen, you are admitted as American citizens. The Clerk will prepare and furnish to you later your certificates evidencing that fact, and may I have the personal pleasure of pressing the hand of each one of you newly admitted citizens today.

HONORABLE J. WATIES WARING, United States District Judge,
to Naturalization Class at Charleston, SC,
23 November 1951.

American History

Those four black girls blown up
in that Alabama church
remind me of five hundred
middle passage blacks,
in a net, under water
in Charleston harbor

so redcoats wouldn't find them.
Can't find what you can't see
Can you?

MICHAEL HARPER

I approach Magnolia Cemetery a little after 5 p.m. The cemetery is situated at the northern end of the town, in an area that
appears to be populated primarily by black people. There are
many other cemeteries around Magnolia, which casts a macabre
aspect of gloom over the whole district. Clearly, there is both
competition and great significance attached to where one is
buried. As I turn off the main street I pass an establishment
which sells tombstones; they sprout like polished teeth in front
of a low wooden building. I drive by a row of one-storey shacks,
outside of which are abandoned armchairs, plastic kitchen
chairs, wooden dining chairs, all of which are occupied by black
people who seem to be idling away the day. I stare at one couple, the man sitting at one end of the porch, his wife at the
other, the pair of them gazing into mid-air, letting the wind turn
thoughts over in their minds. The rhythm of the south; solitary
reflection, no words.

I drive through the tall gates of Magnolia Cemetery, and in
front of me I see a parked mini-van. The sliding door is open and
I am being watched by two men who look like hillbilly extras
from a film set. They contemplate my presence, but they say
nothing. I see a sign which reads 'office', so I park my car and
walk up to the building that the sign appears to be pointing
towards. I knock once, then twice, but there is no answer. Then
I realize that this small solid building is not the office, it is a
mausoleum. I scamper back to the car. As I get in I notice that
the two hillbillies are still watching me. The actual office is one
hundred yards further on, to the right of a small lake, and
beyond a white footbridge which (without arching) spans the
breadth of the water. Ducks float aimlessly, while herons expend
energy by dramatically landing, and then almost immediately

flying off again. A man stands by the steps to the office, and he seems surprised to see me in a 'white' cemetery. However, although he is unable to disguise his surprise, he is polite. He tells me that the office closes at 4.30 p.m., but if I come back tomorrow morning there will be somebody who can help me. They have a computer in the basement, he says, where you simply punch in the name of a person and the location of the grave will magically appear. I thank him and walk back to the car knowing that at least the next day's search will be 'efficient'.

I snake along Magnolia's narrow lanes, steering carefully so that the car remains on the asphalt. It is a beautiful cemetery, with an astonishing variety of graves. Some feature a vertical headstone, others are simply horizontal slabs of marble; some are large tombs with a locked door and elaborate grills, while other graves have the most elaborate monuments constructed upon them. Whatever the design, these privileged southern white families all appear determined that they should be grouped together in death. And then, out of the corner of my eye, I catch the name. The bold simplicity of the name 'Waring' on a large, upright slab of marble. I pull the car over to the side of the path and I stare at the single word. The tombstone is set aside from the main body of the cemetery. It is across a path, and behind the grave there is marshland, a profusion of reeds, and then more water.

I get out of my car and walk up to the small plot. I stare at the large slab with its single word, 'Waring'. Beneath the word there is explication:

J. Waties Waring
United States District Judge
July 27 1880 – January 11 1968

Elizabeth Avery Waring
August 10 1895 – October 30 1968

She did not want to live without him. The plot is bounded by a narrow skirting of granite. Along the front edge are inscribed the words 'Perpetual Care J. W. and E. A. Waring'. The whole scene is elegant in its simplicity, and heartbreaking in its loneliness. In the bottom left-hand corner of the plot, above where the judge lies, there is a young magnolia tree which will grow and gain strength as the years pass by. Behind me, and only ten yards away, is an extremely tall monument to the Charleston Light Dragoons which, at this time of the day, casts a powerful shadow. And then I notice the sun beginning to set on the lake. Posted by the lake is the sort of sign that a judge might appreciate.

No Trespassing
No Fishing
No Swimming
Trespassers will be prosecuted

I find it hard to leave Judge Waring and Elizabeth's grave. In the distance I hear the sound of a train's hooter. Charleston was the first place in the United States to boast a train. Always the first with Charleston. The first museum in the United States. The first shot in the civil war. The first place to fly the Union flag. The train passes by and again there is a deep silence, which is only disturbed by the sound of birds singing. The judge and his wife are positioned in Magnolia Cemetery as if to confirm the fact that they were outcasts.

I sit on the back steps of the United States Customs House as the Charleston Festival of African and Caribbean Art continues in full swing. It is now early evening and I am surrounded by a thousand or so people, standing, sitting, walking, eating, drinking, milling about among the booths that sell food and art and artefacts at this 'jammin' in the streets' block party. The participants are mainly older black couples, or young black men and women, but there are also a sizeable number of white faces among the crowd. Night sits easily on everybody's shoulders. The younger blacks and whites wear T-shirts, baggy jeans, and Nikes; they dress alike. The older black couples seem proud, but cautious at this open display of pride in all things African. They remember when a black person could not vote in South Carolina.

New York was not home. Judge Waring and Elizabeth remained active on the lecture circuit and the judge was frequently honoured, particularly by black organizations. Although they had vowed never to return to the south as long as there was segregation, in 1954 the Warings were invited by their black South Carolina friends to a ceremony honouring the judge for his stance on the issue of Civil Rights. On 6 November, they were met at Charleston train station by a crowd of several hundred cheering black people, and escorted by motorcade to the home of Mr and Mrs Cornwell. They stayed with their friends for the duration of their short visit to Charleston, the highlight of which was a ceremony given in the judge's honour at a black elementary school, an event which was attended by over three hundred people. Thereafter, they returned to New York and their 'exile'. The judge continued to make public statements, and to keep abreast of affairs, but the advent of Martin Luther King, Jr meant that life in the south was finally changing for both black and white. The opinion of Judge J. Waties Waring was no longer sought as often as it used to be. In the early 1960s, Elizabeth's health began to decline, to the extent that she seldom ventured out of their New York apartment. The judge also began to experience serious difficulties in both hearing and seeing, and Elizabeth was forced to read aloud to him. In their last years the Warings were somewhat reclusive and they depended upon each other for company.

Judge Waring died peacefully on 11 January 1968, at St

Luke's Hospital, New York. On 17 January he was buried in Magnolia Cemetery in a ceremony attended by less than a dozen whites. However, more than two hundred black people followed the hearse into the cemetery where they insisted on paying their final respects to 'our judge'. In a letter to the *Charleston News and Courier*, Mrs Ruby Cornwell concluded with the words, 'The Judge comes home. We welcome you our judge'. Elizabeth Waring was too ill to attend her husband's funeral, and after his death she entered a nursing home in Massachusetts. However, her will to live had been extinguished. In October of the same year she died, and was buried next to her husband. Sadly, only nine people, including Ruby Cornwell, attended her funeral.

And now the African dancing begins. Five young black women explain the origins of each dance before they dramatically twirl and throw their arms into the air. This is Shango. This is from Senegal. This means we are making a blessing, an offering, praising the sun, the moon. Behind them the moon looms large, and beneath the moon, the sea. Here, in this city which 'processed' nearly one-third of the African population which arrived in the United States, a population who were encouraged to forget Africa, to forget their language, to forget their families, to forget their culture, to forget their dances, five young black women try to remember. Five young black women attempt to liberate their souls and their spirits. Sandy? Margaret? Joan? Susan? Kim? I imagine that they have already taken an African name for themselves. They do not have to share it. Their sinewy bodies weave invisible threads that connect them to the imagined old life.

A night as warm and damp as an indoor swimming-pool. At the conclusion of their dance I walk among the booths and stalls where I am encouraged to buy African clothes, masks, carvings and hats. I notice the slogans on the T-shirts: 'Imported from Africa', 'Black by Popular Demand', 'Danger! Educated Black

Man'. Drums are being pounded. One can pay by American Express. Close to Africa? Closer to America. The female MC can be heard above the drums. There are no 'African-Americans', only 'Africans'. Everybody is 'Brother' or 'Sister'. Here, in Charleston. 'What's happening, brother?' says a man who brushes past me. He raises his palm for me to 'high-five' him. African dancing. Drums. 'What's happening, brother?' The rhythms of Africa floating over Charleston. White men and women dancing behind the United States Customs House. Somewhere in the distance, around the corner and out of sight, Sullivan's Island. And before Sullivan's Island? Africa. And the vessel's European port of departure? Its home port? Its home? White men and women dancing to the rhythms of Africa in the street behind the United States Customs House. Magnolia cemetery on a bright moonlit night, some distance to the north. Home. African drums. The police looking on, guns on their hips. Everybody having a good time. Ghosts walking the streets of Charleston. Ghosts dancing in the streets of Charleston.

EPILOGUE

EXODUS

I am sitting in a large tent whose flaps are peeled back. The wind rises and throws clouds of red dust into the tent causing me to turn away and shield my eyes. The dust of the desert. The wind of the desert. Sudden, unpredictable, and harsh. In the rainy season this land is ankle-deep in cloying mud. Progress is slow; feet plug and unplug. At the moment we are in the dry season; the land is baked hard. The cracks and fissures in the soil suggest a thousand miniature rivers that have been etched upon a rudimentary map.

I sit at a table. Before me is a single plastic cup of water. In the desert one must always drink water. When you feel no thirst, no desire to drink water, then this is the time to drink. The body acts quickly when deprived of water. It betrays you. 'Would you like something to drink?' A cup of water, please. A single plastic cup of water stands before me. Again, I lift my hand to protect my eyes from a swirling cloud of dust. Thirsty landscape. My lips are dry. I lick them and then I take a sip of water.

Nights in the desert are cold and often unbearable. A wide sky, a black canvas speckled with pinpricks of light. A vast, low horizon. A cold wind that rolls like thunder. Hunched shoulders, a shiver along the spine. How can it be so cold? After the unbearable heat of the day, now this? At night, I return to my hotel room in a nearby town. I cater to my insomnia with a duty-free bottle of whisky. Nursemaid to my waking hours. I stare at a flickering screen that brings me news from home. Familiar faces, familiar words, unfamiliar room. Through the window I see a wide sky speckled with pinpricks of light. Out there, somewhere in the desert, they hunch shoulders.

The woman replenishes my cup of water. She apologizes for the heat. I am swallowing mouthfuls of steam. This is not air. I left air behind in another place. I begin to drip with sweat, to accept my fate. I am among them. I want to know why they are here. They are with me in the tent, dressed in their strange, brightly coloured costumes. This is not African dress; this is not local dress; this is the costume of a culture I do not understand. All families dress alike. Fifteen people in purple batik costumes. Twelve people in orange batik costumes. Eight people in green batik costumes. Two-piece costumes. Circus clowns? Uniforms? Groups of costumed African-Americans wander the compound together. Dozens more sit under the shade of my tent; the makeshift dining-room. Hundreds occupy the small camping tents that are scattered about the compound.

She asks me if I want some food. Vegan food will be impossible for me to digest. She is thin, with high cheekbones and a healthy glow to her skin. Vegan food obviously agrees with her. She holds her hand up and signals to her colleague. Just one plate. I sip at my water and look at her. She is originally from Chicago. She left the land of great captivity in 1978. She lives here now with her four children. A teenage daughter appears at the side of the tent. I know it is her daughter. The girl is dressed in a yellow and brown batik costume; like her mother. The daughter is shy. As she speaks she turns one shoe over and onto its outer edge. She scratches short nervous lines in the sand. Apparently, she hopes to work in communications and hair design. Her mother is proud. The daughter leaves her mother alone with her guest.

Since leaving the great captivity, the mother has worked as an assistant teacher and a nutrition specialist. I now understand why she is disappointed by my reluctance to eat. For over twenty years, God has been her life. Growing up in drug-ridden, south-side Chicago she always knew that she wanted to do something with her life. Her plate of food arrives. Tofu yam fritters. Green beans. Never any meat. Never any fish. She smiles and thanks her friend for her trouble. When she first heard about the ideology of the community her spirit opened up to it. She tells me that in Chicago there is a complete break-down of family structure. Here, there is no birth control. There is polygamy. A man can take up to three wives. She waits for me to say something in reply, but I say nothing. She wanted to embrace her legacy and heritage. I take another sip of water. She gestures beyond the open flaps of the tent. People still wan-der about in family groups. We are, she says, descendants of Isaac, Abraham, and Jacob. We are the true children of Israel.

The flag of Israel, and the flag of the small desert town of Dimona fly together in the stiff wind. They mark the outer boundary of this small piece of grass-worn parkland. A police car stands by the roadside. Two bored officers, a man and a woman, sit in the car and look at the cluster of tents and the small wooden stage. There is an inflatable plastic castle on which the children bounce and play. If they choose to, they can ride a tired-looking pony that is being encouraged to describe a pointless circle. The children are supervised. They line up beside the inflatable castle. They line up and wait their turn to ride on the pony. On stage, a disc-jockey plays music. He has a turntable and a selection of long-playing records. Soul. Light jazz. African-American music. African-American people. African-American children. In costumes. Who have come home to the desert. The lost tribes of Israel. Found in Chicago, Washington,

New York. Come hither my children. Return! Here in the desert. Two thousand African-Americans. Free at last.

She finishes her food. This beautiful desert woman from Chicago. Her eyes are clear. Her spirit is pure. She speaks without doubt. Without anxiety. Without ambiguity. Today they are celebrating the New World Passover, which marks the thirty-second anniversary of their departure from the great captivity. They have created a New World Order. Again, the desert wind kicks dust up and into my face. I turn my head away from the celebrations. This rainbow tribe. Eating watermelon. Jets flying overhead. A desert region. A military zone. Two white European stills photographers wander among the returnees. Over thirty years in the desert. They tell me they have come home. To a world that does not recognize them. To a land they cannot tame.

The young girls parade before the Messiah. They are being marshalled by a young man on inline skates. He is part of a group that calls themselves Youth on the Move. The Messiah is seated on a platform atop a wall that is four feet high. He is flanked by his queen, and by the elders of the community. The Messiah is known as Ben Ammi Ben Israel. The Prince of Peace. He used to be known as Ben Carter. He used to work in a foundry in Chicago. The young girls are as young as three and as old as eight. They are majorettes, and they have taken to baton-twirling like true American girls. They are American girls. Except they have never visited the United States. The audience sit around three sides of a concrete playground. As the children twirl their batons, voices shout, 'Don't stop, now.' 'You're a bad thing, sister.' The girls put some hip and waist into their gyrations. On a roof overlooking the proceedings, two men with binoculars keep watch. One is dressed in red, one in white. As the sun slowly sets they fade to black silhouettes. On top of a three-storey building.

We have left the dusty, tent-strewn compound behind and

moved a hundred yards to their permanent settlement. The three-storey budding is their school. Behind the playground, I see a complex of low, one-storey houses. This is where they live, in what was originally an absorption camp for Moroccan immigrants. Shortly after the exodus, the African-Americans were given this run-down complex by the Israeli government. There was no electricity, no plumbing, in fact no conveniences of any kind. Many of the buildings lacked roofs. The children of Israel repaired the complex. These days the African-Americans often live twenty or thirty people to one small house. But their settlement is clean. Flowers grow. There is no filth, no litter. They have made their settlement into a place they can be proud of. Their crowning achievement is the school, for which they received help from the United States government. From the 'black caucus' in Washington, DC. Their former capital.

The Chosen First Fruit are a group of young men aged eighteen to twenty-two. Together with their younger brothers, Youth on the Move, they present their champion: a young man with a middleweight boxing title to his name. The CFF and YOM move as one. They are not Israelis; they are not Africans. They are Americans. 'Soul Train' moves to African drums. The CFF and YOM present their champion to the Messiah, who stands now and acknowledges their 'offering'. He receives the championship belt. The Messiah is dressed in purple, with a purple crocheted hat. His queen remains seated. His two other queens and his sixteen children are elsewhere. Drums continue to be beaten. The Messiah lifts his hands, stills the noise, and speaks. 'It is the sheep that make the shepherd. Without sheep there can be no shepherd. Without people there can be no king. You are the makers of the champion. I simply take this belt in acknowledgement of the greatness of you.' The Messiah is in his sixties. He wears a grey beard and white shoes. He holds the belt aloft and salutes his people. They are a long way from the great captivity. Ben Carter dreamt. The American dream? ('Set

thee up waymarks, make thee high heaps; set thine heart toward
the highway even the way which thou wentest; turn again, O vir-
gin of Israel, turn again to these my cities.' *Jeremiah* 31:21)

There is to be an evening performance. At the Dimona Palace of
Culture. A steeply-raked auditorium is packed to the rafters
with black faces in rainbow costumes. 'Hallelujah!' The cries
cascade through the hall. Call and response. Call and you will be
heard, my child. Saturday night at the Apollo, here in the desert
town of Dimona. Boulevards and palm trees. White houses with
red roofs. Straight lines in the desert. The Palace of Culture is
the centrepiece of their civic world. 'Hallelujah!' There are a
handful of white faces. Journalists. The curious. An old white
woman clutches a guitar. She lives beneath a white straw-
brimmed hat. She stands in the aisle, one arm raised aloft, sway-
ing. She chants, 'Hallelujah!' She is a believer. The Palace of
Culture is full of believers. Tonight. The wind hurtles across the
desert. The sky is choked with stars. The abandoned tents flap
in the wind on the grass-worn parkland up the hill. The playground is now empty. The two men are still on the roof. Still
looking. Believers. And in the middle of row eight is the Messiah
and his queen. He has led his flock. He is leading his flock.

I sit next to the Minister of Information. 'We are the Hebrew
Israelites. Other migratory movements are not spiritual, they
are romantic and cultural. Spirituality is what makes this successful.' He sells me a copy of his book. On stage the singer,
Tekiyah, sings Bob Marley's 'Redemption Song'. The international anthem of the African diaspora. High in the hills of
Jamaica. On the coast of Brazil. In Brooklyn. In every major city
in Europe. And now here in Israel, somebody is singing
'Redemption Song'. Her hands sway above her head. 'How long
shall they kill our prophets?' Tekiyah turns her face to the heavens. Like the others, she is not an Israeli citizen. She has
renounced American citizenship. She is a Hebrew Israelite. She

believes that they, the descendants of the ancient Israelites, were punished by God for disobeying his commandments. That punishment was called slavery and its most vicious manifestation was the 'passage' to the Americas. To the great captivity. But now they are free. We must return the same way that we came. They have returned home, by way of Liberia. 1967. Two years in Africa to cleanse the spirit. Seven died. In 1969, three hundred Hebrew Israelites arrived in Dimona. Now they number over two thousand. Most have been born in the Holy Land. Israel, in northeast Africa. Stateless. Children of God. As many as four families in one house. Black Children of God. The Messiah in the house. Ben Carter, foundry worker. Bob Marley in the air. The desert wind. It is cold outside. I sit next to the Minister of Information and clutch his book.

One of his wives brought him to the tent so that he might meet me. I was sipping at my plastic cup of water. But I immediately recognized the minister. I did not expect him to remember. I reminded him. Cape Coast Cultural Centre. He looked at me with a blank expression. Ghana. Panafest. The exhibition. I saw you by the exhibition. His face lights up. 'Yes, my brother, I was there.' He engineers my hand through a jive-shake. The minister asks me to follow him through the tented camp. Costumed families are clustered together. Some are sprawled in their tents. Some are sitting outside on old sofas or chairs. Home, out of doors. I imagine their living quarters to be cramped. It is only later that I discover just how cramped. Twenty or thirty to one small house. The minister leads me past African-Americans who play chess and backgammon. Children are ubiquitous. Most families contain ten to twelve children, with one 'brother and up to three wives'. We sit on a sagging sofa underneath a tarpaulin shade. This constitutes the Minister's corner of the compound. He then tells me that, like the Messiah, he too has sixteen children by three wives. They are easy to recognize.

A small boy clings to the minister's leg. He is three years old, and he only has eyes for his father. The minister reaches down and gently rubs his hand across the top of his boy's head. The grateful boy looks up at his father, who rewards him with a smile. The boy kicks at the dust and watches it rise, spin and then settle down again, coating his foot a lighter and dustier hue. 'The child is happy,' boasts the minister. I say nothing. The minister tells me that he is from Washington DC and that he served time on Capitol Hill as an intern. His generation were post-Panthers and so he felt lost. Discontented. A few years earlier and he may have 'gone down in a foolish blaze of glory'. He was saved. His family regard the Hebrew Israelites as a nonsensical group of people. It is painful. He has heard all the jokes about them ending up like Jonestown. He has heard all the talk about them being a cult. The Minister is clear. They are not a religion. They have embraced a spiritually principled way of life. Their guiding principles come from the Bible. Members must accept the laws outlined in the first five books of the Bible. The degree to which one embraces the lifestyle defines membership. They believe they are the chosen people and they rightfully belong outside the United States of America. In Israel, northeast Africa.

The bespectacled minister is over six feet tall. He is lean and handsome, although his hair is beginning to turn grey around the edges. He is undoubtedly a charismatic speaker. He is ideal for the job. He points out to me that whereas others have talked, Ben Ammi has actually led his people out of the ghettoes of the United States and 'home' to the promised land. Many failed, including Marcus Garvey. Marcus Garvey never even set foot on the shores of Africa. He travelled the Atlantic rim: from Jamaica to New York, from New York to London. Ben Ammi has led his people from America to Africa, and from Africa 'home' to Israel. The Messiah has reversed the exodus. The minister is proud. All Africans must return to God. Not to religion, but to God. Again the wind begins to kick up the dust and hurl it in my face. I am thirsty. I need to drink, but the minister has omitted to offer me water. Soon I will have to walk to the playground to watch the young girls perform. And then later, the Palace of Culture. What culture? The minister is frustrated. Do I not understand? Their group identity is forged in biblically inspired belief. And further reinforced by their shared diasporan history.

We are interrupted by the public address system. Will all those entered in the jump-rope contest please report to the sidewalk? Similarly, those in the double-Dutch contest, please report to the sidewalk. Now. Girls dressed as majorettes go by. The sounds of Marvin Gaye. The ubiquitous harmonies of black English. ('Where y'all staying?') Cultural baggage. The United States in the blood of the elders. Confusion in the blood of the children. This closed society. On contact with the real world, what? The final irony of life in the great captivity. Burdensome cultural baggage. I'm sorry, sir, but this bag cannot be tucked away under the seat in front. Up ahead. My minister friend shields his eyes from the desert. This landscape, he says. It is beautiful. I look. Then redirect my gaze. I say nothing. There is nothing I can say. You were transported in a wooden vessel across a broad expanse of water to a place which rendered your tongue silent. Look. Listen. Learn. And as you began to speak, you remembered fragments of a former life. Shards of memory. Careful. Some will draw blood. You dressed your memory in the new words of this new country. Remember. There were no round-trip tickets in your part of the ship. Exodus. It is futile to walk into the face of history. As futile as trying to keep the dust from one's eyes in the desert.

A NOTE ON THE TYPE

This book was set in a typeface called Berling. This distinguished letter is a computer version of the original type designed by the Swedish typographer Karl Erik Forsberg (born 1914). Forsberg also designed several other typefaces, including Parad (1936), Lunda (1938), Carolus, and Ericus, but Berling—named after the foundry that produced it, Berlingska Stilgjuteriet of Lund—is the one for which he is best known. Berling, a roman font with the characteristics of an old face, was first used to produce *The Rembrandt Bible* in 1954, which won an award for the most beautiful book of the year.

Composed by NK Graphics, Keene, New Hampshire
Printed and bound by Quebecor, Fairfield, Pennsylvania
Designed by Robert C. Olsson